DAVID O. MCKAY
P9-AGU-396
3293

WOLFGANG BORCHERT

SELECTED READINGS

JAN 7 2003

WITHDRAWN

JUL 0 1 2024
PROPERTY OF:
DAVID O. MCKAY LIBRARY
BYU-IDAHO
REXBURG ID 83460-0405

HOLT SERIES IN GERMAN LITERATURE

John E. Crean, Jr., Editor

WOLFGANG BORCHERT

SELECTED READINGS

Edited by

ANNA OTTEN

Antioch College
Yellow Springs, Ohio

HOLT, RINEHART AND WINSTON, INC.

New York   Toronto   London

By permission of the publisher, the literary selections appearing in this textbook are taken from Wolfgang Borchert, DAS GESAMTWERK © Rowohlt Verlag, Hamburg, 1949. All rights reserved. (IBA)

Cover art: *Die Mütter* (detail). Blatt 6 der Folge „Krieg". Woodcut by Käthe Kollwitz. Klipstein Catalog #182. Prints Division, The New York Public Library, Astor, Lenox and Tilden Foundations.

Cover design by Renate Hiller.

© 1973 by Holt, Rinehart and Winston, Inc.

All rights reserved.

Library of Congress Catalog Card Number 72–84089

ISBN: 0–03–080277–6

Printed in the United States of America

3 4 5 6   065   9 8 7 6 5 4 3 2 1

Borcherts Landsmännern von der Waterkant,
Tonie und Günther

PROPERTY OF:
DAVID O. McKAY LIBRARY
BYU-IDAHO
REXBURG ID 83460-0405

FOREWORD

Why A Series And For What Level

The Holt German Paperback Series was created to fill a need on the foreign language textbook scene. One might wonder, why a series at all, why not just random editions with varying personal editorial criteria? The whole rationale behind a series is to provide the kind of editions which can be used right away in the second year or intermediate level, where serious reading is begun. To produce readable texts which foster good reading habits, to assure consistent editorial procedures and to get together some meaningful and distinctive paperbacks for today's mature students, are the aims we have in mind in presenting our series.

The Single Author—Entire Work Approach

Each volume in the series limits itself to presenting the work of a single modern German author. In some cases this means one longer work such as Dürrenmatt's play, *Die Ehe des Herrn Mississippi* or Hauptmann's short novel, *Der Ketzer von Soana*. In other volumes one can find, for example, several short stories by Heinz Risse, or two short plays by Tankred Dorst, or a choice selection of the prose and poetry of Wolfgang Borchert. Each volume forms in itself a complete entity: the writing is by the same author and any piece included is presented unabridged.

The Anthology: Certain Problems

Anthologies consisting of excerpted works or very short works by many different authors have no doubt enjoyed a measure of popularity in the past decade. An omnibus approach with a smorgasbord menu would seem to offer both swift and varied fare. But such a method of introducing authors and works of literature has revealed some drawbacks both in actual second year teaching as well as in follow-up courses. And in those second year courses reading both a multiple author anthology and a complete, single author work in one semester, a good number of students do considerably better with the single author work, feel they accomplish more (not an unimportant factor) and in general find it easier to assimilate and retain vocabulary more effectively.

We must not forget that after the careful pre-selection of first year vocabulary, students sometimes find overwhelming the tremendous altitude of word sophistication we expect them to attain in second year. The words sometimes come at them too fast and, it would seem, lacking any coherent framework or context. And for a student just about getting accustomed to one author after four or five pages to have to switch abruptly to another, then to another, what context really is he left with to hang on to? Staying with one author for a longer period has the advantage that he will most likely repeat himself more than once in different ways and thus by repetition in familiar contexts enhance the student's vocabulary learning at a crucial stage. And with a longer story as also with several more substantial pieces by an author there is more generous context in which to "place" words—there is simply a larger beginning, middle and end—and such latitude maximizes possibilities for discussion, oral practice and writing.

Introduction to Literature: a Method

Both for the student concluding formal foreign language study as well as for the one who might be going on, our editions suggest a method of how to approach an author. The *Introduction* combines critical insights, biographical background, and pointers on the work, to acquaint the student with what he is about to study.

The text itself is accompanied by a visible, *facing page vocabulary* (in addition to a complete End Vocabulary) for two reasons: (1) to facilitate rapid reading; and (2) to elucidate with more lexical information than mere ad hoc translations the significant "second year words" which students should be learning and remembering. Too often these words just appear translated as footnotes and little editorial effort is made to leave any solid impressions or lasting associations in the student's mind. If words are explained only by ad hoc, purely translational glossing, it will be sheer luck if the word is remembered later; but if a policy of thoughtful, explanatory word study is carried out, as attempted in this series (especially by emphasizing English cognates and related German words), the student has a decent chance to really master these words. The facing page word analysis can serve in its own right as valuable review material. And once a word has been glossed here it is not explained again later in order to stress the cumulative, day-to-day nature of vocabulary build-up.

On the facing pages are also found German *content questions* covering their respective text pages. These differ from the *discussion questions* (following the reading text) in that the former deal strictly with what is happening on a scene-to-scene, chapter-to-chapter basis, whereas the latter, phrased in English, cut across divisions within a work, or compare different works themselves, to deal with themes and message.

Themes, Design, Aims

A student beginning second year language study probably doesn't yet know whether he will go on, either in formal courses or perhaps by independent reading. Each volume in this series has been designed with such a student in mind, in the hope that the themes will catch his interest and the notes will help improve his German. In selecting works we have sought out authors and works with messages as well as those which only raise questions. Today's youth is admirably candid and honest. If we are to reach them, if we are to teach them, we might well turn our attention toward that which troubles our common world, rather than dealing with that which fascinates us alone.

Thus in choosing themes we strive to be *timely* in the truest sense of being *timeless*. Individual editors as well as general editor—by their very collaboration on this project—witness their desire to put the teachable as well as enjoyable into the foreign language classroom.

Acknowledgements

My personal word of thanks is due, firstly, to each of the editors of the individual volumes. They were all most cooperative in getting the material to me on time, and so courteous and friendly throughout the project.

At Holt I owe many thanks to many dedicated and respected publishing colleagues: to Doris Jacoby who worked so closely and so tirelessly with me in the beginning, and to Renate Hiller who saw our series to completion with meticulous care and artistic good taste. I would be remiss, however, were I not to express my gratitude to Eirik Børve, Foreign Language Editor of Rinehart Press, whose warmth and competence brought me into the Holt family and made a publishing house a home.

Honolulu, Hawaii   JOHN E. CREAN, JR.

PREFACE

The stories and poems in this anthology have been selected for students in intermediate German classes who have mastered the basic elements of the language and wish to read literary and timely texts.

The selections are reproduced in their entirety, as they appear in the authorized German editions. Vocabulary and cultural notes are presented on facing pages to facilitate reading. The end vocabulary is virtually complete, except for the usual omissions.

Content questions on the readings are also given on the facing pages, to assist student and teacher in the oral or written reconstruction of the main line of the story. Separate questions are contained in the "Topics for Discussion" section, designed to lead the class beyond pure factual reconstruction into a more subjective consideration of themes, patterns and style.

Sincere thanks are due to the Rowohlt Verlag, Hamburg–Reinbek for permission to reprint the selections. I am also indebted to Dr. John Crean of the Department of European Languages and Literature of the University of Hawaii, Honolulu, for his judicious and kind criticism. I am grateful to Mrs. Gerda Oldham, Miss Irmtraud Wiegel and Miss Cathy Nietsche for their aid in the preparation of the final manuscript.

Yellow Springs, Ohio   ANNA OTTEN

CONTENTS

INTRODUCTION

Wolfgang Borchert's work and life are fragments. He had the misfortune to be eighteen when World War II started. When it ended he was twenty-four, having spent in bleak misery the years that most men believe to be the most joyful and formative of their lives. Such was the fate of his generation, for whom the war years meant hell on earth. Borchert was one of a small number of survivors who found the words to express their experiences. Because of his empathy and skill, he became the spokesman for the millions sacrificed, cut off in the spring of their lives.

All of Borchert's major works bear the imprint of the war and reflect an anguished man, tried almost beyond endurance. Transcending the personal, they are authentic accounts of a generation in a war-time totalitarian state. The dehumanized Third Reich, where men were moved around like puppets on a string, is sketched clearly—a gigantic diabolical machine, an epitome of evil. Borchert's generation was torn from family and home, sent to the front to die in rain, mud or snow. Their lives were wasted. Borchert, who watched hundreds of them live and die in agony, saw the horrid spectacle as an absurdity. It is this impression that he conveys in his best prose works, at times using black humor to make the absurd happenings simultaneously tragic and comic, creating a panoramic view of a world out of joint, with puppet-men caught in its war-machine.

When Borchert was born on May 20, 1921, at Hamburg, his parents could not have foreseen a gloomy future for him. All seemed

1

to be reasonably secure. His father was an elementary school teacher, a quiet, dutiful man. To some, he seemed a bit too rigid and serious, the opposite of his wife. Borchert's mother, a lively, sociable young woman who had come from the village to the big city, had a talent for writing. She wrote stories about life in the country that appeared in magazines and were collected in a book entitled *Sünnroos*.

The boy had much more in common with his mother than with his father. It was she who encouraged him when, at fifteen, he began writing poetry, whereas his father did not spare him sober appraisals and stern criticism. The boy became very attached to his mother. In her presence he was happy, at ease, secure. When he was separated from her, life became bleak and insecure. (Later, at the most desperate moments of his life, he was to cry out for her.) Any love he might have born for women was overshadowed and foredoomed by this deep attachment for her.

Unable to form deep, lasting relationships with anyone except his mother, Borchert the boy and the young man can find only fleeting emotional attachments. These grip him and drain him of energy while they last; but knowing that they will come to an end, he flees, "steals away without farewell," and forever avoids commitment. The "Mother" will be a powerful figure in many guises throughout Borchert's works.

Perhaps the most ambivalent relationship was between father and son. Had the father been a tyrant, like Kafka's for example, the son might have rebelled. But the father was a meek man, unwilling to give directions and, in spite of his sickly constitution, always ready to help the son. Never would he have wished to shape Wolfgang's life. Yet, for the boy the keynote of their relationship was distrust and indifference. He speaks about the "gray, haggard man, my father," someone who had permissively said, "It is good, my boy," when he could have punished. In *Die Hundeblume* (1946) we hear about the father, "of whom he had never particularly taken notice." Whenever the "Father" is mentioned, he appears as the old, gray, helpless figure in whose presence the "Son" feels ill at ease or has a strange feeling of love-hate. This relationship is transferred to God, whom Borchert calls the "Good Lord," who—

if he exists—can do nothing for "his poor, poor children," as Borchert's father had been unable to help him.

For the parents the most trying situation arose when the 17-year-old Wolfgang left school to become an actor. Alarmed by the boy's adamant attitude and fearing the uncertain future of the theater, the parents exerted pressure, and succeeded in apprenticing him to a bookshop owner. Bored by the routine tasks of packing books, young Borchert took actor's training and tap dancing in secret and spent his free time in the company of other aesthetes, discussing contemporary expressionistic literature. He had written poetry since he was 15 and now, at 17, produced prodigiously, following such models as Rilke, Trakl, Benn and Lichtenstein. Given to brief outbursts of ecstasy in what might be termed his "Storm and Stress" period, he wrote down everything that came to his mind, not bothering about rhyme, grammar or syntax. (Later, in *Das ist unser Manifest*, 1947, he would write that he did not want poets "with good grammar." This reflects earlier debates with his father, whose constant criticism he had resented.) Not many of these poems were published, and not even Wolfgang's friends thought too highly of them. Nonetheless, the young man was convinced that he was a poet.

It was at this time, 1939, that Borchert felt separated from the middle-class world around him. His striving for Beauty, Purity and Greatness was no longer reconcilable with the practical bourgeois world bent on material gain and duty to daily tasks. This was confirmation of the artistic impulses that he had sought in the great poets. In addition, it was a confirmation of his own experience, for the rebellion against the father's world was Borchert's own: he was divided between the bourgeois and the artistic worlds in the same love-hatred that he felt for his father. He was also torn between reality and dream, will-to-stay and will-to-part.

At 19, the will-to-part prevails. He joins a traveling theater and traveling all over the Hannover province he enjoys "the best time" of his life as an actor. The euphoria lasts only three months; then he is drafted. It is May, 1941.

What had been vague discontent and longing for absolutes such as Beauty, suddenly assumes clear and concrete form when Borchert enters the army. From that time on, the rigid Third Reich and its dehumanizing impact were the target. He refused to submit, instead was outraged by the complacent bourgeoisie that tolerated such a political machine and by the ruthlessness with which the regime threw its resources into war. Military training struck him as a game with tin soldiers. When he was shipped to the front in blood-red freight cars that stank of cattle, he was nauseated. In the seemingly endless Russian plains, he felt lost. There he saw men falling like "puppets" cut off by an invisible player; or as ugly dark spots in the snow, "bags of rags" in the gleaming whiteness. His days at the front are spent in despair. Dying "for nothing" strikes him as grotesque. At times he fears he will lose his mind; at other times he is driven by a passion for life. Sometimes, to hide his tears, he bursts into bitter laughter. There is scarcely a moment of hope.

It cannot be said that the war and the sickness which subsequently forced him to his bed made Borchert a poet, for he had been one when he entered the army. Yet it is clear that he would not have found his own distinct substance and form without the war experience, and he would not have taken the time to write it down, had not the sickness forced him to rest.

In many of Borchert's stories, not much seems to happen. There is usually a lonely observer—an outsider, outcast or sufferer—who notes what he sees in all its horror. Often the underlying question "Why?" dominates all happenings and leads to an ecstatic outcry of despair. There is also subtle understatement, impotent gesture or desperate laughter (which Borchert uses more effectively than he uses tears). Some stories are gigantic canvasses of a vast sky and earth, where men move to and fro like miniature figures. Some march like thoughtless machines, others shoot automatically "when they see a head," a few look as if they were made of "wood and hunger." In *Vier Soldaten* (1946), a young man trembles so much that he breaks a lamp. Later, four soldiers sit in the cold night without a light, blue-lipped and clinging to their guns. As bullets whistle over their heads, they laugh—a mad, hopeless laughter in a world devoid of sense and hope. In *Der viele viele Schnee*, a sergeant hears a soldier laugh and sing on guard, and assumes that he is mad. The grotesque laughter echoes through the silent woods where the snow glides from the laden branches with a faint sound, like human sighs. The contrast of silent nature and mad, desperate laughter leaves a memorable impression.

In *Jesus macht nicht mehr mit* (1946), a man—the "measure of all things"—has to dig graves and then lie in them to see how they "fit." We learn that he must dig seven or eight graves each day, but that they "never fit." The soil is hard and frozen and the grave-digging soldier asks himself how the dead men can stand it, "even though they are dead." We soon realize that it is *he* who cannot stand it. One day he carefully puts down his shovel and leaves, stepping carefully over the heaped-up dead bodies, for he "does not want to awaken them." The absence of pathos makes this story grotesque, closer to satirical laughter than to tears.

In many of the war stories, a haunting memory is the leitmotif. In *Die Katze war im Schnee erfroren* (1947) it is a burning village, "a red spot in the winter night," that people cannot forget long after spring has come. In *Die lange lange Straße lang* (1947), a lieutenant cannot forget that he had been "responsible for 57 men who were buried at Woronesch." Beckmann, in the drama *Draußen vor der Tür* (1947), cannot find rest because 11 men for whom he was "responsible" had been killed. He wants to give the "Responsibility" back to his commanding officer and die. Grotesque laughter, a longing for "getting out of it all," haunting memories, and death wishes run like leitmotifs through most of Borchert's war stories. The vision is of destruction and meaningless slaughter in an indifferent universe, where God, "if he exists," is silent.

The horrifying experiences which led to these stories proved too much for the sensitive Borchert. It is said that he shot himself in the hand while on a mission so he would be sent home from the front. Letters were found that proved his hostility to the Third Reich and its army. He was put on trial, accused of self-mutilation. The prosecutor demanded his execution, but the Military Court condemned him only to 100 days in solitary confinement, (an experience described in *Die Hundeblume*). After his prison sentence was over, he was sent back to the front to prove that he was worthy of the "mild" punishment. The year was 1942; he was 21 years old.

In his letters from that time, Borchert appears to have become a much more mature man. Also, he had gained more self-confidence as one who was different from the herd. Physically, however, he was not too strong, and the stern Russian winter, for which the soldiers were poorly equipped, broke his health. He suffered from frozen feet, jaundice and spotted fever, and was sent to the infamous military hospital at Smolensk, described in *An diesem Dienstag* (1947). Although he survived and was sent home for a rest, he never really recovered.

From Smolensk, Borchert was sent to a hospital in Germany, where it became clear that he was no longer fit for active duty. It was decided that when he returned to the front he would work at a theater for soldiers. But on the evening before he was to go back Borchert mimicked and ridiculed the then Minister of Propaganda, Goebbels. Borchert was thereupon denounced, condemned as dangerous to the state and imprisoned in Berlin. (A description of the unhappy experience can be found in *Unser kleiner Mozart*, 1947).

In prison he was forced into living with a group, which he disliked, and was able to observe what monotony and hopelessness can do to the human mind. Released in September, 1944, he was returned to active duty.

Borchert spent the following few months at Jena, then traveled to Frankfurt am Main in the spring of 1945. Taken prisoner by the French, he escaped and walked the 600 kilometers to Hamburg, where he arrived sick and exhausted on May 10, just a few days after the official German surrender.

Post-war Hamburg was a city full of ruins and misery. Life was difficult for everyone, particularly those "gray phantoms" who wandered the streets, trying to find their families and jobs. Tired and discouraged by the war experience, post-war Germans wanted to return to social and economic stability, were eager to regain comfort and settle down in a secure routine, had little zeal for adventure or moral renewal. Borchert and many young men of his generation did not fit into this cautious, middle-class mold. They remained "outside" on the street, *Draußen vor der Tür*.

Borchert looked for work as an actor, joined a cabaret and soon after became co-founder of the theater "Die Komödie." When he was asked to assist the producer of *Nathan der Weise* at the "Hamburger Schauspielhaus," it became clear that he was unable to stand the strain of intensive work. Forced to give up all physical activity, he became a shut-in at home or in hospitals for the rest of his life.

Although Borchert was weak and in pain most of the time, his mind remained active and full of creative ideas. He turned to writing, but found that he no longer wanted to write poetry as he had done for years, particularly from 1940 to 1945. No longer could he write beautiful verse, about "*die blaue Blume*" of the Romantics. He needed to come to grips with the stark reality of life as he had experienced it. Nevertheless, there is still very much of the Romantic in the young man who turned to prose in 1946 and was to write all of his prose works in the next two years.

His first story, *Die Hundeblume*, is Romantic in the sense that it deals partly with vague longing and abstract concepts. But Borchert uses a different mode here than in his poetry. He now uses elegant language to describe grotesque occurrences and horrible prison life. Since we are used to this kind of language from the Romantic story, built on harmony of content and expression, Borchert's usage strikes us forcefully. It reflects the absurdity of prison life, where death is met with laughter, dignity turns out to be illusion in the mind of a madman, and common suffering breeds common hatred. Distortion and discord pervade the story so that it reads almost like a parody of the Romantic story, except for the end, where the harmony of Romantic thought and language is recovered, when the prisoner finds the final harmony of death in the maternal earth.

In subsequent stories Borchert moves even farther from his Romantic forebears. He knows that he has much to say, but little time to live. No longer does he wish mainly to write beautiful prose. This had been appropriate in *Die Hundeblume*, written in the contemplative mood of a healthy man shut off from life, a man for whom the hours moved slowly. In some of the stories that follow, the feverish and dissonant pace of life that Borchert had experienced during and shortly after the war is conveyed. Words are accumulated; they fall into place like puppets in a play; they move to form patterns, disperse, form new patterns. At times, they convey the hammering rhythm of machinegun fire or the rhythmic step of a solitary soldier on a deserted street. Many times they are condensed into the urgency of telegraphic style. At other times, they function in patterned repetition.

Borchert's language is varied. Rhetorical language alternates with slang. Local dialect is followed by poetic terms. Musical, harmonious words are juxtaposed with harsh-sounding expressions. Onomatopoetic sounds convey musical quality, as does the structure, when Borchert uses point-counterpoint. Verbal creations are frequent: unusual adjectival compounds, adjectives repeated in sequence and spelled together, whole chains of nouns linked in spelling. It is a highly personal style. Seemingly easy-flowing, it conveys the impression of an ongoing film.

Rarely does this "film" move slowly. Borchert's drama *Draußen vor der Tür* was written in eight hectic days of 1947. The play deals with Beckmann, one of the "gray phantoms" ("einer von *denen*") which wander the streets, one who comes home to a devastated city, to find that he has lost everything. He seeks death in the river, but is carried to the shore. When a young woman tries to help him, he moves deeper into despair and guilt, the latter stemming from the fact that during the war he had been responsible for eleven soldiers who were killed. Now Beckmann wants to give the "responsibility" back to his former colonel, a pleasant, good-humored man who is now a well-to-do citizen. Thinking that Beckmann has lost his mind, the ex-colonel laughs at him and sends him to a cabaret to tell his story so that he can amuse people. But the director of the cabaret, a clever businessman, does not want to employ a beginner. "What have you done so far?" he asks Beckmann. The answer is grotesque in its shortness: "Nothing. War: Was hungry. Was cold. Was shooting: War." Ill at ease, the

director dismisses the applicant. Outside, life is "gray and useless."
Finally, Beckmann goes "home to his mother," only to find that
his parents have committed suicide. The present tenant mourns the
loss of "so much gas, with which they could have cooked their
meals for a month." The callousness of the living and the indifference of "God who sleeps" enrages Beckmann. Falling asleep, he
has a dream. In it, God appears as a decrepit old man, lamenting
the fate of his "boy," his "poor boy." It is then that Beckmann
cries out his accusation: "Where were you, Lord, when the bombs
were falling . . . when eleven men were missing . . . were you at
Stalingrad, Dear Lord? Did you ever take good care of us? . . . We
called out for you. Lord! . . . Where are you?" The old man
cannot help Beckmann. He leaves his questions unanswered.

Though scarcely defined as an individual, Beckmann reflects the
fate of a whole generation unable to return to the bourgeois fold.
His questions were understood and shared by the many who felt as
Borchert did about the war. The play was a great success. When it
was performed as a radio play on February 13, 1947, it made
Borchert famous overnight.

Another "homecoming" is rendered in *Die lange lange Straße
lang*. Again, there is no home. The "gray phantom," Lieutenant
Fischer, wanders on the long, long street, passing places where
people watch football or listen to inspiring music. He reads inscrip-
tions as he passes and watches everyday occurrences. He wants to
catch the "streetcar" whose conductor very much resembles the
"Dear Lord" of *Draußen vor der Tür*. It is not clear whether the
conductor is good or evil: everyone has to pay for a ticket and
"nobody knows where the streetcar goes." All ends, again, with
open questions.

In *Eisenbahnen, nachmittags und nachts* (1946), the question begins
and underlies the story. Nobody knows where the railroads go;
they are simply "on the way." There are some stations along the
way called "brandy, God, bread or girls." We are the railroads,
some of our stations are known, but "nobody knows our heart."

Perhaps the clearest expression of the transitory character of
human life, particularly for Borchert's generation, is found in

Generation ohne Abschied (1946). This generation is "cast out of the security of childhood" into a hostile universe. It has to move on without a moment's respite or the blessing of love. Without farewell, it steals away.

The Borchert hero (or anti-hero, depending on the point-of-view) moves alone, an outcast without God, toward an unknown goal. He is always the same man, longing for love, home or rest in the maternal earth. This is expressed in *Im Mai, im Mai schrie der Kuckuck* (1947), one of Borchert's last stories. The voice of the bird is the poet's inner voice. It "screams for the mother," who "cast him into the world as a stranger among strangers." We are told that poets are outcasts who have no words to express the true nature of the world, no "rhyme for the rattle of a wounded lung," no verse for the sound of machine guns, no means of describing burning villages and "bloodstains in white human skin," no sentences for their "motherless misery." All they can do is "add, draw the sum, enumerate, note." His 200 pages of notes are only "a commentary to the 20,000 invisible pages, the Sisyphus-pages, for which we ignore words, grammar and symbols." All is a "grotesque ode" or a ridiculous epic of our world, our heart, our life.

Borchert's man is abandoned by his "Mother" and becomes the plaything of "God-Father." Whether the Lord is seen as conductor, Dear Lord or organ-grinder does not matter. Borchert's *danse macabre* is led by a boxer, followed by the rich man and the scientist. All are manipulated. When someone wants to revolt, he finds "no face to strike with his fist." Newborn babies lie in the cold, invalids wander the streets, outcasts lie in prison, wars are endlessly fought. Men question why this is so. They receive no answer. Since God, "if he exists," does not answer, all answers have to be sought on the human level.

Borchert's perspective is pessimistic. Only rarely is there a spark of hope, as when a suffering man rises above his fate, knowing it and accepting it. For Borchert (as for Camus), this acceptance is not mere resignation; it is victory, not defeat. In *Ching Ling die Fliege* he shows that man must stand above his fate and discover that "life is more a comedy than a tragedy." Man's struggle to stand above, to be stronger than his fate, underlies all of Borchert's prose works. When a journalist asked him a few days before his death which themes would not bore the contemporary reader, Borchert replied, "Themes about God or No-God, Bread or No-Bread."

Borchert died on November 20, 1947, in Basel, where he had sought a cure for his liver ailment. Although he had won recognition during the last two years of his life for his prose work, he assumed his stature in German letters after his death, a status that should remain as long as men are concerned about "God and Bread," freedom and rebellion, outsider and herd, war and peace—issues common to us all.

Gedichte

[1] **r Leuchtturm** light-house
[3] **r Dorsch** codfish
[6] **ein Schiff in Not** ship in distress

---

1. *Was möchte Borchert sein ?*
2. *Für wen will er es sein ?*
3. *Warum ist das so schwer ?*

Ich möchte Leuchtturm sein
in Nacht und Wind —
für Dorsch und Stint,
für jedes Boot —
5 und ich bin doch selbst
ein Schiff in Not!

s **Abendlied** evening song
[1] **ach** alas
[3] **träumen** to dream;   **sacht** softly, quietly
[4] **das kommt wohl von der dunklen Nacht** that must be because of the dark night
[12] **e Laterne** lantern
[15] **lichterloh brennen** to burn brightly, be ablaze

---

1. *Was soll das Kind tun ?*
2. *Was sagt der Dichter dem Kind über die Sonne ?*
3. *Warum muß die Laterne in der Nacht lichterloh brennen ?*
4. *Wie zeigt der Dichter, daß wir die dunkle Nacht fürchten ?*

ABENDLIED

Warum, ach sag, warum
geht nun die Sonne fort?
Schlaf ein, mein Kind, und träume sacht,
das kommt wohl von der dunklen Nacht,
5 da geht die Sonne fort.

Warum, ach sag, warum
wird unsere Stadt so still?
Schlaf ein, mein Kind, und träume sacht,
das kommt wohl von der dunklen Nacht,
10 weil sie dann schlafen will.

Warum, ach sag, warum
brennt die Laterne so?
Schlaf ein, mein Kind, und träume sacht,
das kommt wohl von der dunklen Nacht,
15 da brennt sie lichterloh!

Warum, ach sag, warum
gehn manche Hand in Hand?
Schlaf ein, mein Kind, und träume sacht,
das kommt wohl von der dunklen Nacht,
20 da geht man Hand in Hand.

Warum, ach sag, warum
ist unser Herz so klein?
Schlaf ein, mein Kind, und träume sacht,
das kommt wohl von der dunklen Nacht,
25 da sind wir ganz allein.

e **Muschel** shell
[1] **blank** bright, polished;   **bunt** colorful
[3] **schlank** slender, slim
[4] **rauschen** to murmur, 'rush'
[6] s **Museum** museum;   **glimmern** to shimmer
[7] r **Hafen** harbor;   e **Kneipe** pub
[10] **horchen** to listen

1. *Wie zeigt der Dichter, daß das Kind der Natur näher ist ?*
2. *Was für Muscheln findet das Kind ?*
3. *Was hört es in den Muscheln ?*
4. *Wo kann man Muscheln sehen ?*

MUSCHELN, MUSCHELN

Muscheln, Muscheln, blank und bunt,
findet man als Kind.
Muscheln, Muscheln, schlank und rund,
darin rauscht der Wind.

5 Darin singt das große Meer —
in Museen sieht man sie glimmern,
auch in alten Hafenkneipen
und in Kinderzimmern.

Muscheln, Muscheln, rund und schlank,
10 horch, was singt der Wind:
Muscheln, Muscheln, bunt und blank,
fand man einst als Kind!

[1] **grinsen** to grin; **glasiggrau** glassy-grey
[2] **s Geflute** tide-stream, flooding
[3] **dem alten Kabeljau ist recht gemischt zu Mute** the old codfish has mixed feelings (feels ill at ease)
[5] **verängstigt** scared; **zum Stalle streben** to press toward the stable; **s Seepferdchen** little sea horse
[6] **r Tintenfisch** squid; **voller Kunst** skillfully
[7] **alabastern** made of alabaster
[8] **zur Tarnung** (in order) to hide; **tintenblau** ink-blue; **r Dunst** haze, veil
[9] **ein·ziehen** to pull in
[10] **mit düsterem Geraune** with gloomy murmur
[11] **er brummt dazwischen (he)rein** he grumbles and throws in
[12] **r Klabautermann** bogeyman; **schlechte Laune haben** to be in a bad mood

1. Wie sieht das Meer vor dem Sturm aus?
2. Wohin fliehen die Fische?
3. Was tut der Tintenfisch?
4. Was machen die Fischer?

Prolog zu einem Sturm

Das Meer grinst grün und glasiggrau,
die Fische fliehn in tieferes Geflute.
Sogar dem alten Kabeljau
ist recht gemischt zu Mute.

5 Verängstigt strebt ein Seepferdchen zum Stalle.
Der Tintenfisch legt voller Kunst
um den Palast aus alabasterner Koralle
zur Tarnung einen tintenblauen Dunst.

Die Fischer ziehn die Netze ein
10 mit düsterem Geraune —
und einer brummt dazwischen rein:
Klabautermann hat schlechte Laune.

e Großstadt metropolis
1 **e Göttin** goddess;   **aus·spucken** to spit out
2 **wüst** desolate
3 **r Atem** breath;   **ein·schlucken** to swallow (down)
5 **e Hure** prostitute, 'whore';   **zu·plinken** (+ *dat.*) to wink at
6 **verderbt** corrupt(ed)
7 **e Lust** joy;   **s Leid** sorrow;   **hinken** to (walk with a) limp
8 **s Erbarmen** pity
11 **r Schoß** lap
12 **orgeln** to play (on) the organ

_____

1. Wie sieht der Dichter die Großstadt ?
2. Wie lebt der Mensch in der großen Stadt ?
3. Was tut sie, wenn wir müde sind ?
4. Was macht der Wind ?

GROSSSTADT

Die Göttin Großstadt hat uns ausgespuckt
in dieses wüste Meer von Stein.
Wir haben ihren Atem eingeschluckt,
dann ließ sie uns allein.

5 Die Hure Großstadt hat uns zugeplinkt —
an ihren weichen und verderbten Armen
sind wir durch Lust und Leid gehinkt
und wollten kein Erbarmen.

Die Mutter Großstadt ist uns mild und groß —
10 und wenn wir leer und müde sind,
nimmt sie uns in den grauen Schoß —
und ewig orgelt über uns der Wind!

r **Kuß** kiss
[2] **erzittern** to tremble
[4] **naß** wet;   **zerknittert** wrinkled
[5] **verächtlich** contemptuous;   **hochgeschoben** pushed up
[7] r **Regentropfen** rain drop;   **zerstieben** (r **Staub** dust) to disperse, scatter
[10] **sinnlos** without reasoning (*here:* sensuously);   **selig** blissful
[11] r **Heiligenschein** halo;   **zerwühlen** to dishevel
[12] **sich ein·spinnen** to form a cocoon (*here:* lantern light reflected in rain drops spins imaginary cocoons in the girl's hair)

---

1. *Was merkt die Frau nicht, weil sie glücklich ist ?*
2. *Wie ist ihr Kleid ?*
3. *Was ist mit dem Regentropfen geschehen ?*
4. *Wie fühlt sich die Frau ?*

DER KUSS

Es regnet — doch sie merkt es kaum,
weil noch ihr Herz vor Glück erzittert:
Im Kuß versank die Welt im Traum.
Ihr Kleid ist naß und ganz zerknittert

5 und so verächtlich hochgeschoben,
als wären ihre Knie für alle da.
Ein Regentropfen, der zu Nichts zerstoben,
der hat gesehn, was niemand sonst noch sah.

So tief hat sie noch nie gefühlt —
10 so sinnlos selig müssen Tiere sein!
Ihr Haar ist wie zu einem Heiligenschein zerwühlt —
Laternen spinnen sich drin ein.

r **Abschied** departure, farewell
[1] r **Kai** quay, pier
[3] **stromabwärts** down-stream
[6] **sich entfernen** to draw away

---

1. *Wo nehmen die beiden Menschen Abschied ?*
2. *Wohin fährt das Schiff ?*
3. *Was sieht man noch eine Weile ?*

ABSCHIED

Das war ein letzter Kuß am Kai —
vorbei.

Stromabwärts und dem Meere zu
fährst du.

5 Ein rotes und ein grünes Licht
entfernen sich . . .

² **r Graben** moat, ditch
⁴ **j-em etw. bei·bringen** to teach s.t. to s.o.
⁹ **s Kalb** calf;   **springen** to jump
¹² **r Fliederbusch** lilac bush;   **r Rasen** lawn
¹⁴ **duften** to smell fragrantly

---

1. Was tut der liebe Gott im Graben ?
2. Was macht er im Stalle ?
3. Weshalb wohnt er auch im Fliederbusch ?

KINDERLIED

Wo wohnt der liebe Gott?
Im Graben, im Graben!
Was macht er da?
Er bringt den Fischlein 's Schwimmen bei,
5 damit sie auch was haben.

Wo wohnt der liebe Gott?
Im Stalle, im Stalle!
Was macht er da?
Er bringt dem Kalb das Springen bei,
10 damit es niemals falle.

Wo wohnt der liebe Gott?
Im Fliederbusch am Rasen!
Was macht er da?
Er bringt ihm wohl das Duften bei
15 für unsre Menschennasen.

e **Erinnerung** remembrance;   e **Hohen Bleichen** name of a street in Hamburg (high bleaching ground, a place once used for drying laundry in the sun)

[1] **weitab** far away;   r **Lärm** noise;   e **Gegenwart** present time

[2] r **Verfall** decay;   **umwittern** to smell of;   **ruhmreich** famous

[3] **rings** all around;   **verstaubt** = **mit Staub bedeckt**

[4] **kokett** flirtatious;   e **Biedermeiertasse** old fashioned cup, in plain style of early 19th century (Victorian)

[5] **darüber wuchtet bleich ein Imperator** above there towers palely an emperor

[6] **doch seiner Büste Würde ist gegipst** but the noble bearing of his bust is made of plaster

[7] **aus·stopfen** to stuff

[8] **beschwipst** (*coll.*) intoxicated

[9] r **Kienspanhalter** stick to hold pine splinters (for lighting purposes);   **Karl der Weise** Charles (V) The Wise (1337–1380), King of France

[10] **blinken** to gleam;   r **Bauch** belly;   e **Falte** wrinkle, 'fold'

[11] e **Zopfperücke** tie-wig;   **leise** slight

[12] **verführerisch** fascinating;   r **Puderhauch** slight odor of powder

[13] **malaiisch** Malayan;   **glotzen** to stare;   **hölzern starre Züge** woodenly rigid facial features

[14] r **Götze** idol;   **fahl** dimly, 'pale';   **erglimmen** to glow faintly;   r **Mulatte** mulatto

[15] **verrosten** to rust;   e **Waffe** weapon

[16] **klirren** to clash, clang;   **weich** soft, gentle

[17] r **Totenwurm** death-watch beetle;   e **Barockkommode** baroque chest (of drawers)

[18] **aus·dörren** to dry up

[19] **betrübt** depressed;   **summen** to hum, buzz;   e **Fliege** fly

[20] **hocken** to squat;   **Arthur Schopenhauer** (1788–1860) German philosopher;   **Schopenhauers dreizehn Bände** the thirteen volumes of Schopenhauer's works

---

1. Wo stehen die Biedermeiertassen ?
2. Was für Augen hat der Südseealligator ?
3. Wie riecht die Zopfperücke ?
4. Weswegen ist die Fliege betrübt ?

ANTIQUITÄTEN

Erinnerung an die Hohen Bleichen

Weitab vom Lärm der großen Gegenwart,
verfallumwittert, ruhmreich und verlassen,
stehn stille Dinge rings, verstaubt, apart
ein paar kokette Biedermeiertassen.

5 Darüber wuchtet bleich ein Imperator,
doch seiner Büste Würde ist gegipst.
Ein ausgestopfter Südseealligator
grinst glasig grünen Auges wie beschwipst.

Der bronzne Kienspanhalter Karls des Weisen
10 blinkt über Buddhas Bauch und seinen Falten.
Die Zopfperücke hat noch einen leisen
verführerischen Puderhauch behalten.

Malaiisch glotzt mit hölzern starren Zügen
ein Götze. Fahl erglimmen Zähne von Mulatten.
15 Verrostet träumen Waffen von den Kriegen
und klirren leis in Rembrandts weichem Schatten.

Der Totenwurm in der Barockkommode
tickt zeitlos in den ausgedörrten Wänden.
Betrübt summt eine Fliege ihre Ode —
20 das macht, sie hockt auf Schopenhauers dreizehn
                          Bänden.

5 r große Buchstabe capital letter
6 e Brille eyeglasses;   r Rand rim
8 e Tafel blackboard
10 Der Alte Fritz Frederick the Great (1712–1786), King of Prussia;   r Trinkbecher drinking cup
11 s Blech tin;   die Dicke Berta "Fat Berta," howitzer used in World War I;   bis to
13 e Zungenspitze tip of the tongue;   an·stoßen to nudge
15 e Grube ditch
16 r Haken check mark, 'hook'
17 r Satz sentence;   sauber neat(ly)
19 r Schulhof school playgrounds;   e Nebelkrähe hooded crow;   weggeworfen thrown away
21 befehlen (zu) to order (to appear before)
22 r Schal scarf;   ab·nehmen to take off
24 sowas (coll.) = so etwas such things
26 Da kommen Sie nicht mit durch. You won't get away with it.
27 an etw. (acc.) gewöhnt sein to be accustomed to s.t.
28 glatt without ado;   j-en stehen lassen to let s.o. cool his heels;   r Hauptmann captain
29 verwundet wounded

---

1. Wo sind die Mädchen?
2. Was üben die Kinder?
3. Wie schreibt Ulla das Wort "Krieg"?
4. Was denkt sie über die Lehrerin?
5. Wohin wird Leutnant Ehlers gerufen?
6. Was wird ihm befohlen?
7. Was erfahren wir über die zweite Kompanie?

An diesem Dienstag

Die Woche hat einen Dienstag.
Das Jahr ein halbes Hundert.
Der Krieg hat viele Dienstage.

An diesem Dienstag
5 übten sie in der Schule die großen Buchstaben. Die Lehrerin hatte
eine Brille mit dicken Gläsern. Die hatten keinen Rand. Sie waren
so dick, daß die Augen ganz leise aussahen.
Zweiundvierzig Mädchen saßen vor der schwarzen Tafel und schrieben mit großen Buchstaben:
10 DER ALTE FRITZ HATTE EINEN TRINKBECHER AUS
BLECH. DIE DICKE BERTA SCHOSS BIS PARIS. IM KRIEGE
SIND ALLE VÄTER SOLDAT.
Ulla kam mit der Zungenspitze bis an die Nase. Da stieß die Lehrerin sie an. Du hast Krieg mit ch geschrieben, Ulla. Krieg wird
15 mit g geschrieben. G wie Grube. Wie oft habe ich das schon gesagt.
Die Lehrerin nahm ein Buch und machte einen Haken hinter Ullas
Namen. Zu morgen schreibst du den Satz zehnmal ab, schön sauber,
verstehst du? Ja, sagte Ulla und dachte: Die mit ihrer Brille.
Auf dem Schulhof fraßen die Nebelkrähen das weggeworfene Brot.

20 An diesem Dienstag
wurde Leutnant Ehlers zum Bataillonskommandeur befohlen.
Sie müssen den roten Schal abnehmen, Herr Ehlers.
Herr Major?
Doch, Ehlers. In der Zweiten ist sowas nicht beliebt.
25 Ich komme in die zweite Kompanie?
Ja, und die lieben sowas nicht. Da kommen Sie nicht durch. Die
Zweite ist an das Korrekte gewöhnt. Mit dem roten Schal läßt die
Kompanie Sie glatt stehen. Hauptmann Hesse trug sowas nicht.
Ist Hesse verwundet?

[1] **nee** (*coll.*) = **nein** no;   **sich melden** to report
[2] **flau** slack
[3] **na ja** oh well
[4] **fertig werden** to make out, manage well
[5] **erziehen** to train
[6] **türlich** = **natürlich**
[7] **vorsichtig** careful
[8] **anständig** respectable;   **r Scharfschütze** sharpshooter;   **r Zeigefinger** index finger, trigger-finger
[9] **jucken** to itch;   **s Glühwürmchen** glow worm;   **herum·schwirren** to fly about; **vorig** last
[10] **r Kopfschuß** head wound
[14] **an·stecken** to light
[18] **Severinchen** diminutive of family name (endearment)
[20] **rauchen** to smoke;   **knabbern** to nibble
[21] **r Handschuh** glove;   **e Jungens** (*coll.*) the "boys"
[22] **draußen** out there
[23] **Hölderlin, Friedrich** (1770–1843) German poet
[24] **r Unsinn** nonsense;   **freundlich** cheerful
[30] **e Bahre** stretcher;   **e Entlausungsanstalt** delousing center
[34] **scheren** to shear;   **r Sanitäter** medical orderly
[35] **s Spinnenbein** spiderleg;   **r Knöchel** knuckle;   **ab·reiben** to rub (down)
[36] **e Apotheke** pharmacy

---

1. *Was hören wir über Hauptmann Hesse ?*

Nee, er hat sich krank gemeldet. Fühlte sich nicht gut, sagte er. Seit er Hauptmann ist, ist er ein bißchen flau geworden, der Hesse. Versteh ich nicht. War sonst immer so korrekt. Na ja, Ehlers, sehen Sie zu, daß Sie mit der Kompanie fertig werden. Hesse hat die Leute gut
5 erzogen. Und den Schal nehmen Sie ab, klar?
Türlich, Herr Major.
Und passen Sie auf, daß die Leute mit den Zigaretten vorsichtig sind. Da muß ja jedem anständigen Scharfschützen der Zeigefinger jucken, wenn er diese Glühwürmchen herumschwirren sieht. Vorige
10 Woche hatten wir fünf Kopfschüsse. Also passen Sie ein bißchen auf, ja?
Jawohl, Herr Major.
Auf dem Wege zur zweiten Kompanie nahm Leutnant Ehlers den roten Schal ab. Er steckte ein Zigarette an. Kompanieführer Ehlers,
15 sagte er laut.
Da schoß es.

An diesem Dienstag
sagte Herr Hansen zu Fräulein Severin:
Wir müssen dem Hesse auch mal wieder was schicken, Severinchen.
20 Was zu rauchen, was zu knabbern. Ein bißchen Literatur. Ein Paar Handschuhe oder sowas. Die Jungens haben einen verdammt schlechten Winter draußen. Ich kenne das. Vielen Dank.
Hölderlin vielleicht, Herr Hansen?
Unsinn, Severinchen, Unsinn. Nein, ruhig ein bißchen freundlicher.
25 Wilhelm Busch oder so. Hesse war doch mehr für das Leichte. Lacht doch gern, das wissen Sie doch. Mein Gott, Severinchen, was kann dieser Hesse lachen!
Ja, das kann er, sagte Fräulein Severin.

An diesem Dienstag
30 trugen sie Hauptmann Hesse auf einer Bahre in die Entlausungsanstalt. An der Tür war ein Schild:
OB GENERAL, OB GRENADIER:
DIE HAARE BLEIBEN HIER.
Er wurde geschoren. Der Sanitäter hatte lange dünne Finger. Wie
35 Spinnenbeine. An den Knöcheln waren sie etwas gerötet. Sie rieben ihn mit etwas ab, das roch nach Apotheke. Dann fühlten die Spinnenbeine nach seinem Puls und schrieben in ein dickes Buch: Tem-

[1] **ohne Besinnung** unconscious;   **Fleckfieberverdacht** suspected of Typhus ('spotted fever')

[2] **s Seuchenlazarett** isolation hospital;   **Smolensk** industrial city in USSR

[4] **r Träger** stretcherbearer;   **heraus·pendeln** to roll outside

[5] **hin und her** back and forth;   **e Stufe** step

[6] **r Russe** Russian

[7] **r Schnupfen** headcold

[10] **wedeln** to wave

[11] **40 Grad Kälte** 40° below zero

[12] **neun . . . gedauert** it took the letter nine days to come

[15] **die Jungs** dialect for **die Jungen**

[17] **r Oberfeldarzt** head medical officer;   **r Chefarzt** senior medical officer

[20] **scheußlich** horrible

[24] **e Zauberflöte** The Magic Flute, opera by W. A. Mozart (1756–1791)

[27] **etw. durch·halten** to endure s.t.

[28] **r Unterarzt** junior surgeon

[29] **krumm** bent over;   **s Rußland** Russia

[31] **sich schämen** to be ashamed

[33] **poltern** to rattle

[34] **bumsen** to bang, bump

[35] **hin·legen** to put down

---

1. Was müssen die Sanitäter tun ?
2. Was schreiben sie über Hauptmann Hesse in ihr Buch ?
3. Weshalb freut sich Frau Hesse über den Brief ?
4. Warum kann sich die Nachbarin nicht auch freuen ?
5. Wo befindet sich das Seuchenlazarett ?
6. Was schreibt Schwester Elisabeth an ihre Eltern ?
7. Was erfahren wir über den Unterarzt ?
8. Warum will er Hauptmann Hesse nichts mehr geben ?

peratur 41,6. Puls 116. Ohne Besinnung. Fleckfieberverdacht. Der
Sanitäter machte das dicke Buch zu. Seuchenlazarett Smolensk
stand da drauf. Und darunter: Vierzehnhundert Betten.
Die Träger nahmen die Bahre hoch. Auf der Treppe pendelte sein
5 Kopf aus den Decken heraus und immer hin und her bei jeder Stufe.
Und kurzgeschoren. Und dabei hatte er immer über die Russen ge-
lacht. Der eine Träger hatte Schnupfen.

An diesem Dienstag
klingelte Frau Hesse bei ihrer Nachbarin. Als die Tür aufging,
10 wedelte sie mit dem Brief. Er ist Hauptmann geworden. Hauptmann und Kompaniechef, schreibt er. Und sie haben über 40 Grad
Kälte. Neun Tage hat der Brief gedauert. An Frau Hauptmann
Hesse hat er oben drauf geschrieben.
Sie hielt den Brief hoch. Aber die Nachbarin sah nicht hin. 40 Grad
15 Kälte, sagte sie, die armen Jungs. 40 Grad Kälte.

An diesem Dienstag
fragte der Oberfeldarzt den Chefarzt des Seuchenlazarettes Smolensk: Wieviel sind es jeden Tag?
Ein halbes Dutzend.
20 Scheußlich, sagte der Oberfeldarzt.
Ja, scheußlich, sagte der Chefarzt.
Dabei sahen sie sich nicht an.

An diesem Dienstag
spielten sie die Zauberflöte. Frau Hesse hatte sich die Lippen rot
25 gemacht.

An diesem Dienstag
schrieb Schwester Elisabeth an ihre Eltern: Ohne Gott hält man
das gar nicht durch. Aber als der Unterarzt kam, stand sie auf.
Er ging so krumm, als trüge er ganz Rußland durch den Saal.
30 Soll ich ihm noch was geben? fragte die Schwester.
Nein, sagte der Unterarzt. Er sagte das so leise, als ob er sich
schämte.
Dann trugen sie Hauptmann Hesse hinaus. Draußen polterte es.
Die bumsen immer so. Warum können sie die Toten nicht langsam
35 hinlegen. Jedesmal lassen sie sie so auf die Erde bumsen. Das sagte

[2] **zicke zacke juppheidi** colloquial expressions evoking smart and dashing behavior
[3] **schneidig** dashing
[6] **stolpern** to stumble
[9] **malen** to print; **s Schreibheft** copy book

einer. Und sein Nachbar sang leise:
                    Zicke zacke juppheidi
                    Schneidig ist die Infanterie.
Der Unterarzt ging von Bett zu Bett. Jeden Tag. Tag und Nacht.
5 Tagelang. Nächte durch. Krumm ging er. Er trug ganz Rußland
durch den Saal. Draußen stolperten zwei Krankenträger mit einer
leeren Bahre davon. Nummer 4, sagte der eine. Er hatte Schnupfen.

An diesem Dienstag
saß Ulla abends und malte in ihr Schreibheft mit großen Buch-
10 staben:
            IM KRIEG SIND ALLE VÄTER SOLDAT.
            IM KRIEG SIND ALLE VÄTER SOLDAT.
Zehnmal schrieb sie das. Mit großen Buchstaben. Und Krieg mit
G. Wie Grube.

e Ratte rat
1 hohl hollow, empty; vereinsamt isolated; gähnen to yawn
2 s Staubgewölk dust cloud; flimmern to shimmer; steilgereckt erect
3 r Schornsteinrest remains of a chimney; e Schuttwüste desert of rubble; dösen
  to doze
4 mit einmal all at once
6 blinzeln to peek
7 ärmlich shabbily; behost (e Hosen) clad in pants
8 krumm bowlegged
9 s Geblinzel peek
10 r Korb basket
13 s Haargestrüpp thicket of hair
16 r Stock stick
17 mutig courageous(ly)
18 auf etw. (acc.) auf·passen to watch out for s.t.
20 ab·setzen to set down; wischen to wipe
21 r Hosenboden seat of trousers; hin und her back and forth
22 verächtlich contemptuously
28 zu·klappen to snap shut
29 Pah! exclamation expressing slight disdain; geringschätzig disdainfully
30 s Kaninchenfutter rabbit food
31 Donnerwetter! What do you know!; verwundert astonished; ein fixer Kerl a
  clever fellow

---

1. Um welche Tageszeit spielt sich die Geschichte ab?
2. Wo ist der Junge?
3. Warum kommt der Mann dorthin?
4. Weswegen hat der Junge einen Stock?
5. Wie findet der Mann heraus, daß der Junge intelligent ist?

Nachts schlafen die Ratten doch

Das hohle Fenster in der vereinsamten Mauer gähnte blaurot voll früher Abendsonne. Staubgewölke flimmerte zwischen den steilgereckten Schornsteinresten. Die Schuttwüste döste.

Er hatte die Augen zu. Mit einmal wurde es noch dunkler. Er
5 merkte, daß jemand gekommen war und nun vor ihm stand, dunkel, leise. Jetzt haben sie mich! dachte er. Aber als er ein bißchen blinzelte, sah er nur zwei etwas ärmlich behoste Beine. Die standen ziemlich krumm vor ihm, daß er zwischen ihnen hindurchsehen konnte. Er riskierte ein kleines Geblinzel an den Hosenbeinen hoch und erkannte
10 einen älteren Mann. Der hatte ein Messer und einen Korb in der Hand. Und etwas Erde an den Fingerspitzen.

Du schläfst hier wohl, was? fragte der Mann und sah von oben auf das Haargestrüpp herunter. Jürgen blinzelte zwischen den Beinen des Mannes hindurch in die Sonne und sagte: Nein, ich schlafe nicht.
15 Ich muß hier aufpassen. Der Mann nickte: So, dafür hast du wohl den großen Stock da?

Ja, antwortete Jürgen mutig und hielt den Stock fest.

Worauf paßt du denn auf?

Das kann ich nicht sagen. Er hielt die Hände fest um den Stock.
20 Wohl auf Geld, was? Der Mann setzte den Korb ab und wischte das Messer an seinem Hosenboden hin und her.

Nein, auf Geld überhaupt nicht, sagte Jürgen verächtlich. Auf ganz etwas anderes.

Na, was denn?
25 Ich kann es nicht sagen. Was anderes eben.

Na, denn nicht, dann sage ich dir natürlich auch nicht, was ich hier im Korb habe. Der Mann stieß mit dem Fuß an den Korb und klappte das Messer zu.

Pah, kann mir denken, was in dem Korb ist, meinte Jürgen gering-
30 schätzig, Kaninchenfutter.

Donnerwetter, ja! sagte der Mann verwundert, bist ja ein fixer Kerl. Wie alt bist du denn?

41

[2] **Oha!** exclamation; *here:* admiration
[8] **stimmen** to be correct;   **s Kaninchen** rabbit
[13] **immerzu** = **die ganze Zeit**
[15] **r Sonnabend** Saturday;   **flüstern** to whisper
[18] **e Blechschachtel** tin box
[20] **an·fassen** to clutch;   **zaghaft** timidly;   **ich drehe** I roll (my own cigarettes)
[23] **an·sehen** to look at;   **vor allem** especially
[24] **aus·suchen** to choose
[27] **sich auf·richten** to straighten up
[28] **schade** it's a shame;   **um·drehen** to turn around
[29] **verraten** to betray
[38] **auf etw.** (*acc.*) **zeigen** to point at s.t.
[39] **zusammengesackt** collapsed;   **eine Bombe kriegen** to get bombed

---

1. *Wie alt ist der Junge?*
2. *Was hat das Kind zu essen?*
3. *Was erzählt der Mann über die Kaninchen?*
4. *Weshalb ist der Kleine plötzlich bereit zu sagen, warum er aufpassen muß?*
5. *Was sagt er über die Ratten?*

Neun.

Oha, denk mal an, neun also. Dann weißt du ja auch, wieviel drei mal neun sind, wie?

Klar, sagte Jürgen und um Zeit zu gewinnen, sagte er noch: Das ist ja ganz leicht. Und er sah durch die Beine des Mannes hindurch. Dreimal neun, nicht? fragte er noch mal, siebenundzwanzig. Das wußte ich gleich.

Stimmt, sagte der Mann, genau soviel Kaninchen habe ich.

Jürgen machte einen runden Mund: Siebenundzwanzig?

Du kannst sie sehen. Viele sind noch ganz jung. Willst du?

Ich kann doch nicht. Ich muß doch aufpassen, sagte Jürgen unsicher.

Immerzu? fragte der Mann, nachts auch?

Nachts auch. Immerzu. Immer. Jürgen sah an den krummen Beinen hoch. Seit Sonnabend schon, flüsterte er.

Aber gehst du denn gar nicht nach Hause? Du mußt doch essen.

Jürgen hob einen Stein hoch. Da lag ein halbes Brot. Und eine Blechschachtel.

Du rauchst? fragte der Mann, hast du denn eine Pfeife?

Jürgen faßte seinen Stock fest an und sagte zaghaft: Ich drehe. Pfeife mag ich nicht.

Schade, der Mann bückte sich zu seinem Korb, die Kaninchen hättest du ruhig mal ansehen können. Vor allem die Jungen. Vielleicht hättest du dir eines ausgesucht. Aber du kannst hier ja nicht weg.

Nein, sagte Jürgen traurig, nein, nein.

Der Mann nahm den Korb und richtete sich auf. Na ja, wenn du hierbleiben mußt — schade. Und er drehte sich um. Wenn du mich nicht verrätst, sagte Jürgen da schnell, es ist wegen den Ratten.

Die krummen Beine kamen einen Schritt zurück: Wegen den Ratten?

Ja, die essen doch von Toten. Von Menschen. Da leben sie doch von.

Wer sagt das?

Unser Lehrer.

Und du paßt nun auf die Ratten auf? fragte der Mann.

Auf die doch nicht! Und dann sagte er ganz leise: Mein Bruder, der liegt nämlich da unten. Da. Jürgen zeigte mit dem Stock auf die zusammengesackten Mauern. Unser Haus kriegte eine Bombe. Mit

² **erst vier** just four
⁷ **aus·sehen** to look;   **müde** tired
¹³ **e Kuhle** hole;   **r Schutt** debris
¹⁶ **füttern** to feed
¹⁷ **ab·holen** to call for, pick up
¹⁹ **lauter** just plain
²² **weg·steigen** to climb away;   **r Mauerrest** remains of a wall
²³ **ein·packen** to pack up (and leave)
²⁴ **kriegen** (*coll.*) to get
²⁸ **r Kaninchenstall** rabbit hutch
³¹ **bestimmt** for sure;   **s Brett** board
³² **e Kiste** crate
³³ **auf etw.** (*acc.*) **zu·laufen** to walk towards s.t.
³⁶ **schwenken** to swing;   **aufgeregt** excitedly

---

1. Was erfahren wir über seine Familie?
2. Wie überzeugt ihn der Mann, daß er nachts nicht aufzupassen braucht?
3. Unter welcher Bedingung ist Jürgen bereit später wegzugehen?
4. Warum will der Mann mit Jürgens Vater sprechen?
5. Weshalb hört der Mann die letzten Worte des Jungen nicht mehr?
6. Welche Farbe hat das Kaninchenfutter?

einmal war das Licht weg im Keller. Und er auch. Wir haben noch
gerufen. Er war viel kleiner als ich. Erst vier. Er muß hier ja noch
sein. Er ist doch viel kleiner als ich.

Der Mann sah von oben auf das Haargestrüpp. Aber dann sagte
5 er plötzlich: Ja, hat euer Lehrer euch denn nicht gesagt, daß die
Ratten nachts schlafen?

Nein, flüsterte Jürgen und sah mit einmal ganz müde aus, das hat
er nicht gesagt.

Na, sagte der Mann, das ist aber ein Lehrer, wenn er das nicht mal
10 weiß. Nachts schlafen die Ratten doch. Nachts kannst du ruhig
nach Hause gehen. Nachts schlafen sie immer. Wenn es dunkel
wird, schon.

Jürgen machte mit seinem Stock kleine Kuhlen in den Schutt.

Lauter kleine Betten sind das, dachte er, alles kleine Betten. Da
15 sagte der Mann (und seine krummen Beine waren ganz unruhig
dabei): Weißt du was? Jetzt füttere ich schnell meine Kaninchen
und wenn es dunkel wird, hole ich dich ab. Vielleicht kann ich eins
mitbringen. Ein kleines oder, was meinst du?

Jürgen machte kleine Kuhlen in den Schutt. Lauter kleine Kanin-
20 chen. Weiße, graue, weißgraue. Ich weiß nicht, sagte er leise und sah
auf die krummen Beine, wenn sie wirklich nachts schlafen.

Der Mann stieg über die Mauerreste weg auf die Straße. Natürlich,
sagte er von da, euer Lehrer soll einpacken, wenn er das nicht mal weiß.

Da stand Jürgen auf und fragte: Wenn ich eins kriegen kann?
25 Ein weißes vielleicht?

Ich will mal versuchen, rief der Mann schon im Weggehen, aber
du mußt hier solange warten. Ich gehe dann mit dir nach Hause,
weißt du? Ich muß deinem Vater doch sagen, wie so ein Kaninchenstall gebaut wird. Denn das müßt ihr ja wissen.

30 Ja, rief Jürgen, ich warte. Ich muß ja noch aufpassen, bis es dunkel
wird. Ich warte bestimmt. Und er rief: Wir haben auch noch Bretter
zu Hause. Kistenbretter, rief er.

Aber das hörte der Mann schon nicht mehr. Er lief mit seinen
krummen Beinen auf die Sonne zu. Die war schon rot vom Abend
35 und Jürgen konnte sehen, wie sie durch die Beine hindurchschien,
so krumm waren sie. Und der Korb schwenkte aufgeregt hin und
her. Kaninchenfutter war da drin. Grünes Kaninchenfutter, das war
etwas grau vom Schutt.

¹ **r Kegler** bowler
² **e Kugel** ball
³ **r Kegel** bowling pin
⁵ **e Kegelbahn** bowling alley;   **donnern** to thunder
⁸ **geräumig** spacious;   **gemütlich** comfortable;   **s Grab** grave;   **aus·halten** to endure
⁹ **s Gewehr** gun;   **erfinden** to invent
¹² **auf j-en schießen** to shoot at s.o.
¹³ **befehlen** to command
¹⁴ **erschießen** to shoot dead
¹⁵ **belohnen** to reward
¹⁷ **ab** away
¹⁸ **heraus·kucken** (*coll.*) (kucken = gucken) to peep out
²⁵ **kaputt** *here:* shot off
³² **allmählich** gradually
³⁵ **davon** from that;   **auf·wachen** to wake up

---

1. *Wer sind die Kegler, die Kugel und die Kegel ?*
2. *Woran erinnert das Loch in der Erde ?*
3. *Wofür ist das Gewehr erfunden worden ?*
4. *Auf wen schießen die beiden Männer ?*
5. *Warum schießen sie auf ihn ?*

Wir sind die Kegler.
Und wir selbst sind die Kugel.
Aber wir sind auch die Kegel,
die stürzen.
5 Die Kegelbahn, auf der es donnert,
ist unser Herz.

Die Kegelbahn

Zwei Männer hatten ein Loch in die Erde gemacht. Es war ganz
geräumig und beinahe gemütlich. Wie ein Grab. Man hielt es aus.
Vor sich hatten sie ein Gewehr. Das hatte einer erfunden, damit
10 man damit auf Menschen schießen konnte. Meistens kannte man die
Menschen gar nicht. Man verstand nicht mal ihre Sprache. Und sie
hatten einem nichts getan. Aber man mußte mit dem Gewehr auf
sie schießen. Das hatte einer befohlen. Und damit man recht viele
von ihnen erschießen konnte, hatte einer erfunden, daß das Gewehr
15 mehr als sechzigmal in der Minute schoß. Dafür war er belohnt worden.
Etwas weiter ab von den beiden Männern war ein anderes Loch.
Da kuckte ein Kopf raus, der einem Menschen gehörte. Er hatte
eine Nase, die Parfum riechen konnte. Augen, die eine Stadt oder
20 eine Blume sehen konnten. Er hatte einen Mund, mit dem konnte
er Brot essen und Inge sagen oder Mutter. Diesen Kopf sahen die
beiden Männer, denen man das Gewehr gegeben hatte.
Schieß, sagte der eine.
Der schoß.
25 Da war der Kopf kaputt. Er konnte nicht mehr Parfum riechen,
keine Stadt mehr sehen und nicht mehr Inge sagen. Nie mehr.
Die beiden Männer waren viele Monate in dem Loch. Sie machten
viele Köpfe kaputt. Und die gehörten immer Menschen, die sie gar
nicht kannten. Die ihnen nichts getan hatten und die sie nicht mal
30 verstanden. Aber einer hatte das Gewehr erfunden, das mehr als
sechzigmal schoß in der Minute. Und einer hatte es befohlen.
Allmählich hatten die beiden Männer so viele Köpfe kaputt gemacht, daß man einen großen Berg daraus machen konnte. Und
wenn die beiden Männer schliefen, fingen die Köpfe an zu rollen.
35 Wie auf einer Kegelbahn. Mit leisem Donner. Davon wachten die
beiden Männer auf.
Aber man hat es doch befohlen, flüsterte der eine.

[2] **stöhnen** to groan
[3] **manchmal** sometimes;   **Spaß machen** to be fun
[6] **richtig Spaß** downright fun
[10] **e Entschuldigung** excuse;   **es gibt ihn nicht (es gibt** + *acc.* there is) he does not exist
[14] **uns gibt es** we do exist
[19] **mit etw. an·sitzen** to be stuck, saddled with s.t.
[21] **fertigmachen!** get ready!;   **los·gehen** to start up

---

1. *Wer ist verantwortlich ?*
2. *Was wäre die einzige Entschuldigung Gottes ?*
3. *Warum können die beiden Männer nicht schlafen ?*

Aber wir haben es getan, schrie der andere.

Aber es war furchtbar, stöhnte der eine.

Aber manchmal hat es auch Spaß gemacht, lachte der andere.

Nein, schrie der Flüsternde.

5 Doch, flüsterte der andere, manchmal hat es Spaß gemacht. Das ist es ja. Richtig Spaß.

Stunden saßen sie in der Nacht. Sie schliefen nicht. Dann sagte der eine:

Aber Gott hat uns so gemacht.

10 Aber Gott hat eine Entschuldigung, sagte der andere, es gibt ihn nicht.

Es gibt ihn nicht? fragte der erste.

Das ist seine einzige Entschuldigung, antwortete der zweite.

Aber uns — uns gibt es, flüsterte der erste.

15 Ja, uns gibt es, flüsterte der andere.

Die beiden Männer, denen man befohlen hatte, recht viele Köpfe kaputt zu machen, schliefen nicht in der Nacht. Denn die Köpfe machten leisen Donner.

Dann sagte der eine: Und wir sitzen nun damit an.

20 Ja, sagte der andere, wir sitzen nun damit an.

Da rief einer: Fertigmachen. Es geht wieder los.

Die beiden Männer standen auf und nahmen das Gewehr.

Und immer, wenn sie einen Menschen sahen, schossen sie auf ihn. Und immer war das ein Mensch, den sie gar nicht kannten. Und 25 der ihnen nichts getan hatte. Aber sie schossen auf ihn. Dazu hatte einer das Gewehr erfunden. Er war dafür belohnt worden.

Und einer — einer hatte es befohlen.

[3,4] *see p. 38,* glosses [2,3]

[6] **ich habe gelegen** I fell to the ground

[7] **e Straßenbahn** street car, trolley

[12] **Woronesch** city in Russia;   **keine Ahnung haben** to have no idea

[17] **rumpeln** to rumble;   **r Lastwagen** truck;   **e Tonne** barrel;   **s Kopfsteinpflaster** cobble stones

[18] **e Kanonenorgel** cannon-fire (The poet compares it to organ playing.)

[19] **hinterher = nachher**

[20] **r Autoschlosser** auto mechanic;   **r Beamte** civil servant;   **r Verkäufer** salesman; **r Friseur** barber

[21] **r Bauer** farmer;   **r Schuljunge** school boy

[27] **ne = eine;   e Null** zero

---

1. Wo ist Fischer?

2. Wohin will er gehen?

3. An wen denkt er?

4. Welche Berufe hatten die bei Woronesch begrabenen Soldaten?

Die lange lange Straße lang

Links zwei drei vier links zwei drei vier links zwei weiter, Fischer!
drei vier links zwei vorwärts, Fischer! schneidig, Fischer! drei vier
atme, Fischer! weiter, Fischer, immer weiter zickezacke zwei drei
vier schneidig ist die Infantrie zickezackejuppheidi schneidig ist die
5 Infantrie die Infantrie — — —
Ich bin unterwegs. Zweimal hab ich schon gelegen. Ich will zur
Straßenbahn. Ich muß mit. Zweimal hab ich schon gelegen. Ich hab
Hunger. Aber mit muß ich. Muß. Ich muß zur Straßenbahn. Ich
muß mit. Zweimal hab ich schon drei vier links zwei drei vier aber
10 mit muß ich drei vier zickezacke zacke drei vier juppheidi ist die
Infantrie die Infantrie Infantrie fantrie fantrie — — — 57 haben sie
bei Woronesch begraben. 57, die hatten keine Ahnung, vorher nicht
und nachher nicht. Vorher haben sie noch gesungen. Zickezackejuppheidi. Und einer hat nach Hause geschrieben: — — — dann kaufen
15 wir uns ein Grammophon. Aber dann haben viertausend Meter weiter
ab die Andern auf Befehl auf einen Knopf gedrückt. Da hat es ge-
rumpelt wie ein alter Lastwagen mit leeren Tonnen über Kopfsteinpflaster: Kanonenorgel. Dann haben sie 57 bei Woronesch begraben.
Vorher haben sie noch gesungen. Hinterher haben sie nichts mehr
20 gesagt. 9 Autoschlosser, 2 Gärtner, 5 Beamte, 6 Verkäufer, 1 Friseur,
17 Bauern, 2 Lehrer, 1 Pastor, 6 Arbeiter, 1 Musiker, 7 Schuljungen.
7 Schuljungen. Die haben sie bei Woronesch begraben. Sie hatten
keine Ahnung. 57.
Und mich haben sie vergessen. Ich war noch nicht ganz tot. Jupp-
25 heidi. Ich war noch ein bißchen lebendig. Aber die andern, die haben
sie bei Woronesch begraben. 57. 57. Mach noch ne Null dran. 570.
Noch ne Null und noch ne Null. 57000. Und noch und noch und
noch. 57000000. Die haben sie bei Woronesch begraben. Sie hatten
keine Ahnung. Sie wollten nicht. Das hatten sie gar nicht gewollt.
30 Und vorher haben sie noch gesungen. Juppheidi. Nachher haben
sie nichts mehr gesagt. Und der eine hat das Grammophon nicht

4 **wunderhübsch** magnificently beautiful
9 **elend** miserable
11 **wär(e)n** were
12 **s Geräusch** noise
14 **s Kopfkissen** pillow;   **grummeln** (*coll.*) to 'grumble'
18 **Aber du . . . geschrien.** In giving birth you cast me forth from you, screaming into the world.
20 **blaudunkel** blue-dark
25 **davon·schlurfen** to shuffle along;   **e Latsche** (*coll.*) slipper (down at heels)
27 **j-en auf·halten** to stop s.o.;   **e Wand** wall
30 **wanken** to tremble;   **e Welle** wave
32 **rums** (*interj.*) *here:* sound of something that collapses
34 **hin·kommen** to get there

---

1. *Woraus sehen wir, daß Fischer beinahe eine Marschiermaschine ist ?*
2. *Weshalb hat er vor den Nächten Angst ?*
3. *Wen macht er dafür verantwortlich, daß er jetzt allein ist ?*
4. *Was denkt er, wenn er ein Geräusch hört ?*
5. *Weshalb wankt der Boden ?*

gekauft. Sie haben ihn bei Woronesch und die andern 56 auch begraben. 57 Stück. Nur ich. Ich, ich war noch nicht ganz tot. Ich muß
zur Straßenbahn. Die Straße ist grau. Aber die Straßenbahn ist gelb.
Ganz wunderhübsch gelb. Da muß ich mit. Nur daß die Straße so
5 grau ist. So grau und so grau. Zweimal hab ich schon zickezacke
vorwärts, Fischer! drei vier links zwei links zwei gelegen drei vier
weiter, Fischer! Zickezacke juppheidi schneidig ist die Infantrie
schneidig, Fischer! weiter, Fischer! links zwei drei vier wenn nur der
Hunger der elende Hunger immer der elende links zwei drei vier
10 links zwei links zwei links zwei — — —
   Wenn bloß die Nächte nicht wärn. Wenn bloß die Nächte nicht
wärn. Jedes Geräusch ist ein Tier. Jeder Schatten ist ein schwarzer
Mann. Nie wird man die Angst vor den schwarzen Männern los.
Auf dem Kopfkissen grummeln die ganze Nacht die Kanonen: Der
15 Puls. Du hättest mich nie allein lassen sollen, Mutter. Jetzt finden
wir uns nicht wieder. Nie wieder. Nie hättest du das tun sollen. Du
hast doch die Nächte gekannt. Du hast doch gewußt von den Nächten. Aber du hast mich von dir geschrien. Aus dir heraus und in diese
Welt mit den Nächten hineingeschrien. Und seitdem ist jedes Ge-
20 räusch ein Tier in der Nacht. Und in den blaudunklen Ecken warten
die schwarzen Männer. Mutter Mutter! in allen Ecken stehn die
schwarzen Männer. Und jedes Geräusch ist ein Tier. Jedes Geräusch
ist ein Tier. Und das Kopfkissen ist so heiß. Die ganze Nacht grummeln die Kanonen darauf. Und dann haben sie 57 bei Woronesch
25 begraben. Und die Uhr schlurft wie ein altes Weib auf Latschen davon
davon davon. Sie schlurft und schlurft und schlurft und keiner keiner
hält sie auf. Und die Wände kommen immer näher. Und die Decke
kommt immer tiefer. Und der Boden der Boden der wankt von der
Welle Welt. Mutter Mutter! warum hast du mich allein gelassen,
30 warum? Wankt von der Welle. Wankt von der Welt. 57. Rums.
Und ich will zur Straßenbahn. Die Kanonen haben gegrummelt.
Der Boden wankt. Rums. 57. Und ich bin noch ein bißchen lebendig.
Und ich will zur Straßenbahn. Die ist gelb in der grauen Straße.
Wunderhübsch gelb in der grauen. Aber ich komm ja nicht hin.
35 Zweimal hab ich schon gelegen. Denn ich hab Hunger. Und davon
wankt der Boden. Wankt so wunderhübsch gelb von der Welle Welt.
Welt. Wankt von der Hungerwelt. Wankt so welthungrig und stras-
senbahngelb.
   Eben hat einer zu mir gesagt: Guten Tag, Herr Fischer. Bin ich

[10] **Schritt halten** to keep in step, keep pace
[16] **e Mülleimerallee** (**r Eimer** pail) garbage can alley;   **s Aschkastenspalier** street lined
with ash or dust bins
[17] **r Rinnstein** gutter;   **glacis** (*Old French* glacier, to slide) a gentle slope, particularly the
exterior slope or wall of the ditch around fortifications;   **e Champs-Ruinés** (*French*)
ruined fields (recalls Champs-Elysées, elegant street in Paris);   **r Muttschuttschlagin-
dutt** *i.e.* **r Mutt** (*dial.*) mud;   **r Schutt** rubble;   **schlag ihn tot** kill him
[18] **e Trümmer** (pl.) debris
[25] **s Löffelchen** little spoon (-full)
[39] **juppvorbei schneidig** hoop-la, dashing

1. Was ist der Unterschied zwischen „Herrn Fischer" und „Leutnant Fischer"?
2. Was sieht Herr Fischer an der Straße?
3. Was möchte das kleine Mädchen vom lieben Gott?
4. Weshalb kann ihm der liebe Gott nichts geben?
5. Wie geht es der Mutter des kleinen Mädchens?

Herr Fischer? Kann ich Herr Fischer sein, einfach wieder Herr
Fischer? Ich war doch Leutnant Fischer. Kann ich denn wieder
Herr Fischer sein? Bin ich Herr Fischer? Guten Tag, hat der gesagt.
Aber der weiß nicht, daß ich Leutnant Fischer war. Einen guten Tag
hat er gewünscht — für Leutnant Fischer gibt es keine guten Tage
mehr. Das hat er nicht gewußt.
    Und Herr Fischer geht die Straße lang. Die lange Straße lang.
Die ist grau. Er will zur Straßenbahn. Die ist gelb. So wunderhübsch
gelb. Links zwei, Herr Fischer. Links zwei drei vier. Herr Fischer
hat Hunger. Er hält nicht mehr Schritt. Er will doch noch mit, denn
die Straßenbahn ist so wunderhübsch gelb in dem Grau. Zweimal
hat Herr Fischer schon gelegen. Aber Leutnant Fischer kommandiert: Links zwei drei vier vorwärts, Herr Fischer! Weiter, Herr
Fischer! Schneidig, Herr Fischer, kommandiert Leutnant Fischer.
Und Herr Fischer marschiert die graue Straße lang, die graue graue
lange Straße lang. Die Mülleimerallee. Das Aschkastenspalier. Das
Rinnsteinglacis. Die Champs-Ruinés. Den Muttschuttschlagindutt-
broadway. Die Trümmerparade. Und Leutnant Fischer kommandiert.
Links zwei links zwei. Und Herr Fischer Herr Fischer marschiert,
links zwei links zwei links zwei links vorbei vorbei vorbei — — —
    Das kleine Mädchen hat Beine, die sind wie Finger so dünn.
Wie Finger im Winter. So dünn und so rot und so blau und so dünn.
Links zwei drei vier machen die Beine. Das kleine Mädchen sagt
immerzu und Herr Fischer marschiert nebenan das sagt immerzu:
Lieber Gott, gib mir Suppe. Lieber Gott, gib mir Suppe. Ein Löffel-
chen nur. Ein Löffelchen nur. Ein Löffelchen nur. Die Mutter hat
Haare, die sind schon tot. Lange schon tot. Die Mutter sagt: Der
liebe Gott kann dir keine Suppe geben, er kann es doch nicht. Warum
kann der liebe Gott mir keine Suppe geben? Er hat doch keinen
Löffel. Den hat er nicht. Das kleine Mädchen geht auf seinen Finger-
beinen, den dünnen blauen Winterbeinen, neben der Mutter. Herr
Fischer geht nebenan. Von der Mutter sind die Haare schon tot.
Sie sind schon ganz fremd um den Kopf. Und das kleine Mädchen
tanzt rundherum um die Mutter herum um Herrn Fischer herum
rundherum: Er hat ja keinen Löffel. Er hat ja keinen Löffel. Er hat
ja keinen nicht mal einen hat ja keinen Löffel. So tanzt das kleine
Mädchen rundherum. Und Herr Fischer marschiert hinteran. Wankt
nebenan auf der Welle Welt. Wankt von der Welle Welt. Aber Leutnant Fischer kommandiert: Links zwei juppvorbei schneidig, Herr

[12] **verraten** to betray
[13] **aus sich aus·stoßen** to expel (from oneself)
[15] **s Klavier** piano
[17] **r Geburtstag** birthday
[18] **e Heldengedenkfeier** heroes' memorial day celebration
[19] **es gibt** (+ *acc.*) there is
[20] **s Lazarett** (military) hospital
[21] **aus sein** to be over
[24] **tuten** to "toot";   **hoch·kucken** = **hoch·gucken** (*coll.*) to look up
[29] **riechen** to smell;   **s Dach** roof
[33] **schubsen** (*coll.*) (*cf.* **schieben** to shove) to push
[39] **pennen** (*coll.*) to take a nap

---

1. *Wie alt ist Herr Fischer ?*
2. *Wann spielte immer jemand Klavier ?*
3. *Weshalb sagt Timm, daß die Lokomotive weint ?*
4. *Wer hat den Alten vom Wagen geschubst ?*
5. *Was sagt Herr Fischer darüber ?*

Fischer, links zwei und das kleine Mädchen singt dabei: Er hat ja
keinen Löffel. Er hat ja keinen Löffel. Und zweimal hat Herr Fischer
schon gelegen. Vor Hunger gelegen. Er hat ja keinen Löffel. Und
der andere kommandiert: Juppheidi juppheidi die Infantrie die In-
5 fantrie die Infantrie — — —
      57 haben sie bei Woronesch begraben. Ich bin Leutnant Fischer.
Mich haben sie vergessen. Ich war noch nicht ganz tot. Zweimal
hab ich schon gelegen. Jetzt bin ich Herr Fischer. Ich bin 25 Jahre
alt. 25 mal 57. Und die haben sie bei Woronesch begraben. Nur ich,
10 ich, ich bin noch unterwegs. Ich muß die Straßenbahn noch kriegen.
Hunger hab ich. Aber der liebe Gott hat keinen Löffel. Er hat ja keinen
Löffel. Ich bin 25 mal 57. Mein Vater hat mich verraten und meine
Mutter hat mich ausgestoßen aus sich. Sie hat mich allein geschrien.
So furchtbar allein. So allein. Jetzt gehe ich die lange Straße lang.
15 Die wankt von der Welle der Welt. Aber immer spielt einer Klavier.
Immer spielt einer Klavier. Als mein Vater meine Mutter sah — spielte
einer Klavier. Als ich Geburtstag hatte — spielte einer Klavier. Bei
der Heldengedenkfeier in der Schule — spielte einer Klavier. Als
wir dann selbst Helden werden durften, als es den Krieg gab —
20 spielte einer Klavier. Im Lazarett — spielte dann einer Klavier.
Als der Krieg aus war — spielte immer noch einer Klavier. Immer
spielt einer. Immer spielt einer Klavier. Die ganze lange Straße
lang.
      Die Lokomotive tutet. Timm sagt, sie weint. Wenn man hoch-
25 kuckt, zittern die Sterne. Immerzu tutet die Lokomotive. Aber Timm
sagt, sie weint. Immerzu. Die ganze Nacht. Die ganze lange Nacht
nun schon. Sie weint, das tut einem im Magen weh, wenn sie so weint,
sagt Timm. Sie weint wie Kinder, sagt er. Wir haben einen Wagen
mit Holz. Das riecht wie Wald. Unser Wagen hat kein Dach. Die
30 Sterne zittern, wenn man hochkuckt. Da tutet sie wieder. Hörst
du? sagt Timm, sie weint wieder. Ich versteh nicht, warum die Lokomotive weint. Timm sagt es. Wie Kinder, sagt er. Timm sagt, ich
hätte den Alten nicht vom Wagen schubsen sollen. Ich hab den
Alten nicht vom Wagen geschubst. Du hättest es nicht tun sollen,
35 sagt Timm. Ich habe es nicht getan. Sie weint, hörst du, wie sie weint,
sagt Timm, du hättest es nicht tun sollen. Ich hab den Alten nicht
vom Wagen geschubst. Sie weint nicht. Sie tutet. Lokomotiven tuten.
Sie weint, sagt Timm. Er ist von selbst vom Wagen gefallen. Ganz
von selbst, der Alte. Er hat gepennt, Timm, gepennt hat er, sag ich

⁵ j-en in den Hintern treten to boot s.o. in the "rear end"
⁷ schleppen to carry, drag
⁹ j-en an·gucken = j-en ansehen
¹¹ sich an·hören to sound
¹⁴ rütteln to jolt; e Schienen (*pl.*) tracks
²⁰ wegen (+ *gen.; here: dat.*[*coll.*]) because of
²² r Nagel nail
²³ r Schmied smith; zählen to count
²⁴ Vati (*coll.*) = Vater "daddy"
²⁶ (sich) biegen to bend, buckle (from the weight)
³⁴ blank shiny
³⁹ ich bin über = übriggeblieben left over (from war)

---

1. *Was hat Timm dem Alten getan ?*
2. *Weshalb hält der kleine Junge die Hände auf ?*
3. *Was für Finger hat er ?*
4. *Was für Hände hat der Schmied ?*
5. *Was will der Schmied wissen ?*

dir. Da ist er von selbst vom Wagen gefallen. Du hättest es nicht tun
sollen. Sie weint. Die ganze Nacht nun schon. Timm sagt, man soll
keine alten Männer vom Wagen schubsen. Ich hab es nicht getan.
Er hat gepennt. Du hättest es nicht tun sollen, sagt Timm. Timm sagt,
5 er hat in Rußland mal einen Alten in den Hintern getreten. Weil
er so langsam war. Und er nahm immer so wenig auf einmal.
Sie waren beim Munitionsschleppen. Da hat Timm den Alten in
den Hintern getreten. Da hat der Alte sich umgedreht. Ganz langsam,
sagt Timm, und er hat ihn ganz traurig angekuckt. Gar nichts weiter.
10 Aber er hat ein Gesicht gehabt wie sein Vater. Genau wie sein Vater.
Das sagt Timm. Die Lokomotive tutet. Manchmal hört es sich an,
als ob sie schreit. Timm meint sogar, sie weint. Vielleicht hat Timm
recht. Aber ich hab den Alten nicht vom Wagen geschubst. Er hat
gepennt. Da ist er von selbst. Es rüttelt ja ziemlich auf den Schienen.
15 Wenn man hochkuckt, zittern die Sterne. Der Wagen wankt von der
Welle Welt. Sie tutet. Schrein tut sie. Schrein, daß die Sterne zittern.
Von der Welle Welt.

Aber ich bin noch unterwegs. Zwei drei vier. Zur Straßenbahn.
Zweimal hab ich schon gelegen. Der Boden wankt von der Welle
20 Welt. Wegen dem Hunger. Aber ich bin unterwegs. Ich bin schon so
lange so lange unterwegs. Die lange Straße lang. Die Straße.

Der kleine Junge hält die Hände auf. Ich soll die Nägel holen.
Der Schmied zählt die Nägel. Drei Mann? fragt er.

Vati sagt, für drei Mann.
25 Die Nägel fallen in die Hände. Der Schmied hat dicke breite
Finger. Der kleine Junge ganz dünne, die sich biegen von den großen
Nägeln.

Ist der, der sagt, er ist Gottes Sohn, auch dabei?

Der kleine Junge nickt.
30 Sagt er immer noch, daß er Gottes Sohn ist?

Der kleine Junge nickt. Der Schmied nimmt die Nägel noch mal.
Dann läßt er sie wieder in die Hände fallen. Die kleinen Hände,
biegen sich davon. Dann sagt der Schmied: Na ja.

Der kleine Junge geht weg. Die Nägel sind schön blank. Der kleine
35 Junge läuft. Da machen die Nägel ein Geräusch. Der Schmied nimmt
den Hammer. Na ja, sagt der Schmied. Dann hört der kleine Junge
hinter sich: Pink Pank Pink Pank. Er schlägt wieder, denkt der kleine
Junge. Nägel macht er, viele blanke Nägel.

57 haben sie bei Woronesch begraben. Ich bin über. Aber ich hab

[1] s **Reich** realm
[18] **frieren** to freeze
[20] r **Ortsvorsteher** chief magistrate of a place
[24] r **Pfarrer** priest, pastor
[28] r **Schulmeister** schoolteacher
[35] **sich (he)rum·drehen** to turn (oneself) around;   **j-en um·bringen** to kill s.o.
[37] r **Minister** = r **Verteidigungsminister** Secretary of Defense

---

1. *Wonach fragen die 57 Leutnant Fischer ?*
2. *Von wem bekommen sie auch keine Antwort ?*
3. *Wer bringt den General um ?*

Hunger. Mein Reich ist von dieser dieser Welt. Und der Schmied
hat die Nägel umsonst gemacht, juppheidi, umsonst gemacht, die
Infantrie, umsonst die schönen blanken Nägel. Denn 57 haben sie
bei Woronesch begraben. Pink Pank macht der Schmied. Pink Pank
5 bei Woronesch. Pink Pank. 57 mal Pink Pank. Pink Pank macht
der Schmied. Pink Pank macht die Infantrie. Pink Pank machen
die Kanonen. Und das Klavier spielt immerzu Pink Pank Pink Pank
Pink Pank — — —
  57 kommen jede Nacht nach Deutschland. 9 Autoschlosser, 2
10 Gärtner, 5 Beamte, 6 Verkäufer, 1 Friseur, 17 Bauern, 2 Lehrer,
1 Pastor, 6 Arbeiter, 1 Musiker, 7 Schuljungen. 57 kommen jede
Nacht an mein Bett, 57 fragen jede Nacht:
  Wo ist deine Kompanie? Bei Woronesch, sag ich dann. Begraben,
sag ich dann. Bei Woronesch begraben. 57 fragen Mann für Mann:
15 Warum? Und 57mal bleib ich stumm.
  57 gehen nachts zu ihrem Vater. 57 und Leutnant Fischer. Leutnant Fischer bin ich. 57 fragen nachts ihren Vater: Vater, warum?
und der Vater bleibt 57mal stumm. Und er friert in seinem Hemd.
Aber er kommt mit.
20 57 gehen nachts zum Ortsvorsteher. 57 und der Vater und ich.
57 fragen nachts den Ortsvorsteher: Ortsvorsteher, warum? Und
der Ortsvorsteher bleibt 57mal stumm. Und er friert in seinem
Hemd. Aber er kommt mit.
  57 gehen nachts zum Pfarrer. 57 und der Vater und der Ortsvor-
25 steher und ich. 57 fragen nachts den Pfarrer: Pfarrer, warum? Und
der Pfarrer bleibt 57mal stumm. Und er friert in seinem Hemd.
Aber er kommt mit.
  57 gehen nachts zum Schulmeister. 57 und der Vater und der Ortsvorsteher und der Pfarrer und ich. 57 fragen nachts den Schulmeister:
30 Schulmeister, warum? Und der Schulmeister bleibt 57mal stumm.
Und er friert in seinem Hemd. Aber er kommt mit.
  57 gehen nachts zum General. 57 und der Vater und der Ortsvorsteher und der Pfarrer und der Schulmeister und ich. 57 fragen
nachts den General: General, warum? Und der General — der
35 General dreht sich nicht einmal rum. Da bringt der Vater ihn um.
Und der Pfarrer? Der Pfarrer bleibt stumm.
  57 gehen nachts zum Minister. 57 und der Vater und der Ortsvorsteher und der Pfarrer und der Schulmeister und ich. 57 fragen
nachts den Minister: Minister, warum? Da hat der Minister sich sehr

[1] **sich erschrecken** to frighten oneself; **r Sektkorb** (r **Sekt** champagne; **r Korb** basket) champagne bucket (for cooling); **verstecken** to hide
[2] **prosten** to drink to s.o.'s health, toast s.o.
[9] **die Ewigkeit durch** throughout eternity
[24] **s Milchgeschäft** dairy store; **r Vorgarten** front yard; **r Kuhgeruch (riechen)** smell of cows
[26] **r Zahnarzt** (r **Zahn** tooth) dentist
[27] **Sonnabends nur nach Vereinbarung** Saturdays only by arrangement
[29] **doof** (*coll.*) stupid, dumb
[31] **e Bratkartoffel** fried potato
[32] **r Klavierunterricht** piano lessons
[34] **r Pflasterstein** paving-stone
[36] **r Benzinfleck** gasoline stain
[37] **flau** dull, slack; **s Emaille** enamel
[38] **beheben** to eliminate

---

1. Was antwortet der Minister?
2. Warum muß Leutnant Fischer auf der langen Straße unterwegs sein?
3. Woraus sehen wir, daß Leutnant Fischer und Herr Fischer nicht dasselbe wollen?
4. Was für Geschäfte gibt es an der Straße?

erschreckt. Er hatte sich so schön hinterm Sektkorb versteckt, hinterm Sekt. Und da hebt er sein Glas und prostet nach Süden und Norden und Westen und Osten. Und dann sagt er: Deutschland, Kameraden, Deutschland! Darum! Da sehen die 57 sich um. Stumm.
5 So lange und stumm. Und sie sehen nach Süden und Norden und Westen und Osten. Und dann fragen sie leise: Deutschland? Darum? Dann drehen die 57 sich rum. Und sehen sich niemals mehr um. 57 legen sich bei Woronesch wieder ins Grab. Sie haben alte arme Gesichter. Wie Frauen. Wie Mütter. Und sie sagen die Ewigkeit
10 durch: Darum? Darum? Darum? 57 haben sie bei Woronesch begraben. Ich bin über. Ich bin Leutnant Fischer. Ich bin 25. Ich will noch zur Straßenbahn. Ich will mit. Ich bin schon lange lange unterwegs. Nur Hunger hab ich. Aber ich muß. 57 fragen: Warum? Und ich bin über. Und ich bin schon lange die lange lange Straße
15 unterwegs.

Unterwegs. Ein Mann. Herr Fischer. Ich bin es. Leutnant steht drüben und kommandiert: Links zwei drei vier links zwei drei vier zickzacke juppheidi zwei drei vier links zwei drei vier die Infantrie die Infantrie pink pank pink pank drei vier pink pank drei vier pink
20 pank pink pank die lange Straße lang pink pank immer lang immer rum warum warum warum pink pank pink pank bei Woronesch darum bei Woronesch darum pink pank die lange lange Straße lang. Ein Mensch. 25. Ich. Die Straße. Die lange lange. Ich. Haus Haus Haus Wand Wand Milchgeschäft Vorgarten Kuhgeruch Haus-
25 tür.

Zahnarzt
Sonnabends nur nach Vereinbarung

Wand Wand Wand

Hilde Bauer ist doof

30 Leutnant Fischer ist dumm. 57 fragen: warum. Wand Wand Tür Fenster Glas Glas Glas Laterne alte Frau rote rote Augen Bratkartoffelgeruch Haus Haus Klavierunterricht pink pank die ganze Straße lang die Nägel sind so blank Kanonen sind so lang pink pank die ganze Straße lang Kind Kind Hund Ball Auto Pflasterstein Pflaster-
35 stein Kopfsteinköpfe Köpfe pink pank Stein Stein grau grau violett Benzinfleck grau grau die lange lange Straße lang Stein Stein grau blau flau flau so grau Wand Wand grüne Emaille

Schlechte Augen schnell behoben
Optiker Terboben

40

Im 2. Stockwerk oben

[1] e Seele soul
[2] hupen to honk;   pupen to fart ('poop')
[7] Skat a card game
[10] bieder honest, upright
[11] passen (*French:* passer) to pass, i.e. not move in a card game
[14] mauern to risk nothing (cards)
[16] Ramsch haben a play in the game of Skat where all players pass
[17] man los! (*coll.*) go to it!
[18] s Kreuz cross, club (cards);   heilig sacrosanct (*here:* club is trump card);   aus·spielen
to lead (cards)
[25] r Trumpf trump card
[25] (ab·)wimmeln to try to get rid of
[30] e Faust fist

---

1. *Woraus sehen wir, daß der Tod immer gegenwärtig ist?*
2. *Was erfahren wir über die Männer, die Skat spielen?*
3. *Woran erinnert sich Fischer, wenn sie ihre Fäuste auf den Tisch donnern lassen?*
4. *Wer ist auf den drei Bildern der Mutter?*
5. *Wohin stellt sie sie abends?*

Wand Wand Wand Stein Hund Hund hebt Bein Baum Seele Hunde-
traum Auto hupt noch Hund pupt doch Pflaster rot Hund tot Hund
tot Hund tot Wand Wand Wand die lange Straße lang Fenster Wand
Fenster Fenster Fenster Lampen Leute Licht Männer immer noch
5 Männer blanke Gesichter wie Nägel so blank so wunderhübsch
blank — — —
   Vor hundert Jahren spielten sie Skat. Vor hundert Jahren spielten
sie schon. Und jetzt jetzt spielen sie noch. Und in hundert Jahren dann
spielen sie auch immer noch. Immer noch Skat. Die drei Männer.
10 Mit blanken biederen Gesichtern.
   Passe.
   Karl, sag mehr.
   Ich passe auch.
   Also dann — — ihr habt gemauert, meine Herren.
15 Du hättest ja auch passen können, dann hätten wir einen schönen
Ramsch gehabt.
   Man los. Man los. Wie heißt er?
   Das Kreuz ist heilig. Wer spielt aus?
   Immer der fragt.
20 Einmal hat es die Mutter erlaubt. Und noch mal Trumpf!
   Was, Karl, du hast kein Kreuz mehr?
   Diesmal nicht.
   Na, dann wollen wir mal auf die Dörfer gehen. Ein Herz hat
jeder.
25 Trumpf! Nun wimmel, Karl, was du bei der Seele hast. Acht-
undzwanzig.
   Und noch einmal Trumpf!
   Vor hundert Jahren spielten sie schon. Spielten sie Skat. Und in
hundert Jahren, dann spielen sie noch. Spielen sie immer noch Skat
30 mit blanken biederen Gesichtern. Und wenn sie ihre Fäuste auf den
Tisch donnern lassen, dann donnert es. Wie Kanonen. Wie 57 Kanonen.
   Aber ein Fenster weiter sitzt eine Mutter. Die hat drei Bilder vor
sich. Drei Männer in Uniform. Links steht ihr Mann. Rechts steht
35 ihr Sohn. Und in der Mitte steht der General. Der General von ihrem
Mann und ihrem Sohn. Und wenn die Mutter abends zu Bett geht,
dann stellt sie die Bilder, daß sie sie sieht, wenn sie liegt. Den Sohn.
Und den Mann. Und in der Mitte den General. Und dann liest sie
die Briefe, die der General schrieb. 1917. Für Deutschland. — steht

[9] **Pyramidon** brand name of a headache remedy
[11] **s Geschäft** business
[15] **r Laden** store;   **florieren** to 'flourish,' thrive
[25] **e Ackerkrume** top soil
[30] **durch·streichen** to cross out
[35] **lindern** to appease;   **r Haß** hatred

1. Was steht in den Briefen, die die Mutter liest ?
2. Was verkauft der Mann in der dunklen Ecke ?
3. Wer kauft seine Ware ?
4. Weshalb ist der Mann glücklich ?
5. Was steht in dem Gedicht ?

auf dem einen. 1940. Für Deutschland. — steht auf dem anderen.
Mehr liest die Mutter nicht. Ihre Augen sind ganz rot. Sind so rot.
Aber ich bin über. Juppheidi. Für Deutschland. Ich bin noch
unterwegs. Zur Straßenbahn. Zweimal hab ich schon gelegen. Wegen
5 dem Hunger. Juppheidi. Aber ich muß hin. Der Leutnant kommandiert. Ich bin schon unterwegs. Schon lange lange unterwegs.
  Da steht ein Mann in einer dunklen Ecke. Immer stehen Männer
in den dunklen Ecken. Immer stehn dunkle Männer in den Ecken.
Einer steht da und hält einen Kasten und einen Hut. Pyramidon!
10 bellt der Mann. Pyramidon! 20 Tabletten genügen. Der Mann
grinst, denn das Geschäft geht gut. Das Geschäft geht so gut. 57
Frauen, rotäugige Frauen, die kaufen Pyramidon. Mach eine Null
dran. 570. Noch eine und noch eine. 57000. Und noch und noch und
noch. 57000000. Das Geschäft geht gut. Der Mann bellt: Pyramidon.
15 Er grinst, der Laden floriert: 57 Frauen, rotäugige Frauen, die kaufen Pyramidon. Der Kasten wird leer. Und der Hut wird voll. Und
der Mann grinst. Er kann gut grinsen. Er hat keine Augen. Er ist
glücklich: Er hat keine Augen. Er sieht die Frauen nicht. Sieht die
57 Frauen nicht. Die 57 rotäugigen Frauen.
20 Nur ich bin über. Aber ich bin schon unterwegs. Und die Straße
ist lang. So fürchterlich lang. Aber ich will zur Straßenbahn. Ich
bin schon unterwegs. Schon lange lange unterwegs.
  In einem Zimmer sitzt ein Mann. Der Mann schreibt mit Tinte
auf weißem Papier. Und er sagt in das Zimmer hinein:
25   Auf dem Braun der Ackerkrume
        weht hellgrün ein Gras.
        Eine blaue Blume
        ist vom Morgen naß.
  Er schreibt es auf das weiße Papier. Er liest es ins leere Zimmer
30 hinein. Er streicht es mit Tinte wieder durch. Er sagt in das Zimmer
hinein:
        Auf dem Braun der Ackerkrume
        weht hellgrün ein Gras.
        Eine blaue Blume
35   lindert allen Haß.
  Der Mann schreibt es hin. Er liest es in das leere Zimmer hinein.
Er streicht es wieder durch. Dann sagt er in das Zimmer hinein:
        Auf dem Braun der Ackerkrume
        weht hellgrün ein Gras.

[16] **graulich** grayish
[17] **eisig** icy
[20] **r Obergefreite** private first class (PFC)
[21] **e Krücke** crutch
[22] **zielen (auf** + *acc.*) to aim (at)
[23] **r Iwan** popular name for Russians
[24] **geschafft** done (*here:* killed, in the sense of "done-in" or "done away with");   **MG** = **Maschinengewehr** automatic rifle
[27] **s Maul** snout, mouth (of animals)

---

1. *Wie unterschied sich die Landschaft bei Woronesch von der des Gedichtes?*
2. *Womit hat die Gruppe des Obergefreiten geschossen?*
3. *Wie viele russische Soldaten hat diese Gruppe in einer Nacht getötet?*
4. *An wen denkt Leutnant Fischer, als er die alte Frau sieht, die ihm auf der Bank gegenübersitzt?*

Eine blaue Blume —
Eine blaue Blume —
Eine blaue —
Der Mann steht auf. Er geht um den Tisch herum. Immer um den Tisch herum. Er bleibt stehen:
Eine blaue —
Eine blaue —
Auf dem Braun der Ackerkrume —
Der Mann geht immer um den Tisch herum.

57 haben sie bei Woronesch begraben. Aber die Erde war grau. Und wie Stein. Und da weht kein hellgrünes Gras. Schnee war da. Und der war wie Glas. Und ohne blaue Blume. Millionenmal Schnee. Und keine blaue Blume. Aber der Mann in dem Zimmer weiß das nicht. Er weiß es nie. Er sieht immer die blaue Blume. Überall die blaue Blume. Und dabei haben sie 57 bei Woronesch begraben. Unter glasigem Schnee. Im grauen gräulichen Sand. Ohne Grün. Und ohne Blau. Der Sand war eisig und grau. Und der Schnee war wie Glas. Und der Schnee lindert keinen Haß. Denn 57 haben sie bei Woronesch begraben. 57 begraben. Bei Woronesch begraben.

Das ist noch gar nichts, das ist ja noch gar nichts! sagt der Obergefreite mit der Krücke. Und er legt die Krücke über seine Fußspitze und zielt. Er kneift das eine Auge klein und zielt mit der Krücke über die Fußspitze. Das ist noch gar nichts, sagt er. 86 Iwans haben wir die eine Nacht geschafft. 86 Iwans. Mit einem MG, mein Lieber, mit einem einzigen MG in einer Nacht. Am andern Morgen haben wir sie gezählt. Übereinander lagen sie. 86 Iwans. Einige hatten das Maul noch offen. Viele auch die Augen. Ja, viele hatten die Augen noch offen. In einer Nacht, mein Lieber. Der Obergefreite zielt mit seiner Krücke auf die alte Frau, die ihm auf der Bank gegenübersitzt. Er zielt auf die eine alte Frau und er trifft 86 alte Frauen. Aber die wohnen in Rußland. Davon weiß er nichts. Es ist gut, daß er das nicht weiß. Was sollte er sonst wohl machen? Jetzt, wo es Abend wird?

Nur ich weiß es. Ich bin Leutnant Fischer. 57 haben sie bei Woronesch begraben. Aber ich war nicht ganz tot. Ich bin noch unterwegs. Zweimal hab ich schon gelegen. Vom Hunger. Denn der liebe Gott hat ja keinen Löffel. Aber ich will auf jeden Fall zur Straßenbahn. Wenn nur die Straße nicht so voller Mütter wäre. 57 haben sie bei Woronesch begraben. Und der Obergefreite hat am anderen Morgen

² **Wo sollte er sonst wohl hin?** Where else should he go then?
¹² **bedruckt** printed
¹³ **versichern** to insure
¹⁵ **eWeihnachtsfreude** *lit.* Christmas joy
¹⁶ **e Eintrittserklärung** declaration of membership
¹⁷ **e Lebensversicherung** life insurance (company)
²³ **sich herum·schlagen** to grapple with;   **schluchzen** to sob
³² **heiser** husky, 'hoarse'
³⁴ **zu·machen** to close
³⁵ **auf·machen** to open
³⁶ **verschwimmen** to get blurry;   **r Weltuntergang** end of the world
³⁷ **r Schnaps** hard liquor;   **kratzend** scratching (*here:* of harsh taste)

---

1. *Was steht auf den bunten Plakaten?*
2. *Weshalb sollen sich die Menschen versichern lassen?*
3. *Was haben die 57 toten Soldaten ihren Familien gemacht?*
4. *Was denkt Fischer über Lebensversicherung?*
5. *Wie sieht Evelyn aus?*
6. *Wovon singt sie?*

86 Iwans gezählt. Und 86 Mütter schießt er mit seiner Krücke tot. Aber er weiß es nicht, das ist gut. Wo sollte er sonst wohl hin. Denn der liebe Gott hat ja keinen Löffel. Es ist gut, wenn die Dichter die blauen Blumen blühen lassen. Es ist gut, wenn immer einer Klavier spielt. Es ist gut, wenn sie Skat spielen. Immer spielen sie Skat. Wo sollten sie sonst wohl hin, die alte Frau mit den drei Bildern am Bett, der Obergefreite mit den Krücken und den 86 toten Iwans, die Mutter mit dem kleinen Mädchen, das Suppe haben will, und Timm, der den alten Mann getreten hat? Wo sollten sie sonst wohl hin?

Aber ich muß die lange lange Straße lang. Lang. Wand Wand Tür Laterne Wand Wand Fenster Wand Wand und buntes Papier buntes bedrucktes Papier.

Sind Sie schon versichert?
Sie machen sich und Ihrer Familie
eine Weihnachtsfreude
mit einer Eintrittserklärung in die
URANIA LEBENSVERSICHERUNG

57 haben ihr Leben nicht richtig versichert. Und die 86 toten Iwans auch nicht. Und sie haben ihren Familien keine Weihnachtsfreude gemacht. Rote Augen haben sie ihren Familien gemacht. Weiter nichts, rote Augen. Warum waren sie auch nicht auch nicht in der Urania Lebensversicherung? Und ich kann mich nun mit den roten Augen herumschlagen. Überall die roten rotgeweinten rotgeschluchzten Augen. Die Mutteraugen, die Frauenaugen. Überall die roten rotgeweinten Augen. Warum haben sich die 57 nicht versichern lassen? Nein, sie haben ihren Familien keine Weihnachtsfreude gemacht. Rote Augen. Nur rote Augen. Und dabei steht es doch auf tausend bunten Plakaten: Urania Lebensversicherung Urania Lebensversicherung — —

Evelyn steht in der Sonne und singt. Die Sonne ist bei Evelyn. Man sieht durch das Kleid die Beine und alles. Und Evelyn singt. Durch die Nase singt sie ein wenig und heiser singt sie bißchen. Sie hat heute nacht zu lange im Regen gestanden. Und sie singt, daß mir heiß wird, wenn ich die Augen zumach. Und wenn ich sie aufmach, dann seh ich die Beine bis oben und alles. Und Evelyn singt, daß mir die Augen verschwimmen. Sie singt den süßen Weltuntergang. Die Nacht singt sie und Schnaps, den gefährlich kratzenden Schnaps voll wundem Weltgestöhn. Das Ende singt Evelyn, das Weltende, süß und zwischen nackten schmalen Mädchenbeinen:

[2] **naß** wet; **Wollust** voluptuousness
[3] **Bierflasche** beer bottle
[4] **mondblaß** pale as the moonlight;   **(he)raus·sehen** to peer out
[7] **r Rausch** drunkenness, revelry
[8] **graskalt** as cold as grass
[13] **s Schlachtfeld** battlefield
[14] **r Schuttacker** field full of debris
[15] **s Untergangslied** song about the decline of the world
[19] **r Lehm** clay, 'loam'
[21] **s Massengrab** common grave;   **mädchenheimlich (heimlich** secret, mysterious) girlishly-mysterious
[22] **Mondrausch** intoxication with moonlight
[24] **pflügen** to plow;   **düngen** to fertilize
[27] **s Dasein** existence, being
[33] **r Bahnsteig** station platform
[35] **r Waggon** railroad car;   **r Personenwagen** passenger-car;   **r Güterwagen (e Güter** [*pl.*] goods) freight-car
[38] **das ist schon ganz schön** that's really pretty good
[39] **reichen** to be sufficient;   **womöglich** perhaps

---

1. *Was soll der Mai wieder grün machen ?*
2. *Wo steht Evelyn die ganze Nacht ?*
3. *Weshalb zählt sie die Waggons und die Räder der Züge ?*

heiliger himmlischer heißer Weltuntergang. Ach, Evelyn singt wie
nasses Gras, so schwer von Geruch und Wollust und so grün. So
dunkelgrün, so grün wie leere Bierflaschen neben den Bänken, auf
denen Evelyns Knie abends mondblaß aus dem Kleid raussehen,
5 daß mir heiß wird.

Sing, Evelyn, sing mich tot. Sing den süßen Weltuntergang, sing
einen kratzenden Schnaps, sing einen grasgrünen Rausch. Und
Evelyn drückte meine graskalte Hand zwischen die mondblassen
Knie, daß mir heiß wird.

10 Und Evelyn singt. Komm lieber Mai und mache, singt Evelyn
und hält meine graskalte Hand mit den Knien. Komm lieber Mai
und mache die Gräber wieder grün. Das singt Evelyn. Komm lieber
Mai und mache die Schlachtfelder bierflaschengrün und mache den
Schutt, den riesigen Schuttacker grün wie mein Lied, wie mein
15 schnapssüßes Untergangslied. Und Evelyn singt auf der Bank ein heiseres hektisches Lied, daß mir kalt wird. Komm lieber Mai und mache
die Augen wieder blank, singt Evelyn und hält meine Hand mit
den Knien. Sing, Evelyn, sing mich zurück unters bierflaschengrüne
Gras, wo ich Sand war und Lehm war und Land war. Sing, Evelyn,
20 sing und sing mich über die Schuttäcker und über die Schlachtfelder
und über das Massengrab rüber in deinen süßen heißen mädchen-
heimlichen Mondrausch. Sing, Evelyn, sing, wenn die tausend Kom-
panien durch die Nächte marschieren, dann sing, wenn die tausend
Kanonen die Äcker pflügen und düngen mit Blut. Sing, Evelyn,
25 sing, wenn die Wände die Uhren und Bilder verlieren, dann sing mich
in schapsgrünen Rausch und in deinen süßen Weltuntergang. Sing,
Evelyn, sing mich in dein Mädchendasein hinein, in dein heimliches,
nächtliches Mädchengefühl, das so süß ist, daß mir heiß wird, wieder
heiß wird von Leben. Komm lieber Mai und mache das Gras wieder
30 grün, so bierflaschengrün, so evelyngrün. Sing, Evelyn!

Aber das Mädchen, das singt nicht. Das Mädchen, das zählt,
denn das Mädchen hat einen runden Bauch. Ihr Bauch ist etwas
zu rund. Und nun muß sie die ganze Nacht am Bahnsteig stehen,
weil einer von den 57 nicht versichert war. Und nun zählt sie die
35 ganze Nacht die Waggons. Eine Lokomotive hat 18 Räder. Ein Personenwagen 8. Ein Güterwagen 4. Das Mädchen mit dem runden
Bauch zählt die Waggons und die Räder — die Räder die Räder
die Räder — — — 78, sagt sie einmal, das ist schon ganz schön.
62, sagt sie dann, das reicht womöglich nicht. 110, sagt sie, das reicht.

⁴ **vorbei sein** to have gone by
⁸ **e Eisenbahn** railway train
¹⁴ **entlang kommen** to go along to completion, get over
¹⁶ **los·schreien** to start screaming;   **r Fußballplatz** soccer field
²⁴ **sie haben ihre Haare geordnet** they have combed their hair in place
²⁵ **erschüttern** to move deeply
²⁶ **erbauen** to edify;   **unterhalten** to entertain
³² **nicht weiter kann = nicht weiter·gehen kann**
³⁴ **wacklig** shaky, wobbly
³⁶ **um·wühlen** to move deeply;   **r Magen** stomach;   **um·drehen** to turn upside down
³⁷ **betäuben** to anesthetize, deaden

---

1. Wie viele Wagen hat der Zug, unter den sich das Mädchen wirft?
2. Warum hat sie Selbstmord begangen?
3. Wie schauen die 3000 Menschen aus, die rechts im großen Haus sitzen?
4. Weshalb sind sie dort?
5. Warum steht Leutnant Fischer an der Mauer und kann nicht weiter?
6. Welche symbolische Bedeutung hat das Wort „Wand", das oft im Text vor-
   kommt?

Dann läßt sie sich fallen und fällt vor den Zug. Der Zug hat eine
Lokomotive, 6 Personenwagen und fünf Güterwagen. Das sind 86
Räder. Das reicht. Das Mädchen mit dem runden Bauch ist nicht
mehr da, als der Zug mit seinen 86 Rädern vorbei ist. Sie ist einfach
5 nicht mehr da. Kein bißchen. Kein einziges kleines bißchen ist mehr
von ihr da. Sie hatte keine blaue Blume und keiner spielte für sie
Klavier und keiner mit ihr Skat. Und der liebe Gott hatte keinen
Löffel für sie. Aber die Eisenbahn hatte die vielen schönen Räder.
Wo sollte sie sonst auch hin? Was sollte sie sonst wohl tun? Denn der
10 liebe Gott hatte nicht mal einen Löffel. Und nun ist von ihr nichts
mehr über, gar nichts mehr über.
   Nur ich. Ich bin noch unterwegs. Noch immer unterwegs. Schon
lange, so lang schon lang schon unterwegs. Die Straße ist lang. Ich
komm die Straße und den Hunger nicht entlang. Sie sind beide
15 so lang.
   Hin und wieder schrein sie los. Links auf dem Fußballplatz. Rechts
in dem großen Haus. Da schrein sie manchmal los. Und die Straße
geht da mitten durch. Auf der Straße geh ich. Ich bin Leutnant
Fischer. Ich bin 25. Ich hab Hunger. Ich komm schon von Woro-
20 nesch. Ich bin schon lange unterwegs. Links ist der Fußballplatz.
Und rechts das große Haus. Da sitzen sie drin. 1000. 2000. 3000.
Und keiner sagt ein Wort. Vorne machen sie Musik. Und einige singen. Und die 3000 sagen kein Wort. Sie sind sauber gewaschen.
Sie haben ihre Haare geordnet und reine Hemden haben sie an. So
25 sitzen sie da in dem großen Haus und lassen sich erschüttern. Oder
erbauen. Oder unterhalten. Das kann man nicht unterscheiden. Sie
sitzen und lassen sich sauber gewaschen erschüttern. Aber sie wissen
nicht, daß ich Hunger hab. Das wissen sie nicht. Und daß ich hier
an der Mauer steh — ich, der von Woronesch, der auf der langen
30 Straße mit dem langen Hunger unterwegs ist, schon so lange unterwegs ist — daß ich hier an der Mauer steh, weil ich vor Hunger vor
Hunger nicht weiter kann. Aber das können sie ja nicht wissen. Die
Wand, die dicke dumme Wand ist ja dazwischen. Und davor steh
ich mit wackligen Knien — und dahinter sind sie in sauberer Wäsche
35 und lassen sich Sonntag für Sonntag erschüttern. Für zehn Mark
lassen sie sich die Seele umwühlen und den Magen umdrehen und die
Nerven betäuben. Zehn Mark, das ist so furchtbar viel Geld. Für
meinen Bauch ist das furchtbar viel Geld. Aber dafür steht auch das
Wort PASSION auf den Karten, die sie für zehn Mark bekommen.

¹**Matthäus-Passion** St. Matthew's Passion by Johann Sebastian Bach (1685–1750), German composer and organist;   **r Chor** chorus;   **Barrabas** Barabbas, bandit held in prison when Jesus was arrested. Pontius Pilate was willing to release Jesus at Passover, but the people demanded Barabbas' delivery and Jesus' death.

² **blutrünstig** murderous

⁴ **man sieht ihren Gesichtern gar nicht viel an** you cannot tell much by looking at their faces

⁸ **vorne** up front;   **e Passion** notice juxtaposition with **erleiden** and deliberate reinforcement of passion-suffering;   **erleiden (erlitt, erlitten)** to suffer, endure

⁹ **gedämpft** muted, muffled

¹¹ **sich beherrschen** to control one's feelings;   **keine Frisur . . . vor Qual** nobody's hairdo gets messed up out of anguish and agony

¹³ **geigen** to play on the violin;   **vor·musizieren** to play music (for s.o.)

¹⁴ **r Schreier** screamer;   **die tun ja nur so** they are only pretending, just acting that way

¹⁹ **s Tor** goal (football); also, wordplay on **r Tor,** fool

²² **gegenan·schrei(e)n** to shout back

1. *Was sieht man den Gesichtern der Zuhörer an, wenn der Chor Barrabas schreit ?*
2. *Welches Wort schreien die Tausend auf dem Fußballplatz ?*
3. *Was ruft Leutnant Fischer ?*
4. *Weshalb hat Leutnant Fischer mit all diesen Normalmenschen nichts gemeinsam ?*

MATTHÄUS-PASSION. Aber wenn der große Chor dann BARRA-
BAS schreit BARRABAS blutdurstig blutrünstig schreit, dann fallen
sie nicht von den Bänken, die Tausend in sauberen Hemden. Nein
und sie weinen auch nicht und beten auch nicht und man sieht ihren
5 Gesichtern, sieht ihren Seelen eigentlich gar nicht viel an, wenn
der große Chor BARRABAS schreit. Auf den Billetts steht für
zehn Mark MATTHÄUS-PASSION. Man kann bei der Passion
ganz vorne sitzen, wo die Passion recht laut erlitten wird, oder etwas
weiter hinten, wo nur noch gedämpft gelitten wird. Aber das ist egal.
10 Ihren Gesichtern sieht man nichts an, wenn der große Chor BARRA-
BAS schreit. Alle beherrschen sich gut bei der Passion. Keine Frisur
geht in Unordnung vor Not und vor Qual. Nein, Not und Qual, die
werden ja nur da vorne gesungen und gegeigt, für zehn Mark vor-
musiziert. Und die BARRABAS-Schreier die tun ja nur so, die werden
15 ja schließlich fürs Schreien bezahlt. Und der große Chor schreit
BARRABAS. MUTTER! schreit Leutnant Fischer auf der endlosen
Straße. Leutnant Fischer bin ich. BARRABAS! schreit der große
Chor der Saubergewaschenen. HUNGER! bellt der Bauch von Leutnant Fischer. Leutnant Fischer bin ich. TOR! schreien die Tausend
20 auf dem Fußballplatz. BARRABAS! schreien sie links von der Straße.
TOR schreien sie rechts von der Straße. WORONESCH! schrei ich
dazwischen. Aber die Tausend schrein gegenan. BARRABAS!
schrein sie rechts. TOR! schrein sie links. PASSION spielen sie rechts.
FUSSBALL spielen sie links. Ich steh dazwischen. Ich. Leutnant
25 Fischer. 25 Jahre jung. 57 Millionen Jahre alt. Woronesch-Jahre.
Mütter-Jahre. 57 Millionen Straßen-Jahre alt. Woronesch-Jahre.
Und rechts schrein sie BARRABAS. Und links schrein sie TOR.
Und dazwischen steh ich ohne Mutter allein. Auf der wankenden
Welle Welt ohne Mutter allein. Ich bin 25. Ich kenne die 57, die sie
30 bei Woronesch begraben haben, die 57, die nichts wußten, die nicht
wollten, die kenn ich Tag und Nacht. Und ich kenne die 86 Iwans,
die morgens mit offenen Augen und Mäulern vor dem Maschinengewehr lagen. Ich kenne das kleine Mädchen, das keine Suppe hat
und ich kenne den Obergefreiten mit den Krücken. BARRABAS
35 schrein sie rechts für zehn Mark den Saubergewaschenen ins Ohr.
Aber ich kenne die alte Frau mit den drei Bildern am Bett und das
Mädchen mit dem runden Bauch, das unter die Eisenbahn sprang.
TOR! schrein sie links, tausendmal TOR! Aber ich kenne Timm, der
nicht schlafen kann, weil er den alten Mann getreten hat und ich kenne

[4] **r Pokal** prize cup, trophy;   **s Pokalspiel** cup-tie (sports)
[14] **etw. aus·halten** to endure, to put up with s.t.
[20] **nicht mehr können** to be able to go on no longer
[23] **die sind . . . hinter mir her** they are after me
[29] **r Leierkastenmann** organ-grinder
[30] **"Freut euch des Lebens"** first line of a popular German folk song by the same title
[34] **r Sarg** casket, 'sarcophagus'
[35] **(es klingt) so nach Grab** (it sounds) sepulchral;   **wurmig** wormy;   **erdig** 'earthy'
[36] **s Lämpchen** little lantern
[37] **r Schwindel** 'swindle,' trickery;   **gluhen** to glow, burn;   **e Windel** diaper;   **blühen** blossom (Throughout the last two paragraphs the author parodies the German folk song "Freut euch des Lebens/Weil noch das Lämpchen glüht/Pflücket die Rose/Eh' sie verblüht!")

1. Was ist das Einzige, das Leutnant Fischer hält ?
2. Wer ist hinter ihm her ?
3. Wer macht schneidige Musik ?
4. Wie singt der alte Mann ?

die 57 rotäugigen Frauen, die bei dem blinden Mann Pyramidon
einkaufen. PYRAMIDON steht für 2 Mark auf der kleinen Schach-
tel. PASSION steht auf den Eintrittskarten rechts von der Straße,
für 10 Mark PASSION. POKALSPIEL steht auf den blauen, den
5 blumenblauen Billets für 4 Mark auf der linken Seite der Straße.
BARRABAS! schrein sie rechts. TOR! schrein sie links. Und immer
bellt der blinde Mann: PYRAMIDON! Dazwischen steh ich ganz
allein, ohne Mutter allein, auf der Welle, der wankenden Welle
Welt allein. Mit meinem bellenden Hunger! Und ich kenne die 57
10 von Woronesch. Ich bin Leutnant Fischer. Ich bin 25. Die anderen
schrein TOR und BARRABAS im großen Chor. Nur ich bin über.
Bin so furchtbar über. Aber es ist gut, daß die Saubergewaschenen
die 57 von Woronesch nicht kennen. Wie sollten sie es sonst wohl
aushalten bei Passion und Pokalspiel. Nur ich bin noch unterwegs.
15 Von Woronesch her. Mit Hunger schon lange lange unterwegs.
Denn ich bin über. Die andern haben sie bei Woronesch begraben.
57. Nur mich haben sie vergessen. Warum haben sie mich bloß
vergessen? Nun hab ich nur noch die Wand. Die hält mich. Da muß
ich entlang. TOR! schrein sie hinter mir her. BARRABAS! schrein
20 sie hinter mir her. Die lange lange Straße entlang. Und ich kann schon
lange nicht mehr. Ich kann schon so lange nicht mehr. Und ich hab
nur noch die Wand, denn meine Mutter ist nicht da. Nur die 57
sind da. Die 57 Millionen rotäugigen Mütter, die sind so furchtbar
hinter mir her. Die Straße entlang. Aber Leutnant Fischer komman-
25 diert: Links zwei drei vier links zwei drei vier zickezacke BARRA-
BAS die blaue Blume ist so naß von Tränen und von Blut zickezacke juppheidi begraben ist die Infanterie unterm Fußballplatz unterm Fußballplatz.

Ich kann schon lange nicht mehr, aber der alte Leierkastenmann
30 macht so schneidige Musik. Freut euch des Lebens, singt der alte
Mann die Straße lang. Freut euch, ihr bei Woronesch, juppheidi,
so freut euch doch solange noch die blaue Blume blüht freut euch
des Lebens solange noch der Leierkasten läuft — — —

Der alte Mann singt wie ein Sarg. So leise. Freut euch! singt er,
35 solange noch, singt er, so leise, so nach Grab, so wurmig, so erdig,
so nach Woronesch singt er, freut euch solange noch das Lämpchen
Schwindel glüht! Solange noch die Windel blüht!

Ich bin Leutnant Fischer! schrei ich. Ich bin über. Ich bin schon

[7] **r Hampelmann** (**hampelig** jumpy) puppet;   **e Orgel** organ
[8] **schaukeln** to rock (*here:* to swing)
[10] **schwenken** to swing
[11] **meisterlich** to perfection, masterfully
[13] **regieren** to reign
[17] **r Kittel** smock;   **e Brille** spectacles
[18] **fürchterlich** frightfully
[27] **forschen** to do research
[29] **erfinden** to invent;   **s Pulver** powder
[30] **hoffnungsgrün** green as hope (green, the liturgical color signifying hope)
[34] **pusten** (*coll.*) to puff, blow

---

1. *Was singt der Leierkastenmann?*
2. *Wie benimmt sich der Boxer?*
3. *Was hat der Mann, der regiert?*
4. *Woraus sehen wir, daß der Erfinder gefährlicher ist, als der General?*
5. *Was kann man mit dem grünen Pulver machen?*

lange die lange Straße unterwegs. Und 57 haben sie bei Woronesch
begraben. Die kenn ich.
Freut euch, singt der Leierkastenmann.
Ich bin 25, schrei ich.
5   Freut euch, singt der Leierkastenmann.
Ich hab Hunger, schrei ich.
Freut euch singt er und die bunten Hampelmänner an seiner Orgel
schaukeln. Schöne bunte Hampelmänner hat der Leierkastenmann.
Viele schöne hampelige Männer. Einen Boxer hat der Leierkasten-
10 mann. Der Boxer schwenkt die dicken dummen Fäuste und ruft:
Ich boxe! Und er bewegt sich meisterlich. Einen fetten Mann hat der
Leierkastenmann. Mit einem dicken dummen Sack voll Geld. Ich
regiere, ruft der fette Mann und er bewegt sich meisterlich. Einen
General hat der Leierkastenmann. Mit einer dicken dummen Uni-
15 form. Ich kommandiere, ruft er immerzu, ich kommandiere! Und
er bewegt sich meisterlich. Und einen Dr. Faust hat der Leierkastenmann mit einem weißen weißen Kittel und einer schwarzen Brille.
Und der ruft nicht und schreit nicht. Aber er bewegt sich fürchterlich
so fürchterlich.
20   Freut euch, singt der Leierkastenmann und seine Hampelmänner
schaukeln. Schaukeln fürchterlich. Schöne Hampelmänner hast du,
Leierkastenmann, sag ich. Freut euch, singt der Leierkastenmann.
Aber was macht der Brillenmann, der Brillenmann im weißen Kittel?
frag ich. Er ruft nicht, er boxt nicht, er regiert nicht und er komman-
25 diert nicht. Was macht der Mann im weißen Kittel, er bewegt sich,
bewegt sich so fürchterlich! Freut euch, singt der Leierkastenmann,
er denkt, singt der Leierkastenmann, er denkt und forscht und findet.
Was findet er denn, der Brillenmann, denn er bewegt sich so fürchterlich. Freut euch, singt der Leierkastenmann, er erfindet ein Pulver,
30 ein grünes Pulver, ein hoffnungsgrünes Pulver. Was kann man mit
dem grünen Pulver machen, Leierkastenmann, denn er bewegt sich
fürchterfürchterlich. Freut euch, singt der Leierkastenmann, mit
dem hoffnungsgrünen Pulver kann man mit einem Löffelchen voll
100 Millionen Menschen totmachen, wenn man pustet, wenn man
35 hoffnungsvoll pustet. Und der Brillenmann erfindet und erfindet.
Freut euch doch solange noch, singt der Leierkastenmann. Er erfindet!
schrei ich. Freut euch solange noch, singt der Leierkastenmann,
freut euch doch solange noch.
Ich bin Leutnant Fischer. Ich bin 25. Ich habe dem Leierkasten-

³ **ab·reißen** to tear off
⁵ **ab·drehen** to twist off
⁶ **mittendurch·brechen** to break in the middle, in half
⁷ **mischen** to mix
¹² **faustisch** Faustian
¹⁵ **(e) Angst haben** to be afraid
¹⁷ **e Hütte** hut
¹⁸ **e Rübe** turnip
¹⁹ **r Rhabarber** rhubarb

---

1. *Was tut Leutnant Fischer mit dem Brillenmann ?*
2. *Weshalb tut er es ?*
3. *Wo wohnen die Menschen, solange sie das grüne Pulver noch leben läßt ?*
4. *Wie viele Männer mit weißen Kitteln hat der Leierkastenmann noch ?*
5. *Wer bewegt den Hampelmann im weißen Kittel ?*

mann den Mann im weißen Kittel weggenommen. Freut euch doch
solange noch. Ich hab dem Mann, dem Brillenmann im weißen
Kittel, den Kopf abgerissen! Freut euch doch solange noch. Ich hab
dem weißen Kittelbrillenmann, dem Grünpulvermann, die Arme
5 abgedreht. Freut euch doch solange noch. Ich hab den Hoffnungs-
grünenerfindermann mittendurchgebrochen. Ich hab ihn mittendurchgebrochen. Nun kann er kein Pulver mehr mischen, nun kann
er kein Pulver mehr erfinden. Ich hab ihn mittenmittendurchge-
brochen.
10 Warum hast du meinen schönen Hampelmann kaputt gemacht,
ruft der Leierkastenmann, er war so klug, er war so weise, er war
so faustisch klug und weise und erfinderisch. Warum hast du den
Brillenmann kaputt gemacht, warum? fragt mich der Leierkastenmann.
15 Ich bin 25, schrei ich. Ich bin noch unterwegs, schrei ich. Ich hab
Angst, schrei ich. Darum hab ich den Kittelmann kaputt gemacht.
Wir wohnen in Hütten aus Holz und aus Hoffnung, schrei ich, aber
wir wohnen. Und vor unsern Hütten da wachsen noch Rüben und
Rhabarber. Vor unsern Hütten da wachsen Tomaten und Tabak.
20 Wir haben Angst! schrei ich. Wir wollen leben! schrei ich. In Hütten
aus Holz und aus Hoffnung! Denn die Tomaten und Tabak, die
wachsen doch noch. Die wachsen doch noch. Ich bin 25, schrei ich,
darum hab ich den Brillenmann im weißen Kittel umgebracht. Darum hab ich den Pulvermann kaputt gemacht. Darum darum darum
25 — — — Freut euch, singt da der Leierkastenmann, so freut euch
doch solange noch solange noch solange noch freut euch, singt der
Leierkastenmann und nimmt aus seinem furchtbar großen Kasten
einen neuen Hampelmann mit einer Brille und mit einem weißen
Kittel und mit einem Löffelchen ja Löffelchen voll hoffnungsgrünem
30 Pulver. Freut euch, singt der Leierkastenmann, freut euch solange
noch ich hab doch noch so viele viele weiße Männer so furchtbar-
furchtbar viele. Aber die bewegen sich so fürchterlichfürchterlich,
schrei ich, und ich bin 25 und ich hab Angst und ich wohne in einer
Hütte aus Holz und aus Hoffnung. Und Tomaten und Tabak, die
35 wachsen doch noch.
   Freut euch doch solange noch, singt der Leierkastenmann.
   Aber der bewegt sich doch so fürchterlich, schrei ich.
   Nein, er bewegt sich nicht, er wird er wird doch nur bewegt.
   Und wer bewegt ihn denn, wer wer bewegt ihn denn?

[24] **mit der Straßenbahn** (to go) by streetcar
[35] **r Schoß** lap

---

1. Was will Leutnant Fischer mit dem Leierkastenmann machen?
2. Warum kann er es nicht tun?
3. Welches Gefühl hat Leutnant Fischer, als er durch die Straße läuft?
4. Was fragt er die anderen Menschen, die auch mit der Straßenbahn fahren?
5. Welche Antwort bekommt er?

Ich, sagt da der Leierkastenmann so fürchterlich, ich!

Ich habe Angst, schrei ich und mach aus meiner Hand eine Faust
und schlag sie dem Leierkastenmann dem fürchterlichen Leierkastenmann in das Gesicht. Nein, ich schlag ihn nicht, denn ich kann
5 sein Gesicht das fürchterliche Gesicht nicht finden. Das Gesicht
ist so hoch am Hals. Ich kann mit der Faust nicht heran. Und der
Leierkastenmann der lacht so fürchterfürchterlich. Doch ich find es
nicht ich find es nicht. Denn das Gesicht ist ganz weit weg und lacht
so lacht so fürchterlich. Es lacht so fürchterlich.

10 Durch die Straße läuft ein Mensch. Er hat Angst. Seine Mutter
hat ihn allein gelassen. Nun schrein sie so fürchterlich hinter ihm
her. Warum? schrein 57 von Woronesch her. Warum? Deutschland,
schreit der Minister. Barrabas, schreit der Chor. Pyramidon, ruft
der blinde Mann. Und die andern schrein: Tor. Schrein 57mal Tor.
15 Und der Kittelmann, der weiße Brillenkittelmann, bewegt sich so
fürchterlich. Und erfindet und erfindet und erfindet. Und das kleine
Mädchen hat keinen Löffel. Aber der weiße Mann mit der Brille
hat einen. Der reicht gleich für 100 Millionen. Freut euch, singt der
Leierkastenmann.

20 Ein Mensch läuft durch die Straße. Die lange lange Straße lang.
Er hat Angst. Er läuft mit seiner Angst durch die Welt. Durch die
wankende Welle Welt. Der Mensch bin ich. Ich bin 25. Und ich bin
unterwegs. Bin lange schon und immer noch unterwegs. Ich will
zur Straßenbahn. Ich muß mit der Straßenbahn, denn alle sind hinter
25 mir her. Sind furchtbar hinter mir her. Ein Mensch läuft mit seiner
Angst durch die Straße. Der Mensch bin ich. Ein Mensch läuft vor
dem Schreien davon. Der Mensch bin ich. Ein Mensch glaubt an
Tomaten und Tabak. Der Mensch bin ich. Ein Mensch springt auf
die Straßenbahn, die gelbe gute Straßenbahn. Der Mensch bin ich.
30 Ich fahre mit der Straßenbahn, der guten gelben Straßenbahn.

Wo fahren wir hin? frag ich die andern. Zum Fußballplatz? Zur
Matthäus-Passion? Zu den Hütten aus Holz und aus Hoffnung mit
Tomaten und Tabak? Wo fahren wir hin? frag ich die andern.
Da sagt keiner ein Wort. Aber da sitzt eine Frau, die hat drei Bilder
35 im Schoß. Und da sitzen drei Männer beim Skat nebendran. Und da
sitzt auch der Krückenmann und das kleine Mädchen ohne Suppe
und das Mädchen mit dem runden Bauch. Und einer macht Ge-
dichte. Und einer spielt Klavier. Und 57 marschieren neben der
Straßenbahn her. Zickezackejuppheidi schneidig war die Infantrie

[1] **an der Spitze** at the head, in the front lines
[4] **r Schaffner** conductor
[5] **bezahlen** to pay
[9] **e Sau** sow;   **das weiß keine Sau** (*coll.*) absolutely nobody knows that
[10] **Tingeltangel** (*sound*) cling-clang;   **e Klingel** bell
[12] **unbegreiflich** incomprehensible, inscrutable;   **uralt = sehr alt**
[13] **e Falte** wrinkle, 'fold'

---

1. Wie sieht der Schaffner aus ?

bei Woronesch heijuppheidi. An der Spitze marschiert Leutnant
Fischer. Leutnant Fischer bin ich. Und meine Mutter marschiert
hinterher. Marschiert 57 millionenmal hinter mir her. Wohin fahren
wir denn? frag ich den Schaffner. Da gibt er mir ein hoffnungsgrünes
5 Billet. Matthäus — Pyramidon steht da drauf. Bezahlen müssen
wir alle, sagt er und hält seine Hand auf. Und ich gebe ihm 57 Mann.
Aber wohin fahren wir denn? frag ich die andern. Wir müssen doch
wissen: wohin? Da sagt Timm: Das wissen wir auch nicht. Das weiß
keine Sau. Und alle nicken mit dem Kopf und grummeln: Das weiß
10 keine Sau. Aber wir fahren. Tingeltangel, macht die Klingel der
Straßenbahn und keiner weiß wohin. Aber alle fahren mit. Und der
Schaffner macht ein unbegreifliches Gesicht. Es ist ein uralter Schaffner mit zehntausend Falten. Man kann nicht erkennen, ob es ein böser
oder ein guter Schaffner ist. Aber alle bezahlen bei ihm. Und alle
15 fahren mit. Und keiner weiß: ein guter oder böser. Und keiner weiß:
wohin. Tingeltangel, macht die Klingel der Straßenbahn. Und keiner
weiß. wohin? Und alle fahren: mit. Und keiner weiß — — — und
keiner weiß — — — und keiner weiß — — —

¹ e **Nähmaschine** sewing machine;   r **Eisschrank** refrigerator
² r **Fabrikbesitzer** factory owner
³ r **Erfinder** inventor
⁶ r **Kittel** coat
⁷ **zart** delicate;   r **Buchstabe** letter
⁸ **aus·ziehen** to take off;   **pflegen** to care for, tend
⁹ e **Fensterbank** window sill;   **ein·gehen** to wither
¹⁶ r **Kostenanschlag** estimate (of cost)
¹⁸ e **Kachel** tile
²⁰ **rechtzeitig** opportunely
²¹ e **Schokolade** chocolate;   s **Schießpulver** gunpowder;   **von etw. auf etw.** (*acc.*)
  um·stellen to switch from s.t. to s.t.
²³ r **Duschraum** shower bath
²⁷ r **Bauunternehmer** building contractor

---

1. Was haben alle Leute ?
2. Was will der Erfinder machen ?
3. Welchen Wunsch hat der General ?
4. Welche Einstellung hat der Mann im weißen Kittel zum Tod der Blume und zum
   Menschentod ?
5. Was hat der Fabrikbesitzer früher produziert ?
6. Woraus schließen wir, daß der Krieg ein gutes Geschäft ist?

Lesebuchgeschichten

Alle Leute haben eine Nähmaschine, ein Radio, einen Eisschrank und ein Telefon. Was machen wir nun? fragte der Fabrikbesitzer.
Bomben, sagte der Erfinder.
Krieg, sagte der General.
Wenn es denn gar nicht anders geht, sagte der Fabrikbesitzer.

Der Mann mit dem weißen Kittel schrieb Zahlen auf das Papier.
Er machte ganz kleine zarte Buchstaben dazu.
Dann zog er den weißen Kittel aus und pflegte eine Stunde lang die Blumen auf der Fensterbank. Als er sah, daß eine Blume eingegangen war, wurde er sehr traurig und weinte.
Und auf dem Papier standen die Zahlen. Danach konnte man mit einem halben Gramm in zwei Stunden tausend Menschen totmachen.
Die Sonne schien auf die Blumen.
Und auf das Papier.

Zwei Männer sprachen miteinander.
Kostenanschlag?
Mit Kacheln?
Mit grünen Kacheln natürlich.
Vierzigtausend.
Vierzigtausend? Gut. Ja, mein Lieber, hätte ich mich nicht rechtzeitig von Schokolade auf Schießpulver umgestellt, dann könnte ich Ihnen diese vierzigtausend nicht geben.
Und ich Ihnen keinen Duschraum.
Mit grünen Kacheln.
Mit grünen Kacheln.
Die beiden Männer gingen auseinander.
Es waren ein Fabrikbesitzer und ein Bauunternehmer.
Es war Krieg.

2 **nanu!** well, now!   **r Studienrat** high school teacher;   **r Anzug** suit;   **r Trauerfall** death, *lit.* "mourning case"

3 **keineswegs** not at all;   **e Feier** ceremony

4 **Clausewitz, Carl von** (1780—1831) Prussian general;   **zitieren** to quote, 'cite';   **r Begriff** concept

5 **e Ehre** glory;   **s Vaterland** fatherland;   **Hölderlin, Johann Christian Friedrich** (1770—1843) German poet;   **Langemarck** (Belgium) 1914 attack by German volunteer soldiers

6 **ergreifend** moving

7 **"Der Gott der Eisen wachsen ließ, Der wollte keine Knechte"** from the poem, "Vaterlandslied" by Ernst Moritz Arndt (1769—1860), German poet, historian, and politician

9 **auf·hören** to stop;   **gräßlich** horrible

10 **an·starren** to stare at;   **entsetzen** to shock

13 **donnern** to thunder

17 **ziemlich** fairly;   **schief** cockeyed

22 **drauf·gehen** (*coll.*) to be lost

3 **r Freiwillige** volunteer

31 **'türlich = natürlich**

35 **auseinander·gehen** to part ways

37 **um·fallen** to topple over

---

1. Warum trägt der Studienrat einen dunklen Anzug ?

2. Was wurde bei der Feier gemacht ?

3. Wovon sprechen die beiden Generale, wenn sie viertausend sagen ?

Kegelbahn. Zwei Männer sprachen miteinander.
Nanu, Studienrat, dunklen Anzug an. Trauerfall?
Keineswegs, keineswegs. Feier gehabt. Jungens gehn an die Front.
Kleine Rede gehalten. Sparta erinnert. Clausewitz zitiert. Paar Be-
5 griffe mitgegeben: Ehre, Vaterland, Hölderlin lesen lassen. Langemarck gedacht. Ergreifende Feier. Ganz ergreifend. Jungens haben
gesungen: Gott, der Eisen wachsen ließ. Augen leuchteten. Ergreifend.
Ganz ergreifend.
Mein Gott, Studienrat, hören Sie auf. Das ist ja gräßlich.
10 Der Studienrat starrte die anderen entsetzt an. Er hatte beim Erzählen lauter kleine Kreuze auf das Papier gemacht. Lauter kleine
Kreuze. Er stand auf und lachte. Nahm eine neue Kugel und ließ
sie über die Bahn rollen. Es donnerte leise. Dann stürzten hinten
die Kegel. Sie sahen aus wie kleine Männer.

15 Zwei Männer sprachen miteinander.
Na, wie ist es?
Ziemlich schief.
Wieviel haben Sie noch?
Wenn es gut geht: viertausend.
20 Wieviel können Sie mir geben?
Höchstens achthundert.
Die gehen drauf.
Also tausend.
Danke.
25 Die beiden Männer gingen auseinander.
Sie sprachen von Menschen.
Es waren Generale.
Es war Krieg.

Zwei Männer sprachen miteinander.
30 Freiwilliger?
'türlich.
Wie alt?
Achtzehn. Und du?
Ich auch.
35 Die beiden Männer gingen auseinander.
Es waren zwei Soldaten.
Da fiel der eine um. Er war tot.
Es war Krieg.

² **der** *here:* demonstrative, not relative pronoun
³ **r Richter** judge
⁵ **e Friedenskonferenz** peace conference
⁶ **e Schießbude** shooting gallery;   **Mal schießen, der Herr?** Would the gentleman like to shoot, huh?
⁸ **s Gewehr** gun
⁹ **e Pappe** cardboard
¹² **e Ohrfeige** box on the ears
¹⁶ **r Stock** stick, club
²³ **begraben** to bury
²⁴ **r Regenwurm** earthworm
²⁵ **merken** to notice
²⁷ **r Maulwurf** mole;   **heraus·kucken** (*coll.*) to peer out
²⁸ **beruhigt** with a feeling of relief
³⁰ **e Krähe** crow;   **krächzen** to croak
³² **r Stint** smelt
³⁴ **e Mücke** gnat, 'midge'
³⁶ **manchmal** sometimes

---

1. *Weshalb begreift der Soldat den Richter nicht?*
2. *Warum gibt die Mutter dem Minister eine Ohrfeige?*
3. *Womit schlagen sich die Menschen, wenn sie noch Kinder sind?*
4. *Womit kämpfen sie später?*
5. *Was findet der Regenwurm, der nach hundert Jahren ihre Gräber besucht?*
6. *Was sieht der Maulwurf, der im Jahre 5000 aus der Erde schaut?*

Als der Krieg aus war, kam der Soldat nach Hause. Aber er hatte kein
Brot. Da sah er einen, der hatte Brot. Den schlug er tot.
Du darfst doch keinen totschlagen, sagte der Richter.
Warum nicht, fragte der Soldat.

5 Als die Friedenskonferenz zuende war, gingen die Minister durch
die Stadt. Da kamen sie an einer Schießbude vorbei. Mal schießen,
der Herr? riefen die Mädchen mit den roten Lippen. Da nahmen
die Minister alle ein Gewehr und schossen auf kleine Männer aus
Pappe.
10 Mitten im Schießen kam eine alte Frau und nahm ihnen die Ge-
wehre weg. Als einer der Minister es wiederhaben wollte, gab sie
ihm eine Ohrfeige.
Es war eine Mutter.

Es waren mal zwei Menschen. Als sie zwei Jahre alt waren, da schlu-
15 gen sie sich mit den Händen.
Als sie zwölf waren, schlugen sie sich mit Stöcken und warfen mit
Steinen.
Als sie zweiundzwanzig waren, schossen sie mit Gewehren nach
einander.
20 Als sie zweiundvierzig waren, warfen sie mit Bomben.
Als sie zweiundsechzig waren, nahmen sie Bakterien.
Als sie zweiundachtzig waren, da starben sie. Sie wurden nebeneinander begraben.
Als sich nach hundert Jahren ein Regenwurm durch ihre beiden
25 Gräber fraß, merkte er gar nicht, daß hier zwei verschiedene Menschen begraben waren. Es war dieselbe Erde. Alles dieselbe Erde.

Als im Jahre 5000 ein Maulwurf aus der Erde rauskuckte, da stellte
er beruhigt fest:
Die Bäume sind immer noch Bäume.
30 Die Krähen krächzen noch.
Und die Hunde heben immer noch ihr Bein.
Die Stinte und die Sterne,
das Moos und das Meer
und die Mücken:
35 Sie sind alle dieselben geblieben.
Und manchmal —
manchmal trifft man einen Menschen.

e **Küchenuhr** kitchen clock
[1] **zu·kommen** to approach;   **auf·fallen** to attract attention
[3] **erst** only
[6] **der Reihe nach** down the row
[8] **übrig·bleiben** to be left over
[9] **tellerweiß** white as a plate;   **vor sich hin** in front of him(self);   **ab·tupfen** to dab at, touch
[10] **malen** to paint
[11] **entschuldigend** apologetically
[13] r **Lack** varnish
[14] **hübsch** pretty;   r **Zeiger** hand (clock);   s **Blech** tin
[18] e **Spitze** tip;   **vorsichtig** careful
[19] r **Rand** rim
[22] r **Kinderwagen** stroller
[25] **freudig** cheerfully
[31] **aufgeregt** excitedly

---

1. *Weshalb fiel der junge Mann auf ?*
2. *Woraus sah man, daß er zwanzig Jahre alt war ?*
3. *Was zeigte er den Leuten ?*
4. *Wie sah die Küchenuhr aus ?*
5. *Weshalb versteht die Frau nicht, daß die Küchenuhr dem jungen Menschen so wichtig ist ?*
6. *Warum sehen die Leute auf der Bank ihn nicht an ?*

Die Küchenuhr

Sie sahen ihn schon von weitem auf sich zukommen, denn er fiel auf. Er hatte ein ganz altes Gesicht, aber wie er ging, daran sah man, daß er erst zwanzig war. Er setzte sich mit seinem alten Gesicht zu ihnen auf die Bank. Und dann zeigte er ihnen, was er in der Hand 5 trug.

Das war unsere Küchenuhr, sagte er und sah sie alle der Reihe nach an, die auf der Bank in der Sonne saßen. Ja, ich habe sie noch gefunden. Sie ist übriggeblieben.

Er hielt eine runde tellerweiße Küchenuhr vor sich hin und tupfte 10 mit dem Finger die blaugemalten Zahlen ab.

Sie hat weiter keinen Wert, meinte er entschuldigend, das weiß ich auch. Und sie ist auch nicht so besonders schön. Sie ist nur wie ein Teller, so mit weißem Lack. Aber die blauen Zahlen sehen doch ganz hübsch aus, finde ich. Die Zeiger sind natürlich nur aus Blech. 15 Und nun gehen sie auch nicht mehr. Nein. Innerlich ist sie kaputt, das steht fest. Aber sie sieht noch aus wie immer. Auch wenn sie jetzt nicht mehr geht.

Er machte mit der Fingerspitze einen vorsichtigen Kreis auf dem Rand der Telleruhr entlang. Und er sagte leise: Und sie ist übrig- 20 geblieben.

Die auf der Bank in der Sonne saßen, sahen ihn nicht an. Einer sah auf seine Schuhe und die Frau sah in ihren Kinderwagen. Dann sagte jemand:

Sie haben wohl alles verloren?

25 Ja, ja, sagte er freudig, denken Sie, aber auch alles! Nur sie hier, sie ist übrig. Und er hob die Uhr wieder hoch, als ob die anderen sie noch nicht kannten.

Aber sie geht doch nicht mehr, sagte die Frau.

Nein, nein, das nicht. Kaputt ist sie, das weiß ich wohl. Aber sonst 30 ist sie doch noch ganz wie immer: weiß und blau. Und wieder zeigte er ihnen seine Uhr. Und was das Schönste ist, fuhr er aufgeregt fort,

[1] **das Schönste kommt nämlich noch** the best is yet to come
[2] **denken Sie mal** just imagine
[3] **ausgerechnet** exactly, of all things
[5] **vor·schieben** to push forward
[7] **r Druck** pressure
[8] **überlegen** with an air of superiority
[11] **Das ist nämlich der Witz** that's what is so funny, you see
[17] **zu·nicken** to nod towards
[22] **plötzlich** suddenly
[23] **e Wolljacke** wool jacket;   **r Schal** shawl
[24] **gekachelt (e Kachel** tile) tiled
[28] **s Abendbrot** supper
[29] **aneinander·scheuern (scheuern** to 'scour') to rub against each other
[31] **satt** full
[32] **aus·machen** to put out
[34] **das war ganz selbstverständlich** it went quite without saying
[38] **auf·hören** to stop, cease

---

1. Was glaubt der Mann, als er hört, daß die Uhr um halb drei stehengeblieben ist?
2. Was sagt der junge Mann darüber?
3. Wohin ging er immer gleich, wenn er nach Hause kam?
4. Wer kam dann auch hin?
5. Was tat und sprach die Mutter?

das habe ich Ihnen ja noch überhaupt nicht erzählt. Das Schönste kommt nämlich noch: Denken Sie mal, sie ist um halb drei stehengeblieben. Ausgerechnet um halb drei, denken Sie mal.

Dann wurde Ihr Haus sicher um halb drei getroffen, sagte der
5 Mann und schob wichtig die Unterlippe vor. Das habe ich schon oft gehört. Wenn die Bombe runtergeht, bleiben die Uhren stehen. Das kommt von dem Druck.

Er sah seine Uhr an und schüttelte überlegen den Kopf. Nein, lieber Herr, nein, da irren Sie sich. Das hat mit den Bomben nichts
10 zu tun. Sie müssen nicht immer von den Bomben reden. Nein. Um halb drei war ganz etwas anderes, das wissen Sie nur nicht. Das ist nämlich der Witz, daß sie gerade um halb drei stehengeblieben ist. Und nicht um viertel nach vier oder um sieben. Um halb drei kam ich nämlich immer nach Hause. Nachts, meine ich. Fast immer um
15 halb drei. Das ist ja gerade der Witz.

Er sah die anderen an, aber die hatten ihre Augen von ihm weggenommen. Er fand sie nicht. Da nickte er seiner Uhr zu: Dann hatte ich natürlich Hunger, nicht wahr? Und ich ging immer gleich in die Küche. Da war es dann fast immer halb drei. Und dann, dann
20 kam nämlich meine Mutter. Ich konnte noch so leise die Tür aufmachen, sie hat mich immer gehört. Und wenn ich in der dunklen Küche etwas zu essen suchte, ging plötzlich das Licht an. Dann stand sie da in ihrer Wolljacke und mit einem roten Schal um. Und barfuß. Immer barfuß. Und dabei war unsere Küche gekachelt. Und sie mach-
25 te ihre Augen ganz klein, weil ihr das Licht so hell war. Denn sie hatte ja schon geschlafen. Es war ja Nacht.

So spät wieder, sagte sie dann. Mehr sagte sie nie. Nur: So spät wieder. Und dann machte sie mir das Abendbrot warm und sah zu, wie ich aß. Dabei scheuerte sie immer die Füße aneinander, weil
30 die Kacheln so kalt waren. Schuhe zog sie nachts nie an. Und sie saß so lange bei mir, bis ich satt war. Und dann hörte ich sie noch die Teller wegsetzen, wenn ich in meinem Zimmer schon das Licht ausgemacht hatte. Jede Nacht war es so. Und meistens immer um halb drei. Das war ganz selbstverständlich, fand ich, daß sie mir nachts um
35 halb drei in der Küche das Essen machte. Ich fand das ganz selbstverständlich. Sie tat das ja immer. Und sie hat nie mehr gesagt als: So spät wieder. Aber das sagte sie jedesmal. Und ich dachte, das könnte nie aufhören. Es war mir so selbstverständlich. Das alles war doch immer so gewesen.

[1] **r Atemzug** breath
[4] **richtig** true
[7] **verlegen** self-conscious(ly), embarrassed

---

1. *Was geschah mit den Eltern beim Bombenangriff?*
2. *Welches einzige Ding blieb nachher übrig?*
3. *Wohin sah der Mann, als der junge Mensch seine Geschichte erzählt hatte?*
4. *Woran dachte er dabei?*
5. *Was für eine Bedeutung hat die Küchenuhr für den jungen Menschen mit dem alten Gesicht?*

Einen Atemzug lang war es ganz still auf der Bank. Dann sagte
er leise: Und jetzt? Er sah die anderen an. Aber er fand sie nicht.
Da sagte er der Uhr leise ins weißblaue runde Gesicht: Jetzt, jetzt
weiß ich, daß es das Paradies war. Das richtige Paradies.

5   Auf der Bank war es ganz still. Dann fragte die Frau: Und Ihre
Familie?

Er lächelte sie verlegen an: Ach, Sie meinen meine Eltern? Ja,
die sind auch mit weg. Alles ist weg. Alles, stellen Sie sich vor. Alles
weg.

10 Er lächelte verlegen von einem zum anderen. Aber sie sahen ihn
nicht an.

Da hob er wieder die Uhr hoch und er lachte. Er lachte: Nur sie
hier. Sie ist übrig. Und das Schönste ist ja, daß sie ausgerechnet um
halb drei stehengeblieben ist. Ausgerechnet um halb drei.

15 Dann sagte er nichts mehr. Aber er hatte ein ganz altes Gesicht.
Und der Mann, der neben ihm saß, sah auf seine Schuhe. Aber er
sah seine Schuhe nicht. Er dachte immerzu an das Wort Paradies.

s **Brot** bread (loaf)
[1] **auf·wachen** to awake;   **überlegen** reflect
[3] **horchen** to listen
[6] r **Atem** breath;   **tappen** to grope
[8] r **Küchenschrank** pantry
[11] r **Brotteller** bread plate
[12] **ab·schneiden** to slice
[13] r **Brotkrümel** breadcrumb
[14] s **Tischtuch** tablecloth;   **sauber** clean
[16] e **Fliese** tile
[18] **hier wär** (= **wäre**) **was** there might be something (the matter) here
[22] **tagsüber** during the day
[24] **das liegt an den Haaren** the hair is to blame
[27] **an·ziehen** to put on
[28] **sich erkälten** to catch cold
[29] **lügen** to tell a lie
[30] **verheiratet** married
[32] **sinnlos** senseless(ly)
[34] **vom Tisch stellen** to pick up from the table

---

1. Weshalb wachte die Frau auf ?
2. Was fand sie, als sie mit der Hand über das Bett neben sich fuhr ?
3. Wo traf sie ihren Mann ?
4. Was sah sie auf dem Küchentisch ?
5. Woran liegt es, daß die Frau alt aussieht ?
6. Weswegen sollte der Mann Schuhe anziehen ?

Das Brot

Plötzlich wachte sie auf. Es war halb drei. Sie überlegte, warum
sie aufgewacht war. Ach so! In der Küche hatte jemand gegen einen
Stuhl gestoßen. Sie horchte nach der Küche. Es war still. Es war
zu still und als sie mit der Hand über das Bett neben sich fuhr, fand
5 sie es leer. Das war es, was es so besonders still gemacht hatte:
sein Atem fehlte. Sie stand auf und tappte durch die dunkle Wohnung
zur Küche. In der Küche trafen sie sich. Die Uhr war halb drei.
Sie sah etwas Weißes am Küchenschrank stehen. Sie machte Licht.
Sie standen sich im Hemd gegenüber. Nachts. Um halb drei. In
10 der Küche.

Auf dem Küchentisch stand der Brotteller. Sie sah, daß er sich
Brot abgeschnitten hatte. Das Messer lag noch neben dem Teller.
Und auf der Decke lagen Brotkrümel. Wenn sie abends zu Bett gingen, machte sie immer das Tischtuch sauber. Jeden Abend. Aber
15 nun lagen Krümel auf dem Tuch. Und das Messer lag da. Sie fühlte,
wie die Kälte der Fliesen langsam an ihr hochkroch. Und sie sah
von dem Teller weg.

„Ich dachte, hier wär was", sagte er und sah in der Küche umher.

20 „Ich habe auch was gehört", antwortete sie und dabei fand sie,
daß er nachts im Hemd doch schon recht alt aussah. So alt wie
er war. Dreiundsechzig. Tagsüber sah er manchmal jünger aus. Sie
sieht doch schon alt aus, dachte er, im Hemd sieht sie doch ziemlich
alt aus. Aber das liegt vielleicht an den Haaren. Bei den Frauen
25 liegt das nachts immer an den Haaren. Die machen dann auf einmal
so alt.

„Du hättest Schuhe anziehen sollen. So barfuß auf den kalten
Fliesen. Du erkältest dich noch."

Sie sah ihn nicht an, weil sie nicht ertragen konnte, daß er log.
30 Daß er log, nachdem sie neununddreißig Jahre verheiratet waren.

„Ich dachte, hier wäre was", sagte er noch einmal und sah wieder
so sinnlos von einer Ecke in die andere, „ich hörte hier was. Da dachte
ich, hier wäre was."

„Ich hab auch was gehört. Aber es war wohl nichts." Sie stellte

[1] **schnippen** to flick;   **e Decke** tablecloth
[3] **zu Hilfe kommen** to come to the rescue;   **komm man** (*coll.*) come along
[7] **r Lichtschalter** (**schalten** to switch) light switch
[10] **e Dachrinne** gutter
[12] **klappern** to rattle
[14] **platschen** to make a slapping noise
[20] **unecht** false;   **klingen** to sound
[21] **gähnen** to yawn;   **kriechen** to crawl
[23] **ganz schön . . . kalt** pretty darn cold
[26] **vorsichtig** cautiously;   **kauen** to chew;   **gleichmäßig** evenly
[28] **regelmäßig** regular(ly);   **ein·schlafen** to fall asleep
[29] **j-em etw. hin·schieben** to push toward s.o.
[30] **e Scheibe** slice
[32] **vertragen** to digest;   **iß du man** (*coll.*) just eat
[34] **sich beugen** to bend oneself
[35] **er tat ihr leid** she felt sorry for him
[36] **er sagte auf seinen Teller** he said (looking down) to his plate

---

1. *Was tut die Dachrinne, wenn es windig ist ?*
2. *Wie merkt die Frau, daß der Mann lügt ?*
3. *Was tut die Frau, weil es ihr kalt ist ?*
4. *Was hört sie nach einigen Minuten, als es still war?*
5. *Wodurch zeigt sie am nächsten Abend, daß sie den Mann versteht ?*
6. *Wie begründet sie ihre Handlung ?*

den Teller vom Tisch und schnippte die Krümel von der Decke.

„Nein, es war wohl nichts", echote er unsicher.

Sie kam ihm zu Hilfe: „Komm man. Das war wohl draußen. Komm man zu Bett. Du erkältest dich noch. Auf den kalten Fliesen."

5 Er sah zum Fenster hin. „Ja, das muß wohl draußen gewesen sein. Ich dachte, es wäre hier."

Sie hob die Hand zum Lichtschalter. Ich muß das Licht jetzt ausmachen, sonst muß ich nach dem Teller sehen, dachte sie. Ich darf doch nicht nach dem Teller sehen. „Komm man", sagte sie und mach-
10 te das Licht aus, „das war wohl draußen. Die Dachrinne schlägt immer bei Wind gegen die Wand. Es war sicher die Dachrinne. Bei Wind klappert sie immer."

Sie tappten sich beide über den dunklen Korridor zum Schlafzimmer. Ihre nackten Füße platschten auf den Fußboden.

15 „Wind ist ja," meinte er. „Wind war schon die ganze Nacht."
Als sie im Bett lagen, sagte sie: „Ja, Wind war schon die ganze Nacht. Es war wohl die Dachrinne."

„Ja, ich dachte, es wäre in der Küche. Es war wohl die Dachrinne."
Er sagte das, als ob er schon halb im Schlaf wäre.

20 Aber sie merkte, wie unecht seine Stimme klang, wenn er log.
„Es ist kalt", sagte sie und gähnte leise, „ich krieche unter die Decke. Gute Nacht."

„Nacht", antwortete er und noch: „ja, kalt ist es schon ganz schön."

25 Dann war es still. Nach vielen Minuten hörte sie, daß er leise und vorsichtig kaute. Sie atmete absichtlich tief und gleichmäßig, damit er nicht merken sollte, daß sie noch wach war. Aber sein Kauen war so regelmäßig, daß sie davon langsam einschlief.

Als er am nächsten Abend nach Hause kam, schob sie ihm vier
30 Scheiben Brot hin. Sonst hatte er immer nur drei essen können.

„Du kannst ruhig vier essen", sagte sie und ging von der Lampe weg. „Ich kann dieses Brot nicht so recht vertragen. Iß du man eine mehr. Ich vertrag es nicht so gut."

Sie sah, wie er sich tief über den Teller beugte. Er sah nicht auf.
35 In diesem Augenblick tat er ihr leid.

„Du kannst doch nicht nur zwei Scheiben essen", sagte er auf seinen Teller.

„Doch. Abends vertrag ich das Brot nicht gut. Iß man. Iß man."
Erst nach einer Weile setzte sie sich unter die Lampe an den Tisch.

¹ **tappen** to grope;   **e Vorstadt** suburb, outskirts;   **abgebrochen** disjointedly
² **fehlen** to be absent;   **s Pflaster** pavement
³ **e Planke** fence of boards
⁴ **e Latte** board;   **morsch** decaying;   **auf·seufzen** to groan
⁵ **los·brechen** to break off;   **mürbe** brittle, mellow
⁷ **j-em entgegen·sehen** to look toward s.o.
⁸ **blaßblau** pale blue
⁹ **r Atem** breath
¹⁰ **knochig** bony
¹¹ **ringsum** all around
¹⁴ **r Blechofen** tin stove
¹⁵ **auf·glimmen** to glow, flare up
¹⁶ **winzig** tiny
¹⁹ **zu** *here:* closed
²⁰ **pusten** to blow
²³ **e Haferflocken** rolled oats
²⁵ **ein Kind kriegen** (*coll.*) to have a baby;   **frieren** to freeze
²⁶ **e Faust** fist
²⁸ **kuck** (*coll.*) look
²⁹ **r Heiligenschein** halo
³² **sich hin·setzen** to sit down

---

1. *Wo ist der Mann ?*
2. *Warum läuft er noch so spät herum ?*
3. *Wie schaut die Frau aus ?*
4. *Wie alt ist der dritte Mensch im Zimmer ?*
5. *Wie sieht das Kind aus ?*
6. *Weswegen kommen die drei Männer ins Zimmer ?*

Die drei dunklen Könige

Er tappte durch die dunkle Vorstadt. Die Häuser standen abgebrochen gegen den Himmel. Der Mond fehlte und das Pflaster war erschrocken über den späten Schritt. Dann fand er eine alte Planke. Da trat er mit dem Fuß gegen, bis eine Latte morsch aufseufzte
5 und losbrach. Das Holz roch mürbe und süß. Durch die dunkle Vorstadt tappte er zurück. Sterne waren nicht da.

Als er die Tür aufmachte (sie weinte dabei, die Tür), sahen ihm die blaßblauen Augen seiner Frau entgegen. Sie kamen aus einem müden Gesicht. Ihr Atem hing weiß im Zimmer, so kalt war es. Er
10 beugte sein knochiges Knie und brach das Holz. Das Holz seufzte. Dann roch es mürbe und süß ringsum. Er hielt sich ein Stück davon unter die Nase. Riecht beinahe wie Kuchen, lachte er leise. Nicht, sagten die Augen der Frau, nicht lachen. Er schläft.

Der Mann legte das süße mürbe Holz in den kleinen Blechofen.
15 Da glomm es auf und warf eine Handvoll warmes Licht durch das Zimmer. Die fiel hell auf ein winziges rundes Gesicht und blieb einen Augenblick. Das Gesicht war erst eine Stunde alt, aber es hatte schon alles, was dazugehört: Ohren, Nase, Mund und Augen. Die Augen mußten groß sein, das konnte man sehen, obgleich sie zu waren.
20 Aber der Mund war offen und es pustete leise daraus. Nase und Ohren waren rot. Er lebt, dachte die Mutter. Und das kleine Gesicht schlief.

Da sind noch Haferflocken, sagte der Mann. Ja, antwortete die Frau, das ist gut. Es ist kalt. Der Mann nahm noch von dem süßen
25 weichen Holz. Nun hat sie ihr Kind gekriegt und muß frieren, dachte er. Aber er hatte keinen, dem er dafür die Fäuste ins Gesicht schlagen konnte. Als er die Ofentür aufmachte, fiel wieder eine Handvoll Licht über das schlafende Gesicht. Die Frau sagte leise: Kuck, wie ein Heiligenschein, siehst du? Heiligenschein! dachte er und er hatte
30 keinen, dem er die Fäuste ins Gesicht schlagen konnte.

Dann waren welche an der Tür. Wir sahen das Licht, sagten sie, vom Fenster. Wir wollen uns zehn Minuten hinsetzen.

Aber wir haben ein Kind, sagte der Mann zu ihnen. Da sagten sie

[1] **Nebel aus der Nase stoßen** to blow fog out of their noses
[3] **e Fuße** (*pl.*) **hoch·heben** to put one's feet up
[4] **r Pappkarton** cardboard box
[6] **r Stumpf** stump
[7] **e Manteltasche** coat pocket;   **Zigaretten drehen** to roll cigarettes
[10] **umwickelt** bound up
[11] **r Sack** bag
[12] **schnitzen** to carve
[15] **befühlen** to examine by touch;   **zittern** to tremble
[17] **Zigaretten aus·treten** to stamp out cigarettes
[21] **e Bonbons** (*pl.*) pieces of candy
[23] **gebeugt (beugen)** 'bowed', bent
[24] **stemmen** to set (against);   **kräftig** vigorously
[26] **nicken** to nod;   **nochmal** (= **noch einmal**) once more
[27] **sonderbare Heilige** strange fellows (*lit.* saints)
[28] **brummen** to grumble
[39] **e Weihnachten** (*pl.*) Christmas (eve)

---

1. *Wer sind sie ?*
2. *Warum müssen sie draußen rauchen ?*
3. *Weshalb hat der erste Besucher keine Hände ?*
4. *Warum hat der zweite Mensch umwickelte Füße ?*
5. *Weswegen zittert der dritte Mann ?*
6. *Was für Geschenke bringen sie ?*
7. *Was für ein besonderer Abend ist es ?*

nichts weiter, aber sie kamen doch ins Zimmer, stießen Nebel aus den Nasen und hoben die Füße hoch. Wir sind ganz leise, flüsterten sie und hoben die Füße hoch. Dann fiel das Licht auf sie.

Drei waren es. In drei alten Uniformen. Einer hatte einen Papp-
5 karton, einer einen Sack. Und der dritte hatte keine Hände. Erfroren, sagte er, und hielt die Stümpfe hoch. Dann drehte er dem Mann die Manteltasche hin. Tabak war darin und dünnes Papier. Sie drehten Zigaretten. Aber die Frau sagte: Nicht, das Kind.

Da gingen die vier vor die Tür und ihre Zigaretten waren vier Punkte
10 in der Nacht. Der eine hatte dicke umwickelte Füße. Er nahm ein Stück Holz aus seinem Sack. Ein Esel, sagte er, ich habe sieben Monate daran geschnitzt. Für das Kind. Das sagte er und gab es dem Mann. Was ist mit den Füßen? fragte der Mann. Wasser, sagte der Esel-schnitzer, vom Hunger. Und der andere, der dritte? fragte der Mann
15 und befühlte im Dunkeln den Esel. Der dritte zitterte in seiner Uni-form: Oh, nichts, wisperte er, das sind nur die Nerven. Man hat eben zuviel Angst gehabt. Dann traten sie die Zigaretten aus und gingen wieder hinein.

Sie hoben die Füße hoch und sahen auf das kleine schlafende
20 Gesicht. Der Zitternde nahm aus seinem Pappkarton zwei gelbe Bonbons und sagte dazu: Für die Frau sind die.

Die Frau machte die blassen blauen Augen weit auf, als sie die drei Dunklen über das Kind gebeugt sah. Sie fürchtete sich. Aber da stemmte das Kind seine Beine gegen ihre Brust und schrie so kräf-
25 tig, daß die drei Dunklen die Füße aufhoben und zur Tür schlichen. Hier nickten sie nochmal, dann stiegen sie in die Nacht hinein.

Der Mann sah ihnen nach. Sonderbare Heilige, sagte er zu seiner Frau. Dann machte er die Tür zu. Schöne Heilige sind das, brummte er und sah nach den Haferflocken. Aber er hatte kein Gesicht für
30 seine Fäuste.

Aber das Kind hat geschrien, flüsterte die Frau, ganz stark hat es geschrien. Da sind sie gegangen. Kuck mal, wie lebendig es ist, sagte sie stolz. Das Gesicht machte den Mund auf und schrie.

Weint er? fragte der Mann.
35 Nein, ich glaube, er lacht, antwortete die Frau.

Beinahe wie Kuchen, sagte der Mann und roch an dem Holz, wie Kuchen. Ganz süß.

Heute ist ja auch Weihnachten, sagte die Frau.

Ja, Weihnachten, brummte er und vom Ofen her fiel eine Handvoll
40 Licht hell auf das kleine schlafende Gesicht.

r **Abschied** farewell
[1] e **Bindung** commitment;   e **Tiefe** depth
[2] r **Abgrund** abyss
[3] **schmal** narrow, restricted
[4] **grausam** cruel;   e **Jugend** youth
[5] e **Hemmung** restraint;   e **Behütung** protection;   **ausgestoßen aus dem Laufgitter des Kindseins** *lit.* thrust out of the child's playpen, i.e., the sheltered existence of childhood
[6] **bereiten** to create
[7] **darum** for it;   **verachten** to despise
[9] **um·wirbeln** to whirl about
[11] e **Vergangenheit** past;   **Anerkennung** recognition, appreciation
[13] r **Zigeuner** gipsy;   **mannshoch verschneit** snowed under at a man's height
[18] e **Irrfahrten** (*pl.*) wanderings, vagaries
[22] **aus·kosten** to fully enjoy;   e **Sekunde** second (*time unit*)
[23] e **Flut** flood;   **an·steigen** to mount
[24] r **Damm** dam;   r **Urvater** forefather;   **widerstehen** (+ *dat.*) to withstand
[30] **durch·bluten** to bleed through
[31] **innig** deeply;   **trauernd** mourning;   **tröstend** consoling

---

1. *Wo ist die Heimat der Generation ohne Abschied ?*
2. *Weshalb hat diese Generation keine Bindung ?*
3. *Warum will sie keinen Abschied leben ?*
4. *Weswegen sagen die anderen Menschen, daß diese Generation kein Herz hätte ?*

Generation ohne Abschied

Wir sind die Generation ohne Bindung und ohne Tiefe. Unsere Tiefe ist Abgrund. Wir sind die Generation ohne Glück, ohne Heimat und ohne Abschied. Unsere Sonne ist schmal, unsere Liebe grausam und unsere Jugend ist ohne Jugend. Und wir sind die Gene-
5 ration ohne Grenze, ohne Hemmung und Behütung — ausgestoßen aus dem Laufgitter des Kindseins in eine Welt, die die uns bereitet, die uns darum verachten.

Aber sie gaben uns keinen Gott mit, der unser Herz hätte halten können, wenn die Winde dieser Welt es umwirbelten. So sind wir die
10 Generation ohne Gott, denn wir sind die Generation ohne Bindung, ohne Vergangenheit, ohne Anerkennung.

Und die Winde der Welt, die unsere Füße und unsere Herzen zu Zigeunern auf ihren heißbrennenden und mannshoch verschneiten Straßen gemacht haben, machten uns zu einer Generation ohne
15 Abschied.

Wir sind die Generation ohne Abschied. Wir können keinen Abschied leben, wir dürfen es nicht, denn unserm zigeunernden Herzen geschehen auf den Irrfahrten unserer Füße unendliche Abschiede. Oder soll sich unser Herz binden für eine Nacht, die doch
20 einen Abschied zum Morgen hat? Ertrügen wir den Abschied? Und wollten wir die Abschiede leben wie ihr, die anders sind als wir und den Abschied auskosteten mit allen Sekunden, dann könnte es geschehen, daß unsere Tränen zu einer Flut ansteigen würden, der keine Dämme, und wenn sie von Urvätern gebaut wären, wider-
25 stehen.

Nie werden wir die Kraft haben, den Abschied, der neben jedem Kilometer an den Straßen steht, zu leben, wie ihr ihn gelebt habt.

Sagt uns nicht, weil unser Herz schweigt, unser Herz hätte keine Stimme, denn es spräche keine Bindung und keinen Abschied.
30 Wollte unser Herz jeden Abschied, der uns geschieht, durchbluten, innig, trauernd, tröstend, dann könnte es geschehen, denn unsere

² **empfindlich** (**empfinden** to feel) sensitive
³ **um etw. bitten** to implore, ask for s.t.
⁴ **verleugnen** to renounce, disavow
⁶ **sparen** to save, to spare;   **r Verabschiedete** person who has departed
⁷ **sich davon-stehlen** to steal away;   **r Dieb** thief
⁹ **e Begegnung** encounter;   **e Dauer** permanence, 'endurance'
¹⁰ **sich nähern** to draw near;   **e Lichtsekunde** i.e., the time it takes light to travel a second (*here:* a fraction of a second)
¹¹ **e Spur** trace
¹⁷ **r (e) Verliebte** lover
¹⁹ **s Gut** estate;   **Westfalen** Westphalia;   **genießen** to enjoy (life)
²⁰ **genesen** to convalesce, get well
²² **satter Schlaf** deep (sufficient) sleep;   **e Bleibe** shelter, place to stay
²⁸ **e Heimkehr** return home
³⁰ **aufgehoben sein** to be well looked after

---

1. Wie sind die Begegnungen dieser Generation ?
2. Wo begegnen diese Menschen einander ?
3. Wie ist die Zukunft der Generation ohne Abschied ?

Abschiede sind eine Legion gegen die euren, daß der Schrei unserer
empfindlichen Herzen so groß wird, daß ihr nachts in euren Betten
sitzt und um einen Gott für uns bittet.

Darum sind wir eine Generation ohne Abschied. Wir verleugnen
5 den Abschied, lassen ihn morgens schlafend, wenn wir gehen, verhindern ihn, sparen ihn — sparen ihn uns und den Verabschiedeten.
Wir stehlen uns davon wie Diebe, undankbar dankbar und nehmen
die Liebe mit und lassen den Abschied da.

Wir sind voller Begegnungen, Begegnungen ohne Dauer und ohne
10 Abschied, wie die Sterne. Sie nähern sich, stehen Lichtsekunden
nebeneinander, entfernen sich wieder: ohne Spur, ohne Bindung,
ohne Abschied.

Wir begegnen uns unter der Kathedrale von Smolensk, wir sind
ein Mann und eine Frau—und dann stehlen wir uns davon.

15   Wir begegnen uns in der Normandie und sind wie Eltern und Kind
— und dann stehlen wir uns davon.

Wir begegnen uns eine Nacht am finnischen See und sind Verliebte — und dann stehlen wir uns davon.

Wir begegnen uns auf einem Gut in Westfalen und sind Genies-
20 sende und Genesende—und dann stehlen wir uns davon.

Wir begegnen uns in einem Keller der Stadt und sind Hungernde,
Müde, und bekommen für nichts einen guten satten Schlaf — und
dann stehlen wir uns davon.

Wir begegnen uns auf der Welt und sind Mensch mit Mensch —
25 und dann stehlen wir uns davon, denn wir sind ohne Bindung, ohne
Bleiben und ohne Abschied. Wir sind eine Generation ohne Abschied, die sich davonstiehlt wie Diebe, weil sie Angst hat vor dem
Schrei ihres Herzens. Wir sind eine Generation ohne Heimkehr,
denn wir haben nichts, zu dem wir heimkehren könnten, und wir
30 haben keinen, bei dem unser Herz aufgehoben wäre—so sind wir
eine Generation ohne Abschied geworden und ohne Heimkehr.

Aber wir sind eine Generation der Ankunft. Vielleicht sind wir
eine Generation voller Ankunft auf einem neuen Stern, in einem
neuen Leben. Voller Ankunft unter einer neuen Sonne, zu neuen
35 Herzen. Vielleicht sind wir voller Ankunft zu einem neuen Lieben,
zu einem neuen Lachen, zu einem neuen Gott.

Wir sind eine Generation ohne Abschied, aber wir wissen, daß
alle Ankunft uns gehört.

¹ **krumm** crooked
³ **hin = dorthin (gehen)**
⁴ **r Damm** embankment;   **hämmern** to pound
⁵ **schwarzgrünatmend** black-green breathing;   **sternbestickt** star-embroidered;   **sei-dig** silky;   **samten** velvety
⁶ **fauchen** to puff, (*lit.*) to hiss;   **r Güterzug** freight train
⁷ **unablässig** incessant;   **schwielig** welted, bumpy
⁸ **e Schwelle** tie;   **vorwärts·rumpeln** to jolt on forward;   **unaufhaltsam** incessantly;   **ununterbrochen** uninterrupted
⁹ **brüllen** to roar
¹⁰ **e Diesigkeit** mistiness;   **donnern** to thunder;   **verdämmernd** fading out;   **summen** to buzz
¹¹ **brummen** to hum;   **eilig** hurried
¹² **träge** sluggish
¹³ **an·kündigen** to announce;   **großartig** grandiose
¹⁵ **s Gewitter** storm;   **als ob sie wunder was für Welten umwälzten** as if they would overthrow God knows what worlds
¹⁶ **ähneln** to resemble;   **überraschen** to surprise;   **erregen** to excite
¹⁷ **im Nu** in an instant
¹⁹ **r Ruß** soot;   **verbrannt** singed;   **nebenher** alongside
²⁰ **sich verabschieden** to take (one's) leave
²² **unter** among
²⁴ **verheißungsvoll** promising;   **gierig** eager, avid
²⁵ **sich ereifern** to get excited;   **vielversprechend** promising much
²⁶ **heulen** to howl;   **hohl** hollow(ly)
²⁶ **eingeschüchtert** intimidated
³⁰ **gleichmütig** even tempered

---

1. *Weshalb sind der Strom und die Straße den Eisenbahnen zu langsam?*
2. *Wo fahren sie?*
3. *Wie kündigen sie sich an und wie verabschieden sie sich?*
4. *Wie sehen sie aus?*
5. *Wie fahren sie durch Kleinstadtbahnhöfe?*

Eisenbahnen, nachmittags und nachts

Strom und Straße sind uns zu langsam. Sind uns zu krumm. Denn
wir wollen nach Hause. Wir wissen nicht, wo das ist: Zu Hause.
Aber wir wollen hin. Und Straße und Strom sind uns zu krumm.
Aber auf Brücken und Dämmen hämmern die Bahnen. Durch
5 schwarzgrünatmende Wälder und die sternbestickten seidigen sam-
tenen Nächte fauchen die Güterzüge heran und davon mit dem un-
ablässigen Hintereinander der Räder. Über Millionen schwieliger
Schwellen vorwärtsgerumpelt. Unaufhaltsam. Ununterbrochen: Die
Bahnen. Über Dämme hinhämmernd, über Brücken gebrüllt, aus
10 Diesigkeiten herandonnernd, in Dunkelheiten verdämmernd: Sum-
mende brummende Bahnen. Güterzüge, murmelnd, eilig, irgendwie
träge und ruhlos, sind sie wie wir.
Sie sind wie wir. Sie kündigen sich an, pompös, großartig und schon
aus enorm ferner Ferne, mit einem Schrei. Dann sind sie da wie
15 Gewitter und als ob sie wunder was für Welten umwälzten. Dabei
ähneln sie sich alle und sind immer wieder überraschend und er-
regend. Aber im Nu, kaum daß man begreift, was sie eigentlich wollen,
sind sie vorbei. Und alles ist, als ob sie nicht waren. Höchstens
Ruß und verbranntes Gras nebenher beweisen ihren Weg. Dann
20 verabschieden sie sich, etwas melancholisch und schon aus enorm
ferner Ferne, mit einem Schrei. Wie wir.
Einige unter ihnen singen. Summen und brummen durch unsere
glücklichen Nächte und wir lieben ihren monotonen Gesang, ihren
verheißungsvollen gierigen Rhythmus: Nach Haus — nach Haus
25 — nach Haus. Oder sie ereifern sich vielversprechend durch schla-
fendes Land, heulen hohl über einsame Kleinstadtbahnhöfe mit ein-
geschüchterten schläfrigen Lichtern: Morgen in Brüssel — morgen
in Brüssel. Oder sie wissen noch viel mehr, piano, nur für dich,
und die neben dir sitzen, hören es nicht, piano: Ulla wartet — Ulla
30 wartet — Ulla wartet. Aber es gibt auch gleichmütige unter ihnen,
die endlos sind und weise und den breiten Rhythmus von alten Last-

[1] **r Lastträger** porter;   **knurren** to rumble, growl;   **allerhand** all sorts of things
[2] **e Kette** necklace, chains
[3] **unbegrenzt** unlimited;   **e Pracht (prächtig)** magnificence
[6] **r Kohlenwagen** coal car;   **märchenhaft** fairytale-like, fantastic;   **r Teer** tar
[7] **r Waggon** freight car
[8] **schnarchen** to snore;   **ratlos** helpless
[9] **r Eiswagen** refrigerated car;   **s Grönland** Greenland;   **fischduftend** smelling of fish
[10] **kostbar** precious
[11] **stählern** (made of) steel;   **r Strang** track
[12] **e Schlange** snake
[14] **einsperren** to shut in, imprison;   **unbegreiflich** inconceivable
[15] **r Schatz** treasure
[17] **grausam** 'gruesome';   **unerbittlich** implacable
[19] **häßlich** offensive
[20] **(her)hetzen** to chase after
[21] **grimmig** enraged;   **grollend** growling
[22] **gönnen** to allow
[23] **scheuchen** to frighten
[24] **heiser** hoarse;   **e Wut** rage
[25] **schluchzend** sobbing;   **unbestechlich** incorruptible
[26] **matt** dim;   **s Gestirn (r Stern)** constellation
[27] **s Heimweh** homesickness
[28] **s Verlassene** what one has left behind;   **s Unabwendbare** the unavoidable
[29] **dumpf** muffled
[30] **unselig** wretched;   **mondbeschienene Schienen** moonlit rails (*note internal rhyme*)
[33] **e Rast (rasten)** rest
[34] **s Ziel** goal
[36] **r Vorort** suburb
[37] **versagen** to break down;   **oder mogeln sich . . . Bürger** or they get by for a few more years in retirement—as rainshelters for railroad workers or weekend cottages for city dwellers

---

1. Wonach riechen die Kohlenwagen und die Holzwaggons ?
2. Wie riechen die Eiswagen ?
3. Was für ein Lied singen die Eisenbahnen dem Dichter ?
4. Warum sagt der Dichter, daß die Eisenbahnen wie die Menschen sind ?
5. Wann rasten sie nur ?

trägern haben. Sie murmeln und knurren allerhand vor sich hin und
dabei liegen sie wie niegesehene Ketten in der Landschaft unter
dem Mond, Ketten, unbegrenzt in ihrer Pracht und in ihrem Zauber
und in ihren Farben im blassen Mond: Braunrot, schwarz oder
5 grau, hellblau und weiß: Güterwagen — zwanzig Menschen, vierzig
Pferde — Kohlenwagen, die märchenhaft nach Teer und Parfüm
stinken — Holzwaggons, die atmen wie Wald — Zirkuswagen, hellblau, mit den schnarchenden Athleten im Innern und den ratlosen
Tieren — Eiswagen, grönlandkühl und grönlandweiß, fischduftend.
10 Unbegrenzt sind sie in ihrem Reichtum, und sie liegen wie kostbare
Ketten auf den stählernen Strängen und gleiten wie prächtige seltene
Schlangen im Mondlicht. Und sie erzählen denen, die nachts mit
ihrem Ohr leben und mit ihrem Ohr unterwegs sind, den Kranken
und den Eingesperrten, von der unbegreiflichen Weite der Welt,
15 von ihren Schätzen, von ihrer Süße, ihren Enden und Unendlich-
keiten. Und sie murmeln die, die ohne Schlaf sind, in gute Träume.

Aber es gibt auch grausame, unerbittliche, brutale, die ohne Melodie durch die Nacht hämmern, und ihr Puls will dir nicht wieder aus
den Ohren, denn er ist hart und häßlich, wie der Atem eines bösen
20 asthmatischen Hundes, der hinter dir herhetzt: Immer weiter — nie
zurück — für immer — für immer. Oder grimmiger mit grollenden
Rädern: Alles vorbei — alles vorbei. Und ihr Lied gönnt uns den
Schlaf nicht und scheucht noch grausam die friedlichen Dörfer rechts
oder links aus den Träumen, daß die Hunde heiser werden vor Wut.
25 Und sie rollen schreiend und schluchzend, die Grausamen, Un-
bestechlichen, unter den matten Gestirnen, und selbst der Regen
macht sie nicht milde. In ihrem Schrei schreit das Heimweh, das
Verlorene, Verlassene — schluchzt das Unabwendbare, Getrennte,
Geschehene und Ungewisse. Und sie donnern einen dumpfen Rhyth-
30 mus, unselig und untröstlich, auf den mondbeschienenen Schienen.
Und du vergißt sie nie.

Sie sind wie wir. Keiner garantiert ihren Tod in ihrer Heimat.
Sie sind ohne Ruh und ohne Rast der Nacht, und sie rasten nur,
wenn sie krank sind. Und sie sind ohne Ziel. Vielleicht sind sie in
35 Stettin zu Hause oder in Sofia oder in Florenz. Aber sie zersplittern
zwischen Kopenhagen und Altona oder in einem Vorort von Paris.
Oder sie versagen in Dresden. Oder mogeln sich noch ein paar Jahre
als Altenteil durch — Regenhütten für Streckenarbeiter oder als
Wochenendhäuschen für Bürger.

[2] **kippen** to tip over;   **e Gleise** (*pl.*) rails
[3] **irgendwohin** to someplace or other
[4] **wenn es aus ist** when it's over;   **s Unterwegssein** the process of being underway
[6] **r Bahndamm** railway embankment;   **rußig (r Ruß)** sooty
[7] **r Draht** wire
[8] **erinnern** to remember
[11] **flattern** to stream, 'flutter'
[13] **r Backen** cheek
[16] **pochen** to pound
[17] **verheißen** to promise;   **armmütig** poor, indigent;   **r Häftling** prisoner
[18] **s Gehör** hearing;   **klopfen** to pound
[19] **r Pfiff** whistle;   **überzittern** to vibrate over
[20] **s Gelüst** desire
[22] **beherbergen** to harbor;   **e Ader** vein
[24] **r Abgrund** abyss;   **verschlucken** to swallow
[26] **aus·speien** to spit out
[27] **ausgeliefert (an)** reduced to;   **e Abfahrt** departure
[28] **bleich** faded;   **s Schild** signboard;   **e Stirn** forehead
[29] **furchig** furrowed
[31] **erforen (frieren)** frozen
[32] **r Lippenstift** lipstick;   **r Schnaps** booze, spirits
[35] **r Schienenstrang** stretch of track;   **fleckig** spotted;   **blank** bright
[36] **in etw.** (*acc.*) **ein·teilen** to divide

---

1. Wieviel halten sie und wir aus ?
2. Was geschieht eines Tages ?
3. Was singen die Güterzüge ?
4. Wie heißen die Stationen der Fahrt ?
5. Wie sieht der Dichter die Welt ?
6. Wer ist der Schienenstrang ? Wer sind die Stationen ? Wer ist die Eisenbahn ?

Sie sind wie wir. Sie halten viel mehr aus, als alle geglaubt haben. Aber eines Tages kippen sie aus den Gleisen, stehen still oder verlieren ein wichtiges Organ. Immer wollen sie irgendwohin. Niemals bleiben sie irgendwo. Und wenn es aus ist, was ist ihr Leben? Unter-
5 wegssein. Aber großartig, grausam, grenzenlos. Eisenbahnen, nachmittags, nachts. Die Blumen an den Bahndämmen, mit ihren rußigen Köpfen, die Vögel auf den Drähten, mit rußigen Stimmen, sind mit ihnen befreundet und erinnern sie noch lange.

Und wir bleiben auch stehen, mit erstaunten Augen, wenn es —
10 schon aus enorm ferner Ferne — verheißungsvoll herausschreit. Und wir stehen, mit flatterndem Haar, wenn es da ist wie Gewitter und als ob es wunder was für Welten umwälzte. Und wir stehen noch, mit rußigen Backen, wenn es — schon aus enorm ferner Ferne — schreit. Weit weit ab schreit. Schreit. Eigentlich war es nichts. Oder
15 alles. Wie wir.

Und sie pochen vor den Fenstern der Gefängnisse süßen gefährlich verheißenden Rhythmus. Ohr bist du dann, armmütiger Häftling, unendliches Gehör bist du den klopfenden kommenden Zügen in den Nächten und ihr Schrei und ihr Pfiff überzittert das weiche Dun-
20 kel deiner Zelle mit Schmerz und Gelüst.

Oder sie stürzen brüllend über das Bett, wenn du nachts das Fieber beherbergst. Und die Adern, die mondblauen, vibrieren und nehmen das Lied auf, das Lied der Güterzüge: unterwegs — unterwegs — unterwegs — — Und dein Ohr ist ein Abgrund, der die Welt ver-
25 schluckt.

Unterwegs. Aber immer wieder wirst du auf Bahnhöfe ausgespien, ausgeliefert an Abschied und Abfahrt.

Und die Stationen heben ihre bleichen Schilder wie Stirnen neben deiner dunklen Straße auf. Und sie haben Namen, die furchigen
30 Stirnschilder, Namen, die sind die Welt: Bett heißen sie, Hunger und Mädchen. Ulla oder Carola. Und erfrorene Füße und Tränen. Und Tabak heißen die Stationen, oder Lippenstift oder Schnaps. Oder Gott oder Brot. Und die bleichen Stirnen der Stationen, die Schilder, haben Namen, die heißen: Mädchen.
35 Du bist selber Schienenstrang, rostig, fleckig, silbern, blank, schön und ungewiß. Und du bist in Stationen eingeteilt, zwischen Bahnhöfe gebunden. Und die haben Schilder und da steht dann Mädchen drauf, oder Mond oder Mord. Und das ist dann die Welt.

Eisenbahn bist du, vorübergerumpelt, vorübergeschrien — Schie-

[1] **rostblind** rust tarnished
[3] **giraffeneinsam** lonely as a giraffe;   **s Hirn** brain
[4] **r Hals** neck

nenstrang bist du — alles geschieht auf dir und macht dich rostblind und silberblank.

Mensch bist du, giraffeneinsam ist dein Hirn irgendwo oben am endlosen Hals. Und dein Herz kennt keiner genau.

[1] e **Werkstatt** workshop
[2] **befehlen** to command;   s **Wasserrohr** waterpipe;   r **Kochtopf** cooking pot
[3] r **Stahlhelm** steel helmet;   s **Maschinengewehr** machine gun
[6] r **Ladentisch** (store) counter
[7] s **Zielfernrohr** telescope-sight
[8] r **Scharfschütze** sharpshooter;   **montieren** to assemble
[10] r **Besitzer** owner;   e **Fabrik** factory
[11] s **Puder** powder;   r **Kakao** cocoa;   s **Schießpulver** gunpowder
[14] r **Forscher** scientist, researcher
[15] **erfinden** to invent
[18] e **Stube** = s **Zimmer**
[23] **kriegstauglich schreiben** to declare fit for war
[25] r **Pfarrer** clerygyman;   e **Kanzel** pulpit, 'chancel'
[26] **segnen** to bless;   **heilig sprechen** to proclaim holy
[29] r **Weizen** wheat;   r **Panzer** tank

---

1. *Wozu soll der Mann an der Maschine NEIN sagen ?*
2. *Wozu sollen das Mädchen hinterm Ladentisch und der Fabrikbesitzer NEIN sagen ?*
3. *Worauf sollen der Forscher und der Dichter NEIN antworten ?*
4. *Was müssen der Arzt und der Pfarrer ablehnen ?*

Dann gibt es nur eins!

Du. Mann an der Maschine und Mann in der Werkstatt. Wenn sie dir morgen befehlen, du sollst keine Wasserrohre und keine Kochtöpfe mehr machen—sondern Stahlhelme und Maschinengewehre, dann gibt es nur eins:

5 Sag NEIN!

Du. Mädchen hinterm Ladentisch und Mädchen im Büro. Wenn sie dir morgen befehlen, du sollst Granaten füllen und Zielfernrohre für Scharfschützengewehre montieren, dann gibt es nur eins:

Sag NEIN!

10 Du. Besitzer der Fabrik. Wenn sie dir morgen befehlen, du sollst statt Puder und Kakao Schießpulver verkaufen, dann gibt es nur eins:

Sag NEIN!

Du. Forscher im Laboratorium. Wenn sie dir morgen befehlen,
15 du sollst einen neuen Tod erfinden gegen das alte Leben, dann gibt es nur eins:

Sag NEIN!

Du. Dichter in deiner Stube. Wenn sie dir morgen befehlen, du sollst keine Liebeslieder, du sollst Haßlieder singen, dann gibt es
20 nur eins:

Sag NEIN!

Du. Arzt am Krankenbett. Wenn sie dir morgen befehlen, du sollst die Männer kriegstauglich schreiben, dann gibt es nur eins:

Sag NEIN!

25 Du. Pfarrer auf der Kanzel. Wenn sie dir morgen befehlen, du sollst den Mord segnen und den Krieg heilig sprechen, dann gibt es nur eins:

Sag NEIN!

Du. Kapitän auf dem Dampfer. Wenn sie dir morgen befehlen, du sollst keinen Weizen mehr fahren — sondern Kanonen und Panzer,
30 dann gibt es nur eins:

Sag NEIN!

⁵ **r Schneider** tailor;   **s Brett** board
⁶ **zu·schneiden** to cut out
⁸ **r Richter** judge;   **r Talar** robe
⁹ **s Kriegsgericht** courtmartial
¹⁶ **r Gestellungsbefehl** induction order
²² **r Erdteil** continent
²³ **gebären** to give birth to;   **e Krankenschwester** nurse;   **s Kriegslazarett** military
hospital
²⁴ **e Schlacht (schlachten** to slaughter) battle
³⁰ **lärmend** noisy;   **dampfdunstig** steaming;   **e Hafenstadt** seaport
³¹ **stöhnend** groaningly;   **verstummen** to become silent;   **titanisch** gigantic;   **r Mammutkadaver** mammoth carcass
³² **wasserleichig** like a corpse in the water;   **vereinsamt** solitary;   **e Kaimauer** wharf
wall
³³ **schwanken** to roll;   **algen-, tang- und muschelüberwest** decayed matter covered
with algae, seaweed, and mussels
³⁴ **dröhnen** to 'drone', boom;   **friedhöflich** graveyardlike;   **fischfaulig duftend** smelling of rotten fish;   **mürbe** full of dryrot
³⁵ **siech** sickly
³⁶ **e Straßenbahn** streetcar;   **sinnlos** foolish;   **glanzlos** lacklustre;   **r Käfig** cage
³⁷ **verbeult** battered;   **abgeblättert** stripped;   **verwirrt** tangled;   **s Stahlskelett** steel
skeleton
³⁸ **r Draht** cable;   **morsch** decaying;   **dachdurchlöchert** leaky-roofed
³⁹ **r Schuppen** shed, hangar

---

1. *Was müssen der Kapitän und der Pilot verweigern ?*
2. *Was müssen der Schneider, der Richter und der Mann auf dem Bahnhof
   verneinen ?*
3. *Was sagt Borchert zu den Müttern der Welt ?*
4. *Was würde geschehen, wenn die Mütter nicht NEIN sagen würden ?*

Du. Pilot auf dem Flugfeld. Wenn sie dir morgen befehlen, du sollst Bomben und Phosphor über die Städte tragen, dann gibt es nur eins:
Sag NEIN!
5 Du. Schneider auf deinem Brett. Wenn sie dir morgen befehlen, du sollst Uniformen zuschneiden, dann gibt es nur eins:
Sag NEIN!
Du. Richter im Talar. Wenn sie dir morgen befehlen, du sollst zum Kriegsgericht gehen, dann gibt es nur eins:
10 Sag NEIN!
Du. Mann auf dem Bahnhof. Wenn sie dir mogen befehlen, du sollst das Signal zur Abfahrt geben für den Munitionszug und für den Truppentransport, dann gibt es nur eins:
Sag NEIN!
15 Du. Mann auf dem Dorf und Mann in der Stadt. Wenn sie morgen kommen und dir den Gestellungsbefehl bringen, dann gibt es nur eins:
Sag NEIN!
Du. Mutter in der Normandie und Mutter in der Ukraine, du,
20 Mutter in Frisko und London, du, am Hoangho und am Mississippi, du, Mutter in Neapel und Hamburg und Kairo und Oslo — Mütter in allen Erdteilen, Mütter in der Welt, wenn sie morgen befehlen, ihr sollt Kinder gebären, Krankenschwestern für Kriegslazarette und neue Soldaten für neue Schlachten, Mütter in der Welt, dann
25 gibt es nur eins:
Sagt NEIN! Mütter, sagt NEIN!

Denn wenn ihr nicht NEIN sagt, wenn IHR nicht nein sagt, Mütter, dann:
dann:
30 In den lärmenden dampfdunstigen Hafenstädten werden die grossen Schiffe stöhnend verstummen und wie titanische Mammutkadaver wasserleichig träge gegen die toten vereinsamten Kaimauern schwanken, algen-, tang- und muschelüberwest den früher so schimmernden dröhnenden Leib, friedhöflich fischfaulig duftend, mürbe,
35 siech, gestorben —
die Straßenbahnen werden wie sinnlose glanzlose glasäugige Käfige blöde verbeult und abgeblättert neben den verwirrten Stahlskeletten der Drähte und Gleise liegen, hinter morschen dachdurchlöcherten Schuppen, in verlorenen kraterzerrissenen Straßen —

¹ **schlammgrau** mud-gray;   **dickbreiig** pulpy, viscous;   **bleiern** leaden;   **heranwäl-**
zen to roll in
² **gefräßig** voracious;   **an·wachsen** to grow (up)
³ **s Schauspielhaus** theater
⁴ **gierig** greedy;   **unaufhaltsam** incessantly
⁵ **saftig** succulent;   **verfallen** fallow;   **r Hang** slope;   **verfaulen** to rot
⁶ **verdorrt** withered;   **vertrocknen** to dry up
⁷ **brach·liegen** to lie fallow;   **r Acker** field
⁸ **totsteif** stiff (as a corpse);   **umgekippt** overturned;   **r Melkschemel** milking stool
¹⁰ **genial** ingenious
¹¹ **pilzig verschimmeln** to grow over with mould
¹² **e Kammer** chamber;   **s Kühlhaus** ice house
¹³ **r Speicher** granary, silo;   **s Mehl** flour;   **s Glas** jar;   **e Erdbeere** strawberry
¹⁴ **r Kürbis** pumpkin;   **r Kirschsaft** cherry juice;   **verkommen** to go bad
¹⁵ **umgestürzt** overturned
¹⁶ **ausgelaufen** spilled;   **e Schmierseife** soft soap
¹⁷ **verrostet** rusted;   **r Pflug** plow
¹⁸ **erschlagen** slaughtered;   **s Heer** army;   **qualmend** smoking;   **r Ziegelschornstein**
brick chimney
¹⁹ **e Esse** funnel;   **r Schlot** smokestack;   **stampfen** to crush, stamp upon
²⁰ **zerbröckeln** to crumble away
²² **zerfetzt** torn up;   **s Gedärm** intestines;   **verpestet** poisoned
²³ **giftig** poisonous, spiteful;   **glühen** to glow
²⁴ **wanken** to waver;   **umher·irren** to wander about
²⁵ **unübersehbar** immense;   **r Götze** idol
²⁶ **betonklotzige verödete Städte** deserted cities full of chunks of concrete
²⁷ **dürr** emaciated;   **wahnsinnig** insane;   **lästernd** blasphemous
²⁸ **verrinnen** trickle away;   **geborsten** broken apart
²⁹ **wehen** to drift;   **versickern** to seep away
³⁰ **r Hochbunker** air-raid shelter;   **klatschen** to slap;   **e Blutlache** pool of blood
³¹ **ein·treffen** to come to pass

---

1. *Wo wäre eine große Stille?*
2. *Was geschähe mit dem Wein, dem Reis und den Kartoffeln?*
3. *Wozu dienten die genialen Erfindungen der Ärzte?*
4. *Wo würde der letzte Mensch herumirren?*
5. *Welche Klage würde er herausschreien?*

eine schlammgraue dickbreiige bleierne Stille wird sich heran-
wälzen, gefräßig, wachsend, wird anwachsen in den Schulen und
Universitäten und Schauspielhäusern, auf Sport- und Kinderspiel-
plätzen, grausig und gierig, unaufhaltsam —
5 der sonnige saftige Wein wird an den verfallenen Hängen verfaulen, der Reis wird in der verdorrten Erde vertrocknen, die Kartoffel
wird auf den brachliegenden Äckern erfrieren und die Kühe werden
ihre totsteifen Beine wie umgekippte Melkschemel in den Himmel
strecken —
10 in den Instituten werden die genialen Erfindungen der großen
Ärzte sauer werden, verrotten, pilzig verschimmeln —
in den Küchen, Kammern und Kellern, in den Kühlhäusern und
Speichern werden die letzten Säcke Mehl, die letzten Gläser Erd-
beeren, Kürbis und Kirschsaft verkommen — das Brot unter den
15 umgestürzten Tischen und auf zersplitterten Tellern wird grün werden und die ausgelaufene Butter wird stinken wie Schmierseife, das
Korn auf den Feldern wird neben verrosteten Pflügen hingesunken
sein wie ein erschlagenes Heer und die qualmenden Ziegelschorn-
steine, die Essen und die Schlote der stampfenden Fabriken werden,
20 vom ewigen Gras zugedeckt, zerbröckeln — zerbröckeln — zerbröckeln —
dann wird der letzte Mensch, mit zerfetzten Gedärmen und ver-
pesteter Lunge, antwortlos und einsam unter der giftig glühenden
Sonne und unter wankenden Gestirnen umherirren, einsam zwischen
25 den unübersehbaren Massengräbern und den kalten Götzen der
gigantischen betonklotzigen verödeten Städte, der letzte Mensch,
dürr, wahnsinnig, lästernd, klagend — und seine furchtbare Klage:
WARUM? wird ungehört in der Steppe verrinnen, durch die ge-
borstenen Ruinen wehen, versickern im Schutt der Kirchen, gegen
30 Hochbunker klatschen, in Blutlachen fallen, ungehört, antwortlos,
letzter Tierschrei des letzten Tieres Mensch — all dieses wird ein-
treffen, morgen, morgen vielleicht, vielleicht heute nacht schon,
vielleicht heute nacht, wenn — — wenn — —
wenn ihr nicht NEIN sagt.

² **ab·schließen** to lock
³ **sich** (*dat.*) **vor·stellen** to imagine
⁴ **drinnen** inside
⁵ **etwas Endgültiges, Abschließendes** something definitive, final; **aus·liefern** to surrender
⁷ **unwahrscheinlich** abnormally
⁸ **häßlich** ugly
⁹ **s Eisenblech** sheet-iron; **beschlagen** sheathed
¹⁰ **unnahbar** unapproachable; **sich auf etw.** (*acc.*) **ein·lassen** to accede to a request
¹¹ **inbrünstig** fervent; **s Gebet** prayer; **rühren** to move
¹² **s Wesen** being, existence
¹⁷ **eines der tollsten Abenteuer** one of the maddest adventures
²⁰ **e Ablenkung** distraction
²¹ **entwürdigen** (**e Würde** dignity) to degrade
²⁴ **s Handtuch** towel; **sich auf·hängen** to hang o.s.
²⁵ **e Ader** blood vessel, vein
²⁸ **e Spinne** spider; **s Gerüst** framework
²⁹ **r Hintern** (*coll.*) rear end; **drängen** to press
³⁰ **r Absturz** fall; **auf·fangen** to catch (from falling); **r Faden** thread

---

1. Wie ist die Tür mit der Nummer 432 ?
2. Wo befindet sich die Tür ?
3. Wie ist es, wenn ein Mensch mit sich selbst allein gelassen wird ?
4. Was ist das Entwürdigendste ?

Die Hundeblume

Die Tür ging hinter mir zu. Das hat man wohl öfter, daß eine Tür
hinter einem zugemacht wird — auch daß sie abgeschlossen wird,
kann man sich vorstellen. Haustüren zum Beispiel werden abgeschlossen, und man ist dann entweder drinnen oder draußen. Auch
5 Haustüren haben etwas so Endgültiges, Abschließendes, Ausliefern-
des. Und nun ist die Tür hinter mir zugeschoben, ja, geschoben, denn
es ist eine unwahrscheinlich dicke Tür, die man nicht zuschlagen
kann. Eine häßliche Tür mit der Nummer 432. Das ist das Besondere
an dieser Tür, daß sie eine Nummer hat und mit Eisenblech beschla-
10 gen ist — das macht sie so stolz und unnahbar; denn sie läßt sich auf
nichts ein, und die inbrünstigen Gebete rühren sie nicht.

Und nun hat man mich mit dem Wesen allein gelassen, nein, nicht
nur allein gelassen, zusammen eingesperrt hat man mich mit diesem
Wesen, vor dem ich am meisten Angst habe: Mit mir selbst.

15 Weißt du, wie das ist, wenn du dir selbst überlassen wirst, wenn
du mit dir allein gelassen bist, dir selbst ausgeliefert bist? Ich kann
nicht sagen, daß es unbedingt furchtbar ist, aber es ist eines der toll-
sten Abenteuer, die wir auf dieser Welt haben können: Sich selbst
zu begegnen. So begegnen wie hier in der Zelle 432: nackt, hilflos,
20 konzentriert auf nichts als auf sich selbst, ohne Attribut und Ablenkung und ohne die Möglichkeit einer Tat. Und das ist das Entwürdigendste: Ganz ohne die Möglichkeit zu einer Tat zu sein.
Keine Flasche zum Trinken oder zum Zerschmettern zu haben,
kein Handtuch zum Aufhängen, kein Messer zum Ausbrechen oder
25 zum Aderndurchschneiden, keine Feder zum Schreiben — nichts
zu haben — als sich selbst.

Das ist verdammt wenig in einem leeren Raum mit vier nackten
Wänden. Das ist weniger als die Spinne hat, die sich ein Gerüst
aus dem Hintern drängt und ihr Leben daran riskieren kann, zwi-
30 schen Absturz und Auffangen wagen kann. Welcher Faden fängt
uns auf, wenn wir abstürzen?

⁵ **s Fenstergitter** window-grating
⁶ **kriechen** to crawl, creep
¹⁰ **weichen** to retreat
¹¹ **besoffen** drunk
¹³ **s Ungeheuer** monster
¹⁴ **s Gespenst** ghost
¹⁶ **trudeln** to 'trundle', roll along
¹⁷ **Affe, du!** You ape!
¹⁸ **e Apfelsinenschale** orange peel
²¹ **e Makrele** mackerel
²³ **überwältigen** to overwhelm
²⁴ **e Nuß** nut
²⁵ **von selbst auf·gehen** to open by itself
²⁶ **stürzen** to plunge
²⁸ **r Feldwebel** sergeant;   **r Schwächling** weakling;   **s Netz** net
²⁹ **r Ameiseneifer** antlike zeal
³⁰ **r Hundertdreiundzwanzigpfündige** person weighing 123 lbs.;   **hauchfeines Seil**
very delicate line
³¹ **sich bei j-em bedanken** to express one's thanks to s.o.
³³ **sich an j-en gewöhnen** to get accustomed to s.o.;   **man mutet sich . . . Menschen zu**
one imposes oneself so thoughtlessly on other people
³⁵ **unterhaltsam** entertaining
³⁶ **vergnüglich (s Vergnügen** pleasure**)** diverting;   **merkwürdig** strange
³⁸ **r Zusammenhang (zusammenhanglos** incoherent**)** connection
³⁹ **ab·tropfen** to drop (drip) off

---

1. Was denkt der Gefangene über Gott ?
2. Wie empfindet dieser Mensch die Nacht ?
3. Wie sieht er sich selbst, die Spinne und die Makrele im Verhältnis zu Gott ?
4. Was lehrt ihn die Spinne?
5. Was verlor der Gefangene mit der Zeit ?

Unsere eigene Kraft? Fängt ein Gott uns auf? Gott — ist das die
Kraft, die einen Baum wachsen und einen Vogel fliegen läßt—ist
Gott das Leben? Dann fängt er uns wohl manchmal auf — wenn wir
wollen.

5   Als die Sonne ihre Finger von dem Fenstergitter nahm und die
Nacht aus den Ecken kroch, trat etwas aus dem Dunkel auf mich
zu — und ich dachte, es wäre Gott. Hatte jemand die Tür geöffnet?
War ich nicht mehr allein? Ich fühlte, es ist etwas da, und das atmet
und wächst. Die Zelle wurde zu eng — ich fühlte, daß die Mauern
10 weichen mußten vor diesem, das da war und das ich Gott nannte.

  Du, Nummer 432, Menschlein — laß dich nicht besoffen machen
von der Nacht! Deine Angst ist mit dir in der Zelle, sonst nichts!
Die Angst und die Nacht. Aber die Angst ist ein Ungeheuer, und die
Nacht kann furchtbar werden wie ein Gespenst, wenn wir mit ihr
15 allein sind.

  Da trudelte der Mond über die Dächer und leuchtete die Wände
ab. Affe, du! Die Wände sind so eng wie je, und die Zelle ist leer
wie eine Apfelsinenschale. Gott, den sie den Guten nennen, ist nicht
da. Und was da war, das was sprach, war in dir. Vielleicht war es
20 ein Gott aus dir — du warst es! Denn du bist auch Gott, alle, auch
die Spinne und die Makrele sind Gott. Gott ist das Leben — das
ist alles. Aber das ist so viel, daß er nicht mehr sein kann. Sonst ist
nichts. Aber dieses Nichts überwältigt uns oft.

  Die Zellentür war so zu wie eine Nuß — als ob sie nie offen war,
25 und von der man wußte, daß sie von selbst nicht aufging — daß sie
aufgebrochen werden mußte. So zu war die Tür. Und ich stürzte,
mit mir allein gelassen, ins Bodenlose. Aber da schrie mich die Spinne
an wie ein Feldwebel: Schwächling! Der Wind hatte ihre Netze zerrissen, und sie drängte mit Ameiseneifer ein neues und fing mich,
30 den Hundertdreiundzwanzigpfündigen, in ihren hauchfeinen Seilen.
Ich bedankte mich bei ihr, aber davon nahm sie überhaupt keine
Notiz.

  So gewöhnte ich mich langsam an mich. Man mutet sich so leicht-
fertig andern Menschen zu, und dabei kann man sich kaum selbst
35 ertragen. Ich fand mich aber allmählich doch ganz unterhaltsam und
vergnüglich — ich machte Tag und Nacht die merkwürdigsten Ent-
deckungen an mir.

  Aber ich verlor in der langen Zeit den Zusammenhang mit allem,
mit dem Leben, mit der Welt. Die Tage tropften schnell und regel-

[1] **leer·laufen** to run dry
[4] **e Verzweiflung** despair
[8] **sich auf·tun** to open up;   **e Faust** fist;   **wund** sore
[9] **e Öde** desolation
[11] **eingebildet** imaginary
[12] **schubsen** (*coll.*) to 'shove';   **schlechtrasiert** badly shaven
[15] **s Bellen** barking;   **heiser** hoarse
[16] **r Lederriemen** leather strap;   **r Bauch** belly
[21] **r Kreis** circle;   **erschütternd** moving
[22] **überwinden** to overcome
[23] **blinzeln** to blink
[26] **r Holzpantoffel** wooden clog;   **unbeholfen** clumsy, awkward
[27] **eingeschüchtert** intimidated
[32] **fast ein Fest** almost a party;   **auf die Dauer** in the long run
[33] **kampflos** without struggle
[34] **ab·schweifen** to digress;   **man hat es satt** one is fed up
[36] **r Rundgang** walking around
[37] **e Qual** agony
[38] **verhöhnen** to mock;   **Vordermann und Hintermann** man in front and man behind
(oneself)

---

1. Wie vergingen die Tage ?
2. Was geschieht, wenn ein Gefangener seine Not herausschreit ?
3. Wohin darf der Gefangene täglich gehen und was muß er dort tun ?

mäßig von mir ab. Ich fühlte, wie ich langsam leerlief von der wirk-
lichen Welt und voll wurde von mir selbst. Ich fühlte, daß ich immer
weiter wegging von dieser Welt, die ich eben erst betreten hatte.

Die Wände waren so kalt und tot, daß ich krank wurde vor Ver-
5 zweiflung und Hoffnungslosigkeit. Man schreit wohl ein paar Tage
seine Not raus — aber wenn nichts antwortet, ermüdet man bald.
Man schlägt wohl ein paar Stunden an Wand und Tür — aber wenn
sie sich nicht auftun, sind die Fäuste bald wund, und der kleine
Schmerz ist dann die einzige Lust in dieser Öde.

10 Es gibt doch wohl nichts Endgültiges auf dieser Welt. Denn die
eingebildete Tür hatte sich aufgetan und viele andere dazu, und jede
schubste einen scheuen, schlechtrasierten Mann hinaus in eine lange
Reihe und in einen Hof mit grünem Gras in der Mitte und grauen
Mauern ringsum.

15 Da explodierte ein Bellen um uns und auf uns zu — ein heiseres
Bellen von blauen Hunden mit Lederriemen um den Bauch. Die
hielten uns in Bewegung und waren selbst dauernd in Bewegung
und bellten uns voll Angst. Aber wenn man genug Angst in sich hatte
und ruhiger wurde, erkannte man, daß es Menschen waren in blauen,
20 blassen Uniformen.

Man lief im Kreise. Wenn das Auge das erste erschütternde Wie-
dersehen mit dem Himmel überwunden und sich wieder an die Sonne
gewöhnt hatte, konnte man blinzelnd erkennen, daß viele so zusammenhanglos trotteten und tief atmeten wie man selbst — siebzig,
25 achtzig Mann vielleicht.

Und immer im Kreis — im Rhythmus ihrer Holzpantoffeln, unbeholfen, eingeschüchtert und doch für eine halbe Stunde froher als
sonst. Wenn die blauen Uniformen mit dem Bellen im Gesicht nicht
gewesen wären, hätte man bis in die Ewigkeit so trotten können —
30 ohne Vergangenheit, ohne Zukunft: Ganz genießende Gegenwart:
Atmen, Sehen, Gehen!

So war es zuerst. Fast ein Fest, ein kleines Glück. Aber auf die
Dauer — wenn man monatelang kampflos genießt — beginnt man
abzuschweifen. Das kleine Glück genügt nicht mehr — man hat es
35 satt, und die trüben Tropfen dieser Welt, der wir ausgeliefert sind,
fallen in unser Glas. Und dann kommt der Tag, wo der Rundgang
im Kreis eine Qual wird, wo man sich unter dem hohen Himmel
verhöhnt fühlt und wo man Vordermann und Hintermann nicht

¹ **r Mitleidende (leiden)** fellow sufferer; **empfinden** to feel
² **e Leiche** corpse; **an·ekeln** to disgust
³ **eingelattet als Latte** arrayed one beside the other like laths
⁴ **r Lattenzaun** lath-fence; **verursachen** to cause; **eher . . . als** rather . . . than; **e Übelkeit** nausea
⁶ **j-en mürbe bellen** to bark s.o. down until weak, brittle
⁹ **s Panoptikum** cabinet of curiosities
¹¹ **e Glatze** bald head; **zerfranst** fuzzy
¹² **r Kranz** wreath; **umwildert sein** to be surrounded (in disorderly fashion)
¹³ **fettig** greasy; **r Glanz** glare
¹⁵ **duff** (*Low German*) dull; **matt** dim; **r Stoff** fabric
¹⁶ **dieser nachgemachte Mensch** this imitation man
¹⁸ **e Perücke** wig
¹⁹ **r Gelehrte** scholar; **r Säufer** drunkard; **r Papierkrämer** petty shopkeeper
²⁰ **zäh** tough, stubborn
²¹ **ahnen** to suspect
²⁴ **r Spatz** sparrow
²⁵ **e Dachrinne** gutter
²⁶ **feig(e)** cowardly
³⁰ **heimlich** secret(ly); **r Palast** palace
³³ **begehen** to commit
³⁵ **andauernd** continuous(ly); **quälen (e Qual)** to torment
³⁶ **r Hacken** heel; **mit Absicht** on purpose
³⁷ **spucken** to spit; **viertelpfundweise** by the quarter pound
³⁸ **s Lungenhaschee** minced lung tissue; **zusammen·zucken** to wince

---

1. Wen sieht der Gefangene in dem Hof?
2. Was denkt er über die anderen Gefangenen?
3. Wie schaut der Kopf seines Vordermanns aus?
4. Warum haßt er den Vordermann?
5. Wie quält er ihn?
6. Wie reagiert der Vordermann darauf?

mehr als Brüder und Mitleidende empfindet, sondern als wandernde
Leichen, die nur dazu da sind, uns anzuekeln — und zwischen die
man eingelattet ist als Latte ohne eigenes Gesicht in einem endlosen
Lattenzaun, ach, und sie verursachen einem eher Übelkeit als sonst-
5 was. Das kommt dann, wenn man monatelang kreist zwischen den
grauen Mauern und von den blassen, blauen Uniformen mürbe
gebellt ist.

Der Mann, der vor mir geht, war schon lange tot. Oder er war
aus einem Panoptikum entsprungen, von einem komischen Dämon
10 getrieben, zu tun, als sei er ein normaler Mensch — und dabei war
er bestimmt längst tot. Ja! Nämlich seine Glatze, die von einem zer-
fransten Kranz schmutzig-grauer Haarbüschel umwildert ist, hat
nicht diesen fettigen Glanz von lebendigen Glatzen, in denen sich
Sonne und Regen noch trübe spiegeln können — nein, diese Glatze
15 ist glanzlos, duff und matt wie aus Stoff. Wenn sich dieses Ganze
da vor mir, das ich gar nicht Mensch nennen mag, dieser nachgemachte Mensch, nicht bewegen würde, könnte man diese Glatze
für eine leblose Perücke halten. Und nicht mal die Perücke eines
Gelehrten oder großen Säufers — nein, höchstens die eines Papier-
20 krämers oder Zirkusclowns. Aber zäh ist sie, diese Perücke — sie
kann schon aus Bosheit allein nicht abtreten, weil sie ahnt, daß ich,
ihr Hintermann, sie hasse. Ja, ich hasse sie. Warum muß die Perücke
— ich will nun man den ganzen Mann so nennen, das ist einfacher —
warum muß sie vor mir hergehen und leben, während junge Spatzen,
25 die noch nichts vom Fliegen gewußt haben, sich aus der Dachrinne
zu Tode stürzen? Und ich hasse die Perücke, weil sie feige ist — und
wie feige! Sie fühlt meinen Haß, während sie blöde vor mir hertrottet,
immer im Kreis, im ganz kleinen Kreis zwischen grauen Mauern,
die auch kein Herz für uns haben, denn sonst würden sie eines Nachts
30 heimlich fortwandern und sich um den Palast stellen, in dem unsere
Minister wohnen.

Ich denke schon eine ganze Zeit darüber nach, warum man die
Perücke ins Gefängnis gesperrt hat — was für eine Tat kann sie begangen haben — sie, die zu feige ist, sich nach mir umzudrehen,
35 während ich sie andauernd quäle. Denn ich quäle sie: Ich trete ihr
fortwährend auf die Hacken — mit Absicht natürlich — und mache
mit meinem Mund ein übles Geräusch, als spuckte ich viertelpfundweise Lungenhaschee gegen ihren Rücken. Sie zuckt jedesmal verwundet zusammen. Trotzdem wagt sie es nicht, sich ganz nach

² **ein paar Grad** a few degrees; **s Genick** nape, (back of) neck

⁴ **wagen** to dare

⁵ **Was mag sie ausgefressen haben?** What may she have been up to?; **unterschlagen** to embezzle

⁶ **r Sexualanfall** sexual attack; **öffentliches Ärgernis** public annoyance, outrage

⁷ **berauscht** intoxicated

⁸ **bucklig** hunchbacked; **(he)raus·hüpfen** to 'hop' out

⁹ **e Geilheit** lechery; **stillvergnügt** calm and serene

¹¹ **insgeheim** in secret

¹² **r Mörder** murderer

¹³ **unauffällig** inconspicuous

¹⁴ **j-em ein Bein stellen** to trip s.o. up; **sie wäre . . . vornübergestolpert** she would have stumbled forward on her much too wooden stilts

¹⁷ **r Fahrradschlauch** pneumatic tube of a bicycle wheel

¹⁸ **auseinander·platzen** to burst apart

²⁰ **r Himbeersaft** raspberry juice; **auf der blauseidenen Bluse eines erdolchten Komödianten** on the blue silk blouse of a stabbed comedian

²⁴ **muffig** musty; **mottenpulvriger Geruch** mothball-like smell

²⁵ **e Leidenschaft** passion

²⁶ **milchig** milky white

²⁷ **s Kalb** calf

²⁸ **e Praline** chocolate cream; **r Lebemann** man of the world

²⁹ **r Papierhändler = Papierkrämer; e Hebamme** midwife

³¹ **s Schreibheft** note book; **r Ladentisch** counter

³⁴ **sich entblößen** to expose (o.s.)

³⁶ **verschweigen** to disregard; **ständig** constantly

³⁷ **mit eingeknickten Knien** with bent legs, hobbling

³⁸ **r Juckreiz** irritating itch

---

1. *Weswegen wagt der Gefangene es dennoch nicht, sich umzudrehen?*
2. *Welches Verbrechen könnte er begangen haben?*
3. *Was für eine Stimme könnte der Vordermann haben?*
4. *Wie könnte sein Gesicht aussehen?*
5. *Warum denkt der Gefangene soviel an den Vordermann?*

ihrem Quäler umzusehen — nein, sie ist zu feige dazu. Sie dreht sich nur um ein paar Grad mit steifem Genick in meine Richtung nach hinten, aber die halbe Drehung bis zum Treffen unserer Augenpaare wagt sie nicht.

5 Was mag sie ausgefressen haben? Vielleicht hat sie unterschlagen oder gestohlen? Oder hat sie in einem Sexualanfall öffentliches Ärgernis erregt? Ja, das vielleicht. Einmal war sie berauscht von einem buckligen Eros aus ihrer Feigheit rausgehüpft in eine blöde Geilheit—na, und nun trottete sie vor mir her, stillvergnügt und 10 erschrocken, einmal etwas gewagt zu haben.

Aber ich glaube, jetzt zittert sie insgeheim, weil sie weiß, daß ich hinter ihr gehe, ich, ihr Mörder! Oh, es würde mir leicht sein, sie zu morden, und es könnte ganz unauffällig geschehen. Ich hätte ihr nur das Bein zu stellen brauchen, dann wäre sie mit ihren viel zu staki-15 gen Stelzen vornübergestolpert und hätte sich dabei wahrscheinlich ein Loch in den Kopf gestoßen — und dann wäre ihr die Luft mit einem phlegmatischen pfff . . . entwichen wie einem Fahrradschlauch. Ihr Kopf wäre in der Mitte auseinandergeplatzt wie weißlich-gelbes Wachs, und die wenigen Tropfen rote Tinte daraus hätten lächerlich 20 verlogen gewirkt wie Himbeersaft auf der blauseidenen Bluse eines erdolchten Komödianten.

So haßte ich die Perücke, einen Kerl, dessen Visage ich nie gesehen hatte, dessen Stimme ich nie gehört hatte, von dem ich nur einen muffigen, mottenpulverigen Geruch kannte. Sicher hatte er — die 25 Perücke — eine milde, müde Stimme ohne jede Leidenschaft, so kraftlos wie seine milchigen Finger. Sicher hatte er die vorstehenden Augen eines Kalbes und eine dicke, hängende Unterlippe, die dauernd Pralinen essen möchte. Es war die Maske eines Lebemannes, ohne Größe und mit dem Mut eines Papierhändlers, dessen Hebammen-30 hände oftmals den ganzen Tag nichts getan hatten, als siebzehn Pfennige für ein Schreibheft vom Ladentisch zu streicheln.

Nein, kein Wort mehr über die Perücke! Ich hasse sie wirklich so sehr, daß ich mich leicht in einen Wutausbruch hineinsteigern könnte, bei dem ich mich zu sehr entblößen würde. Genug. Schluß. 35 Ich will nie wieder von ihr reden, nie! —

Aber wenn einer, den du gerne verschweigen möchtest, ständig mit eingeknickten Knien in der Melodie eines Melodramas vor dir hergeht, dann wirst du ihn nicht los. Wie ein Juckreiz im Rücken, wo du mit den Händen nicht ankommst, reizt er dich immer wieder, 40 an ihn zu denken, ihn zu empfinden, ihn zu hassen.

² **einen greulichen Streich spielen** to play a horrible trick
³ **ordinär** vulgar
⁴ **sich aus seinem Blut hoch·wälzen** rise from wallowing in his blood
⁵ **verlegen** embarrassed
⁶ **kopfüber** head over heels;   **e Gefängnismanege** (*French:* manege, a school for teaching horsemanship and for training horses) *here:* a prison seen as such
⁷ **hampeln** (*coll.*) to dither, flounder;   **bockende Esel** stubborn donkeys
⁸ **bis zum Wahnsinn reizen** drive to madness;   **gemachte Angst** pretended fear
¹⁰ **r Scheuerlappen** scouring cloth;   **lüpfen** to stick out, hoist
¹³ **sich auf etw. (acc.) besinnen** to remember s.t.
¹⁷ **hinweg·schwemmen** to carry away
¹⁸ **verwüsten** to ruin, lay 'waste'
²⁰ **Gottfried Keller** (1819–1890) Swiss novelist
²² **unerbittlich** merciless
²⁶ **lendenlahm** weak-kneed;   **wanken** to stagger
²⁷ **r Sekt** champagne;   **auf·schäumen** to bubble up
²⁸ **entsetzlich** horrible
³⁰ **e Nächstenliebe** love of fellow men;   **aufgelegt sein** to be disposed
³² **her·dammeln** (*North German*) to hobble along
³³ **auf j-en angewiesen sein** to be dependent upon s.o.
³⁴ **schmal** narrow
³⁵ **in die . . . mehr hineingehört** into which, according to the laws of anatomy, something more actually belongs
³⁸ **j-em etw. auf·zwingen** to force s.t. on s.o.;   **übernommen** accepted

---

1. *Weswegen wagt der Gefangene es nicht, ihn zu ermorden?*
2. *Was verlangt der Autor vom Leser?*
3. *Weswegen will er das?*
4. *Wohin sehen alle Hintermänner?*

Ich glaube, ich muß die Perücke doch ermorden. Aber ich habe
Angst, der Tote würde mir einen greulichen Streich spielen. Er
würde sich plötzlich mit ordinärem Lachen daran erinnern, daß
er früher ja Zirkusclown war und sich aus seinem Blut hochwälzen.
5 Vielleicht etwas verlegen, als hätte er das Blut nicht halten können
wie andere Leute das Wasser. Kopfüber würde er durch die Gefängnismanege hampeln, hielte womöglich die Wärter für bockende
Esel, die er bis zum Wahnsinn reizen würde, um dann mit gemachter
Angst auf die Mauer zu springen. Von dort aus würde er dann seine
10 Zunge wie einen Scheuerlappen gegen uns lüpfen und auf immer
verschwinden.

Es ist nicht auszudenken, was alles geschehen würde, wenn sich
plötzlich jeder auf das besinnen würde, was er eigentlich ist.

Denke nicht, daß mein Haß auf meinen Vordermann, auf die
15 Perücke, hohl und grundlos ist — oh, man kann in Situationen kommen, wo man so von Haß überläuft und über die eigenen Grenzen
hinweggeschwemmt wird, daß man nachher kaum zu sich selbst
zurückfindet — so hat einen der Haß verwüstet.

Ich weiß, es ist schwer, mir zuzuhören und mit mir zu fühlen.
20 Du sollst auch nicht zuhören, als wenn einer dir etwas von Gottfried
Keller oder Dickens vorliest. Du sollst mit mir gehen, mitgehen in
dem kleinen Kreis zwischen den unerbittlichen Mauern. Nicht in
Gedanken neben mir — nein, körperlich hinter mir als mein Hintermann. Und dann wirst du sehen, wie schnell du mich hassen lernst.
25 Denn wenn du mit uns (ich sage jetzt „uns", weil wir dieses eine alle
gemeinsam haben) in unserm lendenlahmen Kreise wankst, dann
bist du so leer von Liebe, daß der Haß wie Sekt in dir aufschäumt.
Du läßt ihn auch schäumen, nur um diese entsetzliche Leere nicht
mehr zu fühlen. Und glaube nur nicht, daß du mit leerem Magen und
30 leerem Herzen zu besonderen Taten der Nächstenliebe aufgelegt
sein wirst!

So wirst du also als ein von allem Guten Geleerter hinter mir her-
dammeln und monatelang nur auf mich angewiesen sein, auf meinen
schmalen Rücken, den viel zu weichen Nacken und die leere Hose,
35 in die der Anatomie nach eigentlich etwas mehr hineingehört. Am meisten wirst du aber auf meine Beine sehen müssen. Alle Hintermänner
sehen auf die Beine ihres Vordermannes, und der Rhythmus seines
Schrittes wird ihnen aufgezwungen und übernommen, auch wenn
er ihnen fremd und unbequem ist. Ja, und da wird der Haß dich an-

¹ **eifersüchtig** jealous
² **r Gang** gait, stride
³ **e Stilart** style
⁵ **begründen** to justify
⁷ **verspielter Schritt** toying step
⁸ **sich auf etw.** (*acc.*) **ein·stellen** to adjust to s.t.;   **stockend** hesitatingly
⁹ **reell und energisch auf·treten** to walk in a sound and energetic way
¹¹ **zerfahren** absentminded(ly);   **bummeln** to stroll
¹⁵ **sich nach j-em um·sehen** to look around at s.o.
¹⁶ **sich mit j-em verständigen** to come to an understanding with s.o.
¹⁷ **j-en verleugnen** to disavow s.o.
²¹ **j-em ein·heizen** to make it warm for (annoy) s.o.
²² **kochen** *here:* to boil
²⁶ **r Fleck** patch;   **r Rasen** lawn
²⁸ **e Versammlung** gathering;   **r Grashalm** blade of grass
³³ **zu·nicken** to nod, bow to;   **unscheinbar** insignificant
³⁴ **e Miniaturgeisha** a little geisha girl;   **e Wiese** meadow
³⁶ **festgebackt starren** to stare spellbound
³⁹ **auf j-en (etw.) stieren** to stare at s.o. (s.t.)

---

1. Was für einen Gang hat der Gefangene ?
2. Was umkreisen die Gefangenen jeden Morgen?
3. Welche Entdeckung macht der Gefangene eines Tages ?

fallen wie ein eifersüchtiges Weib, wenn du merkst, daß ich keinen
Gang habe. Nein, ich habe keinen Gang. Es gibt tatsächlich Menschen, die keinen Gang haben — sie haben mehrere Stilarten, die
sich nicht miteinander vereinen können zu einer Melodie. Ich bin
5 so einer. Du wirst mich deswegen hassen, ebenso sinnlos und begründet, wie ich die Perücke hassen muß, weil ich ihr Hintermann
bin. Wenn du dich gerade auf meinen etwas unsicheren, verspielten
Schritt eingestellt hast, stellst du stockend fest, daß ich plötzlich ganz
reell und energisch auftrete. Und kaum hast du diesen neuen Typ
10 meines Gehens registriert, da fange ich einige Schritte weiter an,
zerfahren und mutlos zu bummeln. Nein, du wirst keine Freude und
Freundschaft über mich empfinden können. Du mußt mich hassen.
Alle Hintermänner hassen ihre Vordermänner.

Vielleicht würde alles anders werden, wenn sich die Vordermänner
15 mal nach ihren Hintermännern umsehen würden, um sich mit ihnen
zu verständigen. So ist aber jeder Hintermann — er sieht nur seinen
Vordermann und haßt ihn. Aber seinen Hintermann verleugnet er
— da fühlt er sich Vordermann. So ist das in unserm Kreis hinter
den grauen Mauern — so ist es aber wohl anderswo auch, überall
20 vielleicht.

Ich hätte die Perücke doch umbringen sollen. Einmal heizte sie
mir so ein, daß mein Blut an zu kochen fing. Das war, als ich die
Entdeckung machte. Keine große Sache. Nur eine ganz kleine Entdeckung.

25 Habe ich schon gesagt, daß wir jeden Morgen eine halbe Stunde
lang einen kleinen schmutzig-grünen Fleck Rasen umkreisen? In
der Mitte der Manege von diesem seltsamen Zirkus war eine blasse
Versammlung von Grashalmen, blaß und der einzelne Halm ohne
Gesicht. Wie wir in diesem unerträglichen Lattenzaun. Auf der Suche
30 nach Lebendigem, Buntem, lief mein Auge ohne große Hoffnung
eigentlich und zufällig über die paar Hälmchen hin, die sich, als sie
sich angesehen fühlten, unwillkürlich zusammennahmen und mir
zunickten — und da entdeckte ich unter ihnen einen unscheinbaren
gelben Punkt, eine Miniaturgeisha auf einer großen Wiese. Ich war
35 so erschrocken über meine Entdeckung, daß ich glaubte, alle müßten
es gesehen haben, daß meine Augen wie festgebackt auf das gelbe
Etwas starrten, und ich sah schnell und sehr interessiert auf die
Pantoffeln meines Vordermannes. Aber so wie du einem, mit dem
du sprichst, immer auf den Fleck, den er an der Nase hat, stieren

[1] **sich nach etw. sehnen** to yearn for s.t.
[2] **dicht** close
[3] **tat** . . . acted . . .;   **unbefangen** free and easy
[4] **r Löwenzahn** dandelion
[7] **eine Huldigung an etw.** (*acc.*) **dar·bringen** to pay homage to s.t.
[8] **formlich** literally;   **(ich) bildete mir ein, einer . . . Blickes** I imagined that one of
  the blue fellows was following with protruding eyes wherever I looked
[10] **r Wachthund** watch dog
[12] **an etw.** (*dat.*) **teil·nehmen** to share in s.t.
[14] **sich freuen** to be happy
[18] **e Sehnsucht** longing
[19] **schüchtern** timid
[23] **schlau** sly
[26] **tüchtig** considerable;   **r Herdentrieb** herd instinct
[27] **sich täuschen** to deceive o.s.
[28] **latschen** to shuffle
[29] **stur** (*coll.*) stubborn;   **e Spur** track, footprint;   **es gelingt mir** I succeed
[33] **staubig** dusty;   **e Holzpantinen** (*pl.*) wooden clogs
[36] **e Erfüllung** fulfillment;   **e Probe** experiment
[37] **r Strumpf** stocking;   **(he)runter·rutschen** to ride down

---

1. Warum sehnen sich die Augen des Gefangenen nach diesem gelben Punkt?
2. Was für eine Blume ist es ?
3. Wie weit vom Weg steht die Blume ?
4. Weshalb will der Gefangene die Blume in der Zelle haben ?
5. Wie fängt er es an, der Blume näher zu kommen ?
6. Was tun seine Hintermänner aus Herdentrieb ?

mußt und ihn ganz unruhig machst — so sehnten meine Augen sich nach dem gelben Punkt. Als ich jetzt dichter an ihm vorbeikam, tat ich so unbefangen wie möglich. Ich erkannte eine Blume, eine gelbe Blume. Es war ein Löwenzahn — eine kleine gelbe Hunde-
5 blume.

Sie stand ungefähr einen halben Meter links von unserm Weg, von dem Kreis, auf dem wir jeden Morgen eine Huldigung an die frische Luft darbrachten. Ich stand förmlich Angst aus und bildete mir ein, einer der Blauen folge schon mit Stielaugen der Richtung
10 meines Blickes. Aber so sehr unsere Wachthunde gewohnt waren, auf jede individuelle Regung des Lattenzaunes mit wütendem Bellen zu reagieren — niemand hatte an meiner Entdeckung teilgenommen. Die kleine Hundeblume war noch ganz mein Eigentum.

Aber richtig freuen konnte ich mich nur wenige Tage an ihr. Sie
15 sollte mir ganz gehören. Immer wenn unser Rundgang zu Ende ging, mußte ich mich gewaltsam von ihr losreißen, und ich hätte meine tägliche Brotration (und das will was sagen!) dafür gegeben, sie zu besitzen. Die Sehnsucht, etwas Lebendiges in der Zelle zu haben, wurde so mächtig in mir, daß die Blume, die schüchterne kleine Hunde-
20 blume, für mich bald den Wert eines Menschen, einer heimlichen Geliebten bekam: Ich konnte nicht mehr ohne sie leben — da oben zwischen den toten Wänden!

Und dann kam die Sache mit der Perücke. Ich fing es sehr schlau an. Jedesmal, wenn ich an meiner Blume vorbeikam, trat ich so un-
25 auffällig wie möglich einen Fuß breit vom Wege auf den Grasfleck. Wir haben alle einen tüchtigen Teil Herdentrieb in uns, und darauf spekulierte ich. Ich hatte mich nicht getäuscht. Mein Hintermann, sein Hintermann, dessen Hintermann — und so weiter — alle latsch-ten stur und folgsam in meiner Spur. So gelang es mir in vier Tagen,
30 unsern Weg so nahe an meine Hundeblume heranzubringen, daß ich sie mit der Hand hätte erreichen können, wenn ich mich gebückt hätte. Zwar starben einige zwanzig der blassen Grashalme durch mein Unternehmen einen staubigen Tod unter unsern Holzpantinen — aber wer denkt an ein paar zertretene Grashalme, wenn er eine
35 Blume pflücken will!

Ich näherte mich der Erfüllung meines Wunsches. Zur Probe ließ ich einige Male meinen linken Strumpf runterrutschen, bückte mich ärgerlich und harmlos und zog ihn wieder hoch. Niemand fand etwas dabei. Also, morgen denn!

² **feucht** moist
³ **e Aussicht** prospect
⁴ **e Einsamkeit** loneliness
⁶ **s Pantoffelgeklöppel** (*coll.*) slip-slopping of clogs
⁸ **abgefeimt** cunning
⁹ **niederträchtig** vile
¹¹ **rasseln** to clank;   **r Riesenschlüsselbund** gigantic bunch of keys
¹² **r Tatort** scene of the (proposed) crime
¹⁵ **ungeheuer** monstrous
¹⁶ **e Tarantella** a lively Neapolitan folk dance in 6/8 time
¹⁷ **r Nabel** navel
¹⁹ **j-en an·blitzen** to flash a glance at s.o.;   **verdrehen** to turn up (eyes);   **s Kalbsauge** calf's eye
²⁰ **schillern** to be iridescent;   **zusammen·klappen** to collapse
²² **brüllen** to bellow
²⁵ **so selbstverständlich** in such a matter-of-fact manner
²⁷ **gestehen** to confess;   **e Ehrlichkeit** fairness
²⁹ **etw.** (*dat.*) **unterliegen** to be defeated by s.t.
³⁰ **verlaufen** = **verschwinden**
³¹ **e Welle** wave;   **r Strand** beach
³² **haarscharf** very close
³³ **vorbei·pfeifen** to whistle by;   **sich bemühen** to make the effort
³⁴ **j-em etw. gönnen** to grant s.o. s.t.; not to grudge s.o. s.t.;   **nachträglich** subsequently; **vermeintlich** assumed
³⁷ **verlogen** insincere
³⁸ **eigens** specially;   **aus der Hölle beurlaubt** on leave from hell

---

1. Weswegen hat der Gefangene eines Morgens Herzklopfen?
2. Was geschah plötzlich bei der vorletzten Runde?
3. Was sagte der Mann in der blauen Uniform, als er zu dem Liegenden trat?
4. Warum haßt der Gefangene den Vordermann nun nicht mehr?
5. Wie sieht sein neuer Vordermann aus?

Ihr müßt mich nicht auslachen, wenn ich sage, daß ich am nächsten Tag mit Herzklopfen den Hof betrat und feuchte, erregte Hände hatte. Es war auch zu unwahrscheinlich, die Aussicht, nach monatelanger Einsamkeit und Liebelosigkeit unerwartet eine Geliebte in
5 der Zelle zu haben.

Wir hatten unsere tägliche Ration Runden mit monotonem Pantoffelgeklöppel fast beendet — bei der vorletzten Runde sollte es geschehen. Da trat die Perücke in Aktion, und zwar auf die abgefeimteste und niederträchtigste Weise.

10 Wir waren eben in die vorletzte Runde eingebogen, die Blauen rasselten wichtig mit den Riesenschlüsselbunden, und ich näherte mich dem Tatort, von wo meine Blume mir ängstlich entgegensah. Vielleicht war ich nie so erregt wie in diesen Sekunden. Noch zwanzig Schritte. Noch fünfzehn Schritte, noch zehn, fünf . . .

15 Da geschah das Ungeheure! Die Perücke warf plötzlich, als begänne sie eine Tarantella, die dünnen Arme in die Luft, hob das rechte Bein graziös bis an den Nabel und machte auf dem linken Fuß eine Drehung nach hinten. Nie werde ich begreifen, wo sie den Mut hernahm — sie blitzte mich triumphierend an, als wüßte sie alles, verdrehte die Kalbs-
20 augen, bis das Weiße zu schillern anfing, und klappte dann wie eine Marionette zusammen. Oh, nun war es gewiß: er mußte früher Zirkusclown gewesen sein, denn alles brüllte vor Lachen!

Aber da bellten die blauen Uniformen los, und das Lachen war weggewischt, als ob es nie gewesen war. Und einer trat gegen den
25 Liegenden und sagte so selbstverständlich, wie man sagt: es regnet — so sagte er: Er ist tot!

Ich muß noch etwas gestehen — aus Ehrlichkeit gegen mich selbst. In dem Augenblick, als ich mit dem Mann, den ich die Perücke nannte, Auge in Auge war und fühlte, daß er unterlag, nicht mir,
30 nein, dem Leben unterlag — in dieser Sekunde verlief mein Haß wie eine Welle am Strand, und es blieb nichts als ein Gefühl der Leere. Eine Latte war aus dem Zaun gebrochen — der Tod war haarscharf an mir vorbeigepfiffen —, da bemüht man sich schnell, gut zu sein. Und ich gönne der Perücke noch nachträglich den vermeint-
35 lichen Sieg über mich.

Am nächsten Morgen hatte ich einen anderen Vordermann, der mich die Perücke sofort vergessen machte. Er sah verlogen aus wie ein Theologe, aber ich glaube, er war eigens aus der Hölle beurlaubt, mir das Pflücken meiner Blume völlig unmöglich zu machen.

[1] **feixen** (*coll.*) to grin
[2] **s Grinsen** smirk, grin
[3] **jeder Zoll ein Staatsbeamter** every inch a civil servant
[4] **s Berufssoldatengesicht** face of a professional soldier
[5] **verzerren** to distort
[7] **gönnerhaft** condescending
[8] **e Unversöhnlichkeit** implacability
[14] **das war eine Motte** (**e Motte** moth) that was a crazy fellow;   **gerissen** cunning
[17] **e Meute** pack
[18] **umkläffen** (*coll.*) to surround
[19] **aus·üben** to practice
[21] **schnauzenähnlich** snout-like;   **e Angleichung** approximation
[22] **s Tierreich** animal kingdom
[23] **s Standbild** statue
[24] **e Aufschrift** inscription;   **L'Etat c'est moi.** I am the State. (ascribed to Louis XIV [1638–1715], King of France)
[25] **r Schlosser** locksmith
[26] **verunglücken** to have an accident;   **Gott nahm sich seiner an** God took care of him
[28] **auf·pusten** to inflate
[29] **r Luftballon** balloon;   **ungeahnt** never dreamt of
[31] **e Blödheit = e Verrücktheit**
[32] **s Lederkoppel** leather harness (gun belt)
[36] **bissig (beißen)** ferocious(ly);   **auf j-en los·fahren** to rush upon s.o.;   **durchaus ehrlich wirken** give an impression of absolute sincerity
[37] **e Verbeugung** bow, reverence;   **innig-höflich** cordially-polite;   **gut gemeint** well-meant
[38] **Gesegnetes Fest, Herr Wachtmeister!** Blessed Holidays, Mr. Sergeant!
[39] **j-em zürnen** to be angry at s.o.;   **eitel** conceited

---

1. *Warum lachen sogar die blauen Uniformen über den neuen Vordermann?*
2. *Was ist „Saures Grinsen"?*
3. *Wie sehen die blauen Uniformen aus, die die Männer in der Manege bewachen?*
4. *Was für einen Beruf hatte „der Theologe" wirklich?*
5. *Wie grüßt dieser Mann die blauen Uniformen?*
6. *Auf welche Weise reagieren diese?*
7. *Weshalb glauben wir, daß die Gefangenen in einem besonderen Gefängnis sind?*

Er hatte eine impertinente Art aufzufallen. Alles feixte über ihn. Sogar die blaßblauen Hunde konnten ein menschliches Grinsen nicht unterdrücken, was sich ungeheuer merkwürdig ausmachte. Jeder Zoll ein Staatsbeamter — aber die primitive Würde der stumpfen Berufs-
5 soldatengesichter war zu einer Grimasse verzerrt. Sie wollten nicht lachen, bei Gott, nein! Aber sie mußten. Kennst du das Gefühl, das gönnerhafte, wenn du mit jemandem böse bist und ihr seid beide Masken der Unversöhnlichkeit, und nun geschieht irgend etwas Komisches, das euch beide zum Lachen zwingt — ihr wollt nicht
10 lachen, bei Gott, nein! Dann zieht sich das Gesicht aber doch in die Breite und nimmt jenen bekannten Ausdruck an, den man am tref- fendsten mit „Saures Grinsen" benennen könnte. So erging es nun den Blauen, und das war die einzige menschliche Regung, die wir überhaupt an ihnen bemerkten. Ja, dieser Theologe, das war eine
15 Motte! Er war gerissen genug, verrückt zu sein — aber er war nicht so verrückt, daß seine Gerissenheit darunter litt.

Wir waren siebenundsiebzig Mann in der Manege, und eine Meute von zwölf uniformierten Revolverträgern umkläffte uns. Einige mochten zwanzig und mehr Jahre diesen Kläfferdienst ausüben, denn ihre
20 Münder waren im Laufe der Jahre bei vielen tausend Patienten eher schnauzenähnlich geworden. Aber diese Angleichung an das Tierreich hatte nichts von ihrer Einbildung genommen. Man hätte jeden einzelnen von ihnen so wie er war als Standbild benutzen können mit der Aufschrift: L'Etat c'est moi.

25 Der Theologe (später erfuhr ich, daß er eigentlich Schlosser war und bei Arbeiten an einer Kirche verunglückte — Gott nahm sich seiner an!) war so verrückt oder gerissen, daß er ihre Würde voll- kommen respektierte. Was sag ich — respektierte? Er pustete die Würde der blauen Uniformen auf zu einem Luftballon von unge-
30 ahnten Dimensionen, von denen die Träger selbst keine Ahnung hatten. Wenn sie auch über seine Blödheit lachen mußten, ganz heim- lich blähte doch ein gewisser Stolz ihre Bäuche, daß sich die Leder- koppel spannten.

Immer wenn der Theologe einen der Wachthunde passierte, die
35 breitbeinig stehend ihre Macht zum Ausdruck brachten und, sooft es ging, bissig auf uns losfuhren — jedesmal machte er eine durchaus ehrlich wirkende Verbeugung und sage so innig-höflich und gut gemeint: Gesegnetes Fest, Herr Wachtmeister! — daß kein Gott ihm hätte zürnen können — viel weniger die eitlen Luftballons in

[1] **bescheiden** unassuming
[2] **etw.** (*dat.*) **aus·weichen** to avoid s.t.;   **e Ohrfeige** box on the ear
[4] **aus·strahlen** to radiate
[5] **in Anspruch nehmen** to lay claim to, involve
[7] **zärtlich** affectionate;   **ein irrsinniger Kampf** an absurd struggle
[8] **aus tragen** to endure;   **r Angstschweiß** cold sweat;   **aus allen Löchern** from all pores
[10] **r Honig** honey
[11] **alle Muskeln anspannen** to strain all nerves
[12] **nach·tun** to imitate
[13] **s Staatsdenkmal** national monument
[20] **auf·bieten** to summon up
[21] **mildernde Umstände** extenuating circumstances
[22] **etw.** (*dat.*) **gewachsen sein** to be equal to s.t.
[25] **Bismarck, Otto von** (1815–98), German statesman
[26] **r Bückling** = **e Verbeugung**
[28] **ein·richten** to arrange
[30] **ich fischte ihn ganz umständlich** I got hold of it with great difficulties;   **humpeln** to limp
[32] **sich verdunkeln** to cloud over, become overcast
[33] **unverschämt lang** damned tall
[34] **e Vorsehung** providence
[35] **j-em (etw.) nach·helfen** to assist s.o. (s.t.);   **e Gliedmaßen** (*pl.*) limbs
[36] **durcheinander·rudern** to move in confusion;   **s Originelle** peculiarity
[37] **keinerlei Übersicht haben** to have no control at all
[39] **umsinken** to drop down

---

1. *Wovon träumt der Gefangene ?*
2. *Wie sieht der letzte Vordermann aus ?*

Uniform. Und dabei legte er seine Verbeugung so bescheiden an,
daß es immer aussah, als wiche er einer Ohrfeige aus.

Und nun hatte der Teufel diesen Komiker-Theologen zu meinem
Vordermann gemacht, und seine Verrücktheit strahlte so stark aus
5 und nahm mich in Anspruch, daß ich meine neue kleine Geliebte,
meine Hundeblume, beinahe vergaß. Ich konnte ihr kaum einen
zärtlichen Blick zuwerfen, denn ich mußte einen irrsinnigen Kampf
mit meinen Nerven austragen, der mir den Angstschweiß aus allen
Löchern jagte. Jedesmal, wenn der Theologe seine Verbeugung machte
10 und sein „Gesegnetes Fest, Herr Wachtmeister" wie Honig von der
Zunge tropfen ließ — jedesmal mußte ich alle Muskeln anspannen,
es ihm nicht nachzutun. Die Versuchung war so stark, daß ich mehrere
Male den Staatsdenkmälern schon freundlich zunickte und es erst
in der letzten Sekunde fertigbrachte, keine Verbeugung zu machen
15 und stumm zu bleiben.

Wir kreisten täglich etwa eine halbe Stunde im Hof, das waren
täglich zwanzig Runden, und zwölf Uniformen umstanden unsern
Kreis. Der Theologe machte also auf jeden Fall zweihundertund-
vierzig Verbeugungen pro Tag, und zweihundertundvierzigmal mußte
20 ich alle Konzentration aufbieten, nicht verrückt zu werden. Ich
wußte, wenn ich das drei Tage gemacht hätte, würde ich mildernde
Umstände bekommen — dem war ich nicht gewachsen. Ich kam
völlig erschöpft in meine Zelle zurück. Die ganze Nacht aber ging
ich im Traum eine unendliche Reihe blauer Uniformen entlang,
25 die alle wie Bismarck aussahen — die ganze Nacht bot ich diesen
Millionen blaßblauer Bismarcks mit tiefem Bückling ein „Gesegnetes
Fest, Herr Wachtmeister!"

Am nächsten Tag wußte ich es so einzurichten, daß die Reihe an
mir vorbeiging und ich einen andern Vordermann bekam. Ich verlor
30 meinen Pantoffel, fischte ihn ganz umständlich und humpelte in
den Lattenzaun zurück. Gott sei Dank! Vor mir ging die Sonne auf.
Vielmehr — sie verdunkelte sich. Mein neuer Vordermann war so
unverschämt lang, daß meine 1,80 m glatt in seinem Schatten ver-
schwanden. Es gab also doch eine Vorsehung — man mußte ihr nur
35 mit dem Pantoffel nachhelfen. Seine unmenschlich langen Gliedmaßen ruderten sinnlos durcheinander, und das Originelle war, er
kam dabei sogar vorwärts, obgleich er sicher keinerlei Übersicht über
Beine und Arme hatte. Ich liebte ihn beinahe — ja, ich betete, er
möchte nicht plötzlich tot umsinken wie die Perücke oder verrückt

² **die geistige Gesundheit** mental health
⁵ **sich verraten** to give oneself away
⁶ **sein abscheulich näselndes Organ** his abominably nasal tone (speech)
⁷ **r Krake** octopus;   **e Gottesanbeterin** praying mantis
⁸ **verleihen** to confer
¹¹ **r Häftling** prisoner
¹² **rasender Pulsschlag** racing pulse
¹³ **kaschierte Harmlosigkeit** pretended harmlessness
¹⁶ **die sparsamen Sonnenstrahlen** the stingy sunrays
¹⁷ **s Gitter** bars (of prison fence)
¹⁸ **dösen** to doze;   **hellwach** wide awake
¹⁹ **vor Aufregung** out of excitement;   **e Gangart wechseln** to change pace
²¹ **herum·fummeln** (*coll.*) to fumble around with
²² **er fuhr dazwischen auf die Blume zu** in between (meanwhile) he rushed toward the flower
²³ **sie klöppelten in gewohntem Schlendrian** they jogged along in the familiar routine
²⁵ **blasiert** blasé;   **reuig** contrite, penitent;   **s Zeitalter** age
²⁶ **e Grammophonplatte** gramophone record;   **e Raumforschung** space research
²⁷ **hochgemauert** high-set (wall)
²⁹ **r Lichtstrahl** ray, beam (of light)
³⁰ **s Benzin** gasoline
³¹ **r Lippenstift** lipstick
³² **e Pritsche** plank bed
³³ **hinein·saugen** to suck in (draw breath in) eagerly
³⁴ **e Scheibe** disk, orb
³⁶ **e Zärtlichkeit** tenderness, affection
³⁷ **e Anlehnung** dependence;   **ohnegleichen** unique

---

1. Wofür betet der Gefangene ?
2. Warum bekommt der Häftling einen schnelleren Pulsschlag ?
3. Wie gelingt es dem Häftling die Blume abzureißen ?
4. Was tut er mit der Blume in seiner Zelle ?
5. Welches Gefühl erfüllt ihn dabei ?

werden und anfangen, feige Verbeugungen zu machen. Ich betete
für sein langes Leben und seine geistige Gesundheit. Ich fühlte mich
in seinem Schatten so geborgen, daß meine Blicke länger als sonst
die kleine Hundeblume umfingen, ohne daß ich Angst zu haben brauch-
5 te, mich zu verraten. Ich verzieh diesem himmlischen Vordermann
sogar sein abscheulich näselndes Organ, oh, ich verkniff mir großzügig, ihm allerlei Spitznamen wie Oboe, Krake, oder Gottesanbeterin zu verleihen. Ich sah nur noch meine Blume — und ließ
meinen Vordermann so lang und so blöde sein, wie er es wollte!
10 Der Tag war wie alle anderen. Er unterschied sich nur dadurch von
ihnen, daß der Häftling aus Zelle 432 zum Ende der halben Stunde
einen rasenden Pulsschlag bekam und seine Augen den Ausdruck
von kaschierter Harmlosigkeit und schlecht verdeckter Unsicherheit annahmen.
15 Wir bogen in die vorletzte Runde ein — wieder wurden die Schlüssel-
bunde lebendig, und der Lattenzaun döste durch die sparsamen
Sonnenstrahlen wie hinter ewigen Gittern.
Aber was war das? Eine Latte döste ja gar nicht! Sie war hellwach
und wechselte vor Aufregung alle paar Meter die Gangart. Merkte
20 das denn kein Mensch? Nein. Und plötzlich bückte sich die Latte
432, fummelte an ihrem runtergerutschten Strumpf herum und —
fuhr dazwischen blitzschnell mit der einen Hand auf eine erschrockene
kleine Blume zu, riß sie ab — und schon klöppelten wieder siebenundsiebzig Latten in gewohntem Schlendrian in die letzte Runde.

25 Was ist so komisch: Ein blasierter, reuiger Jüngling aus dem Zeitalter der Grammophonplatten und Raumforschung steht in der Ge-
fängniszelle 432 unter dem hochgemauerten Fenster und hält mit
seinen vereinsamten Händen eine kleine gelbe Blume in den schmalen
Lichtstrahl — eine ganz gewöhnliche Hundeblume. Und dann hebt
30 dieser Mensch, der gewohnt war, Pulver, Parfüm und Benzin, Gin
und Lippenstift zu riechen, die Hundeblume an seine hungrige Nase,
die schon monatelang nur das Holz der Pritsche, Staub und Angstschweiß gerochen hat — und er saugt so gierig aus der kleinen gelben
Scheibe ihr Wesen in sich hinein, daß er nur noch aus Nase besteht.
35 Da öffnet sich in ihm etwas und ergießt sich wie Licht in den engen
Raum, etwas, von dem er bisher nie gewußt hat: Eine Zärtlichkeit,
eine Anlehnung und Wärme ohnegleichen erfüllt ihn zu der Blume
und füllt ihn ganz aus.

[3] **keusch** chaste, pure
[4] **r Trost** consolation
[7] **r Wasserbecher** drinking mug
[8] **erschöpft** exhausted
[9] **Angesicht in Angesicht** face to face
[11] **gelöst sein** to be relaxed;   **etw.** (*acc.*) **ab·tun** to do away with s.t.;   **etw.** (*acc.*)
   ab·streifen to get rid of s.t.
[12] **j-en belasten** to weigh upon s.o.;   **e Gefangenschaft** confinement, captivity
[14] **s Christentum** Christianity
[16] **Bali** island in Indonesia;   **r Wilde** savage
[18] **e Kokosnuß** coconut;   **r Kabeljau** codfish;   **r Kolibri** hummingbird
[21] **umspannen** to clutch;   **vertraut** familiar
[22] **s Blech** tin;   **r Trinkbecher** drinking cup
[23] **häufen** to pile up
[24] **sich angewöhnen** (+ *dat.*) to get accustomed to
[25] **e Akelei** columbine (flower)

---

1. *Wonach riecht die Blume ?*
2. *Was streifte er alles ab ?*
3. *Wozu war er noch nie so bereit gewesen ?*
4. *Welchen Gegenstand umspannten seine Hände die ganze Nacht ?*
5. *Was fühlte der Ausgelieferte im Schlaf ?*

Er ertrug den Raum nicht mehr und schloß die Augen und staunte:
Aber du riechst ja nach Erde. Nach Sonne, Meer und Honig, liebes
Lebendiges! Er empfand ihre keusche Kühle wie die Stimme des
Vaters, den er nie sonderlich beachtet hatte und der nun soviel Trost
5 war mit seiner Stille — er empfand sie wie die helle Schulter einer
dunklen Frau.

Er trug sie behutsam wie eine Geliebte zu seinem Wasserbecher,
stellte das erschöpfte kleine Wesen da hinein, und dann brauchte
er mehrere Minuten — so langsam setzte er sich, Angesicht in An-
10 gesicht mit seiner Blume.

Er war so gelöst und glücklich, daß er alles abtat und abstreifte,
was ihn belastete: die Gefangenschaft, das Alleinsein, den Hunger
nach Liebe, die Hilflosigkeit seiner zweiundzwanzig Jahre, die Gegenwart und die Zukunft, die Welt und das Christentum — ja, auch
15 das!

Er war ein brauner Balinese, ein „Wilder" eines „wilden" Volkes,
der das Meer und den Blitz und den Baum fürchtete und anbetete.
Der Kokosnuß, Kabeljau und Kolibri verehrte, bestaunte, fraß und
nicht begriff. So befreit war er, und nie war er so bereit zum Guten
20 gewesen, als er der Blume zuflüsterte . . . werden wie du . . .

Die ganze Nacht umspannten seine glücklichen Hände das ver-
traute Blech seines Trinkbechers, und er fühlte im Schlaf, wie sie
Erde auf ihn häuften, dunkle, gute Erde, und wie er sich der Erde
angewöhnte und wurde wie sie — und wie aus ihm Blumen brachen:
25 Anemonen, Akelei und Löwenzahn — winzige, unscheinbare Sonnen.

[1] e **Etagentür** apartment door;   **ohne viel Aufhebens** without much ado
[5] **aus·halten** to endure;   s **Aneinandervorbeisein** lack of communication (alienation)
[7] **über·wachsen** to outgrow
[8] **weg·schieben** to 'shove' (away) aside
[16] s **Treppenhaus** stairwell, landing;   r **Boden** attic
[17] **überlegen** to deliberate
[18] r **Entschluß** resolution
[19] **vor allem** above all
[20] e **Vorbedingung** preliminary condition
[21] s **Erschießen** shooting;   s **Vergiften** poisoning
[22] e **Blamage** disgrace
[23] **vorwurfsvoll** reproachful;   **mitleidig** sympathetic
[25] **ertränken** to drown;   **pathetisch** theatrical
[26] **aufgeregt** (*used here for* **aufregend**) exciting
[28] **unauffällig** inconspicuous
[29] r **Querbalken** crossbeam;   r **Dachstuhl** roof framework, rafters
[30] r **Wäschekorb** clothesbasket;   e **Leine** rope
[31] **zu·ziehen** to draw shut;   **zögern** to hesitate;   s **Treppengelände(r)** banisters

1. Wie macht der junge Mensch die Tür zu ?
2. Warum will er sich das Leben nehmen ?
3. Was fühlt er, wenn die anderen lachen ?
4. Woran hat er die ganze Nacht gedacht ?
5. Warum will er sich weder erschießen noch vergiften ?
6. Weswegen will er sich nicht ertränken oder aus dem Fenster stürzen ?
7. Wie will er sich am Boden das Leben nehmen ?

Das Holz für morgen

Er machte die Etagentür hinter sich zu. Er machte sie leise und ohne viel Aufhebens hinter sich zu, obgleich er sich das Leben nehmen wollte. Das Leben, das er nicht verstand und in dem er nicht verstanden wurde. Er wurde nicht von denen verstanden, die er liebte.
5 Und gerade das hielt er nicht aus, dieses Aneinandervorbeisein mit denen, die er liebte.

Aber es war noch mehr da, das so groß wurde, daß es alles überwuchs und das sich nicht wegschieben lassen wollte.

Das war, daß er nachts weinen konnte, ohne daß die, die er liebte,
10 ihn hörten. Das war, daß er sah, daß seine Mutter, die er liebte, älter wurde und daß er das sah. Das war, daß er mit den anderen im Zimmer sitzen konnte, mit ihnen lachen konnte und dabei einsamer war als je. Das war, daß die anderen es nicht schießen hörten, wenn er es hörte. Daß sie das nie hören wollten. Das war dieses
15 Aneinandervorbeisein mit denen, die er liebte, das er nicht aushielt. Nun stand er im Treppenhaus und wollte zum Boden hinaufgehen und sich das Leben nehmen. Er hatte die ganze Nacht überlegt, wie er das machen wollte, und er war zu dem Entschluß gekommen, daß er vor allem auf den Boden hinaufgehen müsse, denn da wäre
20 man allein und das war die Vorbedingung für alles andere. Zum Erschießen hatte er nichts und Vergiften war ihm zu unsicher. Keine Blamage wäre größer gewesen, als dann mit Hilfe eines Arztes wieder in das Leben zurückzukommen und die vorwurfsvollen mitleidigen Gesichter der anderen, die so voll Liebe und Angst für ihn waren,
25 ertragen zu müssen. Und sich ertränken, das fand er zu pathetisch, und sich aus dem Fenster stürzen, das fand er zu aufgeregt. Nein, das beste würde sein, man ginge auf den Boden. Da war man allein. Da war es still. Da war alles ganz unauffällig und ohne viel Aufhebens. Und da waren vor allem die Querbalken vom Dachstuhl.
30 Und der Wäschekorb mit der Leine. Als er die Etagentür leise hinter sich zugezogen hatte, faßte er ohne zu zögern nach dem Treppen-

[1] **kegelförmig** tapering;   **s Glasdach** skylight
[2] **r Maschendraht** wire netting
[3] **s Spinngewebe** cobweb;   **blaß** pale
[5] **umfassen** to clasp;   **sauber** clean
[7] **r Strich** line;   **gelblich** yellowish
[11] **s Stockwerk** floor
[12] **ebenfalls** also
[13] **r Farbton** shade
[18] **e Feile** file
[19] **e Faust** fist
[20] **(he)runter·sausen** to dash down
[22] **bremsen** to brake
[23] **s Erdgeschoß** groundfloor;   **e Rille** furrow
[24] **verhören** to interrogate
[25] **e Hauswirtin** landlady
[28] **r Gegenstand** object
[29] **außerdem** moreover;   **verschandeln (e Schande)** to vandalize
[30] **Und dabei war ich es.** And it was me who did it.
[33] **e Mietrechnung** bill for rent
[34] **e Instandsetzungskosten** repair costs
[36] **r Handschuh** glove;   **ersetzen** to replace
[37] **zerreißen** to tear (up)
[38] **r Handwerker** workman;   **hobeln** to plane;   **r Rand** edge;   **glatt** smooth
[39] **r Kitt** putty

---

1. *Was entdeckt er auf dem Treppengeländer ?*
2. *Wie hatte er die tiefe Rille gemacht ?*
3. *Weshalb wurden die Kinder verhört ?*
4. *Was sagte die Hauswirtin ?*
5. *Was wußten die Eltern sofort ?*
6. *Was geschah mit dem Geld, das die Hauswirtin für die Reparatur auf die Mietrechnung geschrieben hatte ?*

geländer und ging langsam nach oben. Das kegelförmige Glasdach
über dem Treppenhaus, das von ganz feinem Maschendraht wie von
Spinnegewebe durchzogen war, ließ einen blassen Himmel hindurch,
der hier oben dicht unter dem Dach am hellsten war.
Fest umfaßte er das saubere hellbraune Treppengeländer und ging
leise und ohne viel Aufhebens nach oben. Da entdeckte er auf dem
Treppengeländer einen breiten weißen Strich, der vielleicht auch etwas gelblich sein konnte. Er blieb stehen und fühlte mit dem Finger
darüber, dreimal, viermal. Dann sah er zurück. Der weiße Strich
ging auf dem ganzen Geländer entlang. Er beugte sich etwas vor. Ja,
man konnte ihn bis tief in die dunkleren Stockwerke nach unten verfolgen. Dort wurde er ebenfalls bräunlicher, aber er blieb doch
einen ganzen Farbton heller als das Holz des Geländers. Er ließ
seinen Finger ein paarmal auf dem weißen Strich entlang fahren,
dann sagte er plötzlich: Das hab ich ja ganz vergessen.
Er setzte sich auf die Treppe. Und jetzt wollte ich mir das Leben
nehmen und hatte das beinahe vergessen. Dabei war ich es doch.
Mit der kleinen Feile, die Karlheinz gehörte. Die habe ich in die
Faust genommen und dann bin ich in vollem Tempo die Treppen
runtergesaust und habe dabei die Feile tief in das weiche Geländer
gedrückt. In den Kurven habe ich besonders stark gedrückt, um zu
bremsen. Als ich unten war, ging über das Treppengeländer vom
Boden bis zum Erdgeschoß eine tiefe, tiefe Rille. Das war ich. Abends
wurden alle Kinder verhört. Die beiden Mädchen unter uns, Karlheinz und ich. Und der nebenan. Die Hauswirtin sagte, das würde
mindestens vierzig Mark kosten. Aber unsere Eltern wußten sofort,
daß es von uns keiner gewesen war. Dazu gehörte ein ganz scharfer
Gegenstand, und den hatte keiner von uns, das wußten sie genau.
Außerdem verschandelte doch kein Kind das Treppengeländer in
seinem eigenen Haus. Und dabei war ich es. Ich mit der kleinen
spitzen Feile. Als keiner von den Familien die vierzig Mark für die
Reparatur des Treppengeländers bezahlen wollte, schrieb die Hauswirtin auf die nächste Mietrechnung je Haushalt fünf Mark mehr
drauf für Instandsetzungskosten des stark demolierten Treppenhauses.
Für dieses Geld wurde dann gleich das ganze Treppenhaus mit Li-
noleum ausgelegt. Und Frau Daus bekam ihren Handschuh ersetzt,
den sie sich an dem aufgesplitterten Geländer zerrissen hatte. Ein
Handwerker kam, hobelte die Ränder der Rille glatt und schmierte
sie dann mit Kitt aus. Vom Boden bis zum Erdgeschoß. Und ich, ich

³ **r Zettel** (piece of) paper
⁶ **falten** to fold
⁷ **e Brusttasche** breast pocket
¹¹ **e Stufe** step; **knarren** to creak
¹² **erledigen** to settle
¹⁷ **s Seifenpulver** soap powder
¹⁸ **extra los sein** to be gone for that very reason
²⁰ **e Erleichterung** relief
²² **j-em Spaß machen** to be fun for s.o.
²⁵ **daß sie mir nicht das Seifenpulver vergißt** (**mir** *coll., added for emphasis*) she must not forget the soap powder (on me)
²⁹ **rutschen** to slide
³¹ **s Geräusch** noise
³² **abwärts** downward
³⁶ **klatschen** to clatter
³⁸ **r Satz** leap

---

1. Was schreibt ihr jetzt der junge Mensch?
2. Was vergißt er dabei ganz?
3. Wen hört er plötzlich sprechen?
4. Warum darf das Seifenpulver nicht vergessen werden?
5. Weswegen soll der Sohn mit dem Wagen weggegangen sein?
6. Weshalb ist es eine Erleichterung für den Vater, daß er wieder da ist?
7. Warum kann sich jetzt der Sohn nicht mehr das Leben nehmen?

war es. Und jetzt wollte ich mir das Leben nehmen und hatte das beinahe vergessen.

Er setzte sich auf die Treppe und nahm einen Zettel. Das mit dem Treppengeländer war ich, schrieb er da drauf. Und dann schrieb er oben drüber: An Frau Kaufmann, Hauswirtin. Er nahm das ganze Geld aus seiner Tasche, es waren zweiundzwanzig Mark, und faltete den Zettel da herum. Er steckte ihn oben in die kleine Brusttasche. Da finden sie ihn bestimmt, dachte er, da müssen sie ihn ja finden. Und er vergaß ganz, daß sich keiner mehr daran erinnern würde. Er vergaß, daß es schon elf Jahre her war, das vergaß er. Er stand auf, die Stufe knarrte ein wenig. Er wollte jetzt auf den Boden gehen. Er hatte das mit dem Treppengeländer erledigt und konnte jetzt nach oben gehen. Da wollte er sich noch einmal laut sagen, daß er es nicht mehr aushielte, das Aneinandervorbeisein mit denen, die er liebte, und dann wollte er es tun. Dann würde er es tun.

Unten ging eine Tür. Er hörte, wie seine Mutter sagte: Und dann sag ihr, sie soll das Seifenpulver nicht vergessen. Daß sie auf keinen Fall das Seifenpulver vergißt. Sag ihr, daß der Junge extra mit dem Wagen los ist, um das Holz zu holen, damit wir morgen waschen können. Sag ihr, das wäre für Vater eine große Erleichterung, daß er nicht mehr mit dem Holzwagen los braucht und daß der Junge wieder da ist. Der Junge ist extra los heute. Vater sagt, das wird ihm Spaß machen. Das hat er die ganzen Jahre nicht tun können. Nun kann er Holz holen. Für uns. Für morgen zum Waschen. Sag ihr das, daß er extra mit dem Wagen los ist und daß sie mir nicht das Seifenpulver vergißt.

Er hörte eine Mädchenstimme antworten. Dann wurde die Tür zugemacht und das Mädchen lief die Treppen hinunter. Er konnte ihre kleine, rutschende Hand das ganze Treppengeländer entlang bis unten verfolgen. Dann hörte er nur ihre Beine noch. Dann war es still. Man hörte das Geräusch, das die Stille machte.

Er ging langsam die Treppe abwärts, langsam Stufe um Stufe abwärts. Ich muß das Holz holen, sagte er, natürlich, das hab ich ja ganz vergessen. Ich muß ja das Holz holen, für morgen.

Er ging immer schneller die Treppen hinunter und ließ seine Hand dabei kurz hintereinander auf das Treppengeländer klatschen. Das Holz, sagte er, ich muß ja das Holz holen. Für uns. Für morgen. Und er sprang die letzten Stufen mit großen Sätzen abwärts.

Ganz oben ließ das dicke Glasdach einen blassen Himmel hindurch. Hier unten aber mußten die Lampen brennen. Jeden Tag. Alle Tage.

¹ **Stubenfliege** housefly
³ **sonderbar** strange, unusual
⁴ **zumindest** at least
⁵ **schon mal** ever;   **Verzeihung!** pardon me!
⁶ **j-em versichern** to assure s.o.
⁷ **s Umgekehrte** reverse
⁸ **im allgemeinen** in general
⁹ **e Verhandlung** trial;   **r Alkoholrausch** alcoholic stupor
¹⁰ **unähnlich** unlike;   **irgendwer** someone or other
¹¹ **e Bemerkung** observation;   **Hamlet mußte auch dran glauben** (*coll.*) Hamlet too
    had to die
¹² **s Dänemark** Denmark
¹⁴ **na, das ist jetzt egal** well, that's all the same now
¹⁷ **hocken** to cringe;   **nieder·schmettern** to crush;   **e Anklage** charge
¹⁸ **zusammen·brechen** to collapse;   **umwogt** surrounded;   **undurchdringlich** im-
    penetrable;   **r Nebel** fog
¹⁹ **seelisch** psychic(al);   **e Düsterkeit** gloom;   **angezogen** dressed, clothed
²¹ **stieren** to stare;   **geradezu fakirhafte Gelassenheit** downright fakir-like composure
    (**r Fakir** member of any religious sect of Islam; *also loosely:* mendicant of other religions,
    yogi)
²¹ **schmucklos** unadorned;   **unmittelbar** direct(ly)
²² **verfinstern** to obscure
²³ **vielmehr** rather
²⁴ **r Tintenklecks** inkblot
²⁵ **s Mathematikheft** math notebook
²⁶ **e Vorzeit** ages past
²⁷ **e Kinderstube** *lit.* nursery (*here:* childhood)
²⁸ **höflich** polite(ly);   **womit** how
²⁹ **e Verachtung** contempt
³⁰ **r Fall** case
³¹ **erwählen** to choose

---

1. *Was will der Autor in dieser Geschichte erzählen?*
2. *Wie ist er ins Gefängnis gekommen?*
3. *Wie sitzt er in seiner Zelle?*
4. *Wohin schaut er?*
5. *Was sieht er dort?*
6. *Was fragt er die Fliege?*
7. *Weswegen nimmt sie von ihm keine Notiz?*

Ching Ling, die Fliege

Sie finden, das ist ein viel zu schöner Name für eine simple Stubenfliege? Oh, dann muß ich Ihnen erzählen, wie die Fliege Ching Ling
zu ihrem sonderbaren Namen gekommen ist, und Sie werden ihn
dann auch zumindest ganz originell finden. Hören Sie bitte.
Haben Sie schon mal im Gefängnis gesessen? Verzeihung, natürlich
nicht! Aber ich kann Ihnen versichern, daß es gar nicht so schwer
ist, hineinzukommen. Das Umgekehrte, nämlich das Herauskommen,
pflegt sich im allgemeinen viel schwieriger zu gestalten. Wie ich bei
der Verhandlung erfuhr, sollte ich in einem dem Alkoholrausch nicht
unähnlichen Zustande irgendwo irgendwann über irgendwen eine
faule Bemerkung gemacht haben. Das soll man nie tun. Hamlet
mußte auch dran glauben, weil er fand, daß im Staate Dänemark
etwas faul sei.
Hamlet durfte das auch nicht tun, wo er doch — na, das ist jetzt
egal. Wichtig ist im Moment, daß Sie erfahren, warum ich die Fliege
Ching Ling nannte.
Ich hockte unter den niederschmetternden Anklagen des Gerichts
völlig zusammengebrochen, umwogt von undurchdringlichen Nebeln
seelischer Düsterkeit, mit leerem Magen und angezogenen Knien
in meiner Zelle und stierte mit geradezu fakirhafter Gelassenheit gegen eine der schmucklosen Wände, als plötzlich unmittelbar vor
meinen verfinsterten Augen eine kleine, ganz gewöhnliche Stubenfliege an der Wand saß. Vielmehr sie stand, denn eine Fliege kann
sich ja gar nicht setzen. So plötzlich war sie da wie ein Tintenklecks
im Mathematikheft.
Blitzschnell erinnerte ich mich der grauen Vorzeit, in die die Tage
meiner Kinderstube einmal gefallen sein müssen, und ich fragte
sie höflich, womit ich ihr dienen könne. Sie nahm gar keine Notiz
von mir und strafte mich mit einer Verachtung, wie es eben nur eine
Fliege kann. Wußte sie von meinem Fall? Aber nein — sie hatte
sich diese ruhige Stelle nur erwählt, um sich ein paar Minuten un-

[1] **ungestört** undisturbed;   **kosmetische Pflege** attention to make-up
[3] **artig** courteously
[4] **ungeniert** unembarassed
[5] **r Reiz** charm;   **bewußt** conscious (of);   **j-en wortlos gewähren lassen** to let s.o. have his own way
[6] **schütteln** to shake;   **verächtlich** contemptuously
[7] **zärtlich** tenderly
[8] **gläsern** glassy;   **glatt** smooth
[9] **durchsichtig** transparent;   **s Ballettröckchen** tutu, ballet skirt;   **zurecht·streichen** (**streichen** to 'stroke') to smooth out
[11] **r Ruck** (**ruckartig**) jerk;   **merkwürdig** remarkable
[12] **nach dem letzten Chic** after the latest fashion;   **auf Taille sitzen** fit well (in the waist);   **eifrig** eager(ly)
[14] **d(a)rauflos** eagerly;   **steinreich** enormously rich
[15] **r Brummer** bluebottle (fly);   **betören** (**r Tor** fool) to infatuate
[16] **lackieren** to varnish;   **mangelnd** lacking, deficient
[17] **e Beleuchtung** lighting
[19] **flüchtig** lightly;   **nach·polieren** to polish over
[20] **verflixt** damn it;   **gestehen** to confess
[21] **r Angstschweiß** cold sweat;   **e Verrenkung** contortion
[22] **s Gelenk** joint
[24] **s Haupthaar** hair on the head
[26] **ohnehin** already;   **stecknadelschlank** as slender as a pin
[27] **massieren** to massage;   **e Spannung** suspense
[28] **schaffen** to achieve;   **e Augenpflege** attention to eyes
[29] **e Wimper** eyelash;   **gründlich** thoroughly;   **aus·bürsten** to brush out;   **nach·ziehen** to pencil (in)
[30] **e Braue** eyebrow;   **unterlassen** to abstain from
[31] **kokett** flirtatious
[32] **anscheinend** apparently;   **über·pudern** to powder over
[33] **selbstgefällig** (self)complacently
[35] **reizen** to provoke
[36] **uralt** primeval;   **männlich** male;   **r Wesenszug** characteristic
[37] **r Jagdtrieb** hunting instinct
[37] **r Rückfall** reversion;   **e Flegeljahre** (*pl.*) adolescence
[38] **heraus·fordern** to provoke;   **s Gebaren** behavior
[39] **e Haltung** posture

---

1. *Warum erinnert die Fliege ihn an eine Tänzerin?*
2. *Was kann der Beobachter nicht feststellen?*
3. *Warum bekommt er Angst, daß sie sich verrenkt?*
4. *Was tut sie, wenn sie den Kopf zwischen die beiden Vorderbeine nimmt?*
5. *Wie macht die Fliege Augenpflege?*

gestört der kosmetischen Pflege hingeben zu können, und dabei
lassen sich Damen im allgemeinen nicht gerne stören. Ich war aber
trotzdem nicht Kavalier genug, um artig wegzusehen, sondern ich
sah ihr ganz ungeniert zu. Und mein kleines Fliegenfräulein schien
sich ihrer Reize durchaus bewußt zu sein; denn sie ließ mich wortlos
gewähren und schüttelte nur einmal kurz und verächtlich mit den
Schultern. Sie fuhr nun mit einigen ihrer Beine zärtlich unter die
gläsernen Flügel und strich sie sorgsam glatt — so wie ungefähr eine
Tänzerin ihr durchsichtiges Ballettröckchen zurechtstreicht — aber
natürlich nicht mit den Beinen. Nachdem sie sich durch einen schnellen
Ruck ihres merkwürdigen Kopfes davon überzeugt hatte, daß die
Flügel nach dem letzten Chic und gut auf Taille saßen, wandte sie
sich eifrig ihren Füßen zu, mani- und pedikürte mit einer Intensität
drauflos, als ob sie heute noch einen Fliegenbaron oder einen stein-
reichen Brummer betören müßte. Nur ob sie ihre Fuß- und Finger-
nägel blau oder rot lackierte, konnte ich wegen der mangelnden
Beleuchtung nicht feststellen. Wieder machte sie diese ruckartige
Bewegung mit ihrem Kopf, und nachdem sie das dritte Bein von links
noch einmal flüchtig nachpoliert hatte, wandte sie sich dem Make-up
ihres Gesichtes zu. Verflixt, ich muß gestehen, daß mir der helle
Angstschweiß ausbrach bei ihren Verrenkungen, denn ich fürchtete
jeden Augenblick, daß sie sich den Kopf aus dem Gelenk drehen
würde — und was ist eine Fliege ohne Kopf? Nachdem sie sich das
kurze Haupthaar energisch mit dem rechten Vorderfuß zurück-
gestrichen hatte, nahm sie den Kopf zwischen die beiden Vorderbeine und fing an, ihren ohnehin schon stecknadelschlanken Hals
zu massieren, daß mir vor Spannung der Atem wegblieb. Aber endlich
hatte sie auch das geschafft, und sie ging zur Augenpflege über. Nachdem sie sich die Wimpern gründlich ausgebürstet hatte, zog sie die
Brauen noch einmal sorgfältig nach, wobei sie es doch nicht unterlassen konnte, mir einen kleinen koketten Seitenblick zuzuwerfen.
Und dann, ein Zittern ging durch ihren Körper — anscheinend puderte
sie sich noch einmal über —, dann war sie fertig und spazierte selbstgefällig einige Schritte vor meiner Nase auf und ab.

Ich weiß nicht, wie es kam — aber das muß mich irgendwie gereizt
haben. Ist es nun ein uralter, typisch männlicher Wesenszug, ist es
der Jagdtrieb oder ist es nur ein Rückfall in die Flegeljahre? Jedenfalls nahm meine Hand bei dem herausfordernden Gebaren der
Fliege unbewußt die bekannte, charakteristische Haltung zum Flie-

¹ **heran·schieben** to move toward;   **mit Vorsicht** with care
² **ahnungslos** unsuspecting;   **r Verstand** mind
⁴ **s sonderbare Gehabe** peculiar behavior;   **rechtfertigen** to justify
⁶ **winzig** tiny
⁸ **schicksalsträchtig** fate-wielding
⁹ **zu·greifen** to grasp (at);   **tappen** to grope
¹⁰ **genarrt (r Narr** fool) duped
¹³ **r Stumpfsinn** dullness;   **zurück·fallen** to relapse
¹⁴ **r Blitz** lightning;   **grauenhaft** horrible;   **e Beklemmung** anguish
¹⁵ **grinsen** to grin;   **blödsinnig** silly
¹⁶ **nachsichtig** indulgent(ly);   **zu·nicken** to nod to;   **r Stiefel** boot
¹⁷ **höhnisch** sneering;   **schleudern** to fling;   **an·sprechen** to address
¹⁸ **sachlich** matter-of-fact
¹⁹ **e Lebensweisheit** practical wisdom;   **fehlen** (+ *dat.*) to be lacking, missing
²¹ **j-em entwischen** to escape (on) s.o.
²⁴ **in die Tiefe reißen** to plunge to the depths;   **begreifen** to comprehend
²⁵ **auf·brausen** to rage up (in answer)
²⁷ **r Einfaltspinsel (einfältig = einfach)** simpleton
²⁸ **e Positur** pose
²⁹ **flüchtig** fleeting(ly);   **auf und davon** up and away
³³ **s Sonnenstäubchen** mote (sunbeam)
³⁵ **nachträglich** subsequently
³⁶ **die glückliche Stimmung** the auspicious mood

---

1. *Was tut die Hand des Beobachters ?*
2. *Wie erklärt er sein sonderbares Gehabe ?*
3. *Warum gelingt es ihm nicht, Schicksal zu sein ?*
4. *Was glaubt er zu sehen ?*
5. *An wen erinnert ihn die sachliche Stimme ?*
6. *Wie weit muß man über seinem Schicksal stehen?*
7. *Worüber muß man lächeln können?*
8. *Weshalb hat der Autor die Fliege „Ching Ling" genannt ?*

genfangen an und schob sich mit Vorsicht näher an das scheinbar
ahnungslose Opfer heran. Und da fing auch mein Verstand an,
einige erklärende Gedanken von sich zu geben. Vielleicht wollte er
das sonderbare Gehabe meiner Hand rechtfertigen. Jedenfalls dachte
5 ich: So wie man mich gefangen hat, so werde ich dich jetzt fangen,
du winzige Fliege — ich will auch mal Schicksal spielen. Ich will
dein Schicksal sein, und gleich werde ich über Tod und Leben entscheiden. Aber so dachte ich nur; denn als meine also schicksals-
trächtige Hand nun plötzlich gottähnlich zugreifen wollte, tappte
10 sie genarrt ins Leere — und der kleine schwarze Tintenklecks saß,
als ob nichts geschehen wäre, nur wenige Zentimeter höher an der
Wand, gerade so hoch, daß ich ihn nicht mehr erreichen konnte.

Resigniert wollte ich wieder in meinen Stumpfsinn zurückfallen,
da durchfuhr es mich wie ein Blitz mit grauenhafter Beklemmung:
15 Hatte die Fliege nicht eben gegrinst und mir mit ihrem blödsinnigen
Kopf nachsichtig zugenickt? Gerade wollte ich ihr meinen Stiefel
mitten in das höhnische Gesicht schleudern, da sprach sie mich an
— mit einer etwas dünnen und sehr sachlichen Stimme, der aber doch
eine gewisse Lebensweisheit nicht fehlte —, sie erinnerte mich an
20 meinen alten Religionslehrer. — Siehst du, sagte sie, du wolltest
mein Schicksal sein und jetzt bin ich dir entwischt, du Dummkopf?
Man muß nämlich über seinem Schicksal stehen, wenn es auch nur
wenige Zentimeter sind, gerade so viel, daß es einen nicht mehr er-
reicht und in die Tiefe reißen kann. Begreifst du das? — Du hast
25 mich ausgelacht, Fliege! brauste ich auf. — Das ist es ja eben, antwortete sie kühl, man muß über sein Schicksal lächeln können. Siehst
du, du Einfaltspinsel, und dann entdeckt man, daß das Leben vielmehr Komödie als Tragödie ist. — Sie setzte sich in Positur, nickte
mir noch einmal flüchtig zu, und damit war sie auf und davon —
30 so plötzlich, wie sie gekommen war.

Ich habe lange darüber nachgedacht, und ich habe gefunden, daß
die Fliege recht hat: Man muß über seinem Schicksal stehen! Ich
habe noch oft an meine kleine Fliege gedacht, die wie ein Sonnenstäubchen in meine Dunkelheit geflogen kam, und ich habe ihr
35 nachträglich noch einen Namen gegeben. Ich habe sie Ching Ling genannt. Das ist chinesisch und heißt: Die glückliche Stimmung.

TOPICS FOR DISCUSSION

1. Which of Borchert's poems have the simplicity and charm of folk songs?

2. How does Borchert indicate in *Muscheln* and *Kinderlied* that childhood is a happy and sheltered time?

3. Which way does Borchert explain night and loneliness in *Abendlied*? Does the young prisoner in *Die Hundeblume* see it that way?

4. What is the element of humor in *Prolog zu einem Sturm* and in *Antiquitäten*?

5. What does the poem *Großstadt* tell us about Borchert's love for the big city?

6. What is Borchert's concept of love in *Der Kuß* and in *Abschied*? Could you conclude that he believes in permanency in love?

7. In *An diesem Dienstag,* the word "Grube" serves as leitmotif. How does the author express it in concrete images?

8. How does Borchert in *An diesem Dienstag* show that military honors mean nothing during the war?

9. Can we conclude that Borchert wants to show how life continues in the ruins and that it is stronger than death in *Nachts schlafen die Ratten doch*? Why?

10. Can we say that the story *Die Kegelbahn* deals with the question of responsibility for the killing in wars? Discuss this question in the framework of the story, and point out others where this problem appears.

11. How does Borchert tell us that Lieutenant Fischer in *Die lange lange Straße lang* cannot become a bourgeois like everyone else?

12. We know that Borchert admired Nietzsche and that he too despised the bourgeois as "herd man." Show how this concept is expressed in *Die lange lange Straße lang.*

13. Borchert uses onomatopoetic words and rhythms to indicate the mode of motion and the speed of events in *Die lange lange Straße lang.* Where in the text does this occur?

14. What does the "streetcar" symbolize and what is its function in the story?

15. When is God mentioned and how is He described?

16. It is known that Borchert was very attached to his mother and felt secure in her presence. Can you find an affirmation of this in the story? How is it expressed?

17. Where in the story are references to the life of Christ?

18. We know that Borchert had love, hatred and guilt feelings for his father. Where in the story are such feelings expressed?

19. The "blue flower," the symbol of Romantic longing, appears twice in the story. How does Borchert indicate that this symbol no longer makes sense in the world as he knows it?

20. In what respect are the lines about "Urania Life Insurance" a cruel satire?

21. "Freut euch des Lebens" is the beginning of a German folk song. Discuss how Borchert uses it in the organ-grinder episode as leit-motif.

22. Whom does the organ-grinder represent and where do we find a similar figure?

23. Which wish does Lieutenant Fischer share with the young father in *Die drei dunklen Könige*?

24. What do the conductor and the organ-grinder have in common?

25. In what guise does evil appear in the story?

26. How is the problem of responsibility treated in *Die lange lange Straße lang*?

27. How does Borchert show in *Lesebuchgeschichten* that during wars everything is reduced to numbers? Show how he puts this idea into images.

28. How does Borchert show in *Lesebuchgeschichten* that one human life—and even the history of mankind—means nothing in relation to eternity?

29. How does Borchert portray simple women of the working class in *Die Küchenuhr, Das Brot,* and *Das Holz für morgen*?

30. What qualities do Borchert's "mothers" have in the stories you have read?

31. What is the significance of the Borchert hero "being cast out of the shelteredness of childhood" in *Generation ohne Abschied* and *Die lange lange Straße lang*?

32. Nietzsche said: "God is dead." Where can you find a similar message in Borchert's stories?

33. What is the attitude toward love in *Generation ohne Abschied*?

34. How does Borchert convey the restlessness of this generation within the structure of the story?

35. In *Im Mai, im Mai schrie der Kuckuck,* the author speaks about a utopian city toward which the outsiders march. In that new city, "teachers and ministers do not lie, . . . mothers do not die, . . . there are no attics where fathers hang themselves because their wives have no bread, . . . there are no blind and one-armed young men . . ." It is a "great city where all hear and see and understand: mon coeur, the night, your heart, the day, der Tag, die Nacht, das Herz." Can you find similar thoughts in another story?

36. How is human life perceived in *Eisenbahnen, nachmittags und nachts*?

37. How can the destruction of the world be avoided, according to *Dann gibt es nur eins* ?

38. How does Borchert imagine the apocalypse?

39. What is the prisoner's view of God in *Die Hundeblume* ?

40. In what respect does the lesson of the spider in *Die Hundeblume* resemble that of the fly in *Ching Ling* ?

41. How does Borchert convey the thought that prison guards are sub-human?

42. By using words like "manège" and "clowns," Borchert conveys the idea that he sees the prison as a circus. How does he succeed in creating people who fit into it? Whom can you describe in particular?

43. Can you give other instances when Borchert chooses words that designate places of public amusement, for instance "bowling alley" or "puppet theater," to describe tragic situations? What kind of an effect does he achieve this way?

44. How does Borchert succeed in showing how ridiculous the "primitive dignity" and conceit of the prison guards is?

45. What does the yellow flower symbolize and for what did the blue flower stand in *Die lange lange Straße lang* ?

46. In which stories does Borchert use a style that is typical of a school-boy's report? To what effect?

47. In which story, where the decision has to be made whether to live or to die, is the absence of pathos particularly striking?

48. How does Borchert portray simple people?

49. Which ideas recur in Borchert's stories?

50. What similar characteristics do the protagonists of all Borchert's stories share? How do they differ, if at all?

VOCABULARY

A

ab away, down, off
ab·drehen to pull out
s Abendbrot supper
s Abendlied, -er evening song
e Abfahrt, -en departure
abgeblättert stripped
abgebrochen disjointedly
abgefeimt cunning
r Abgrund, ˮe abyss
ab·holen to call for
ab·lehnen to refuse
e Ablenkung, -en distraction
ab·reiben ie, ie to rub
ab·reißen i, i to tear off, to pluck
abscheulich abominable
r Abschied farewell
ab·schließen o, o to lock
ab·schneiden i, i to slice
ab·schweifen to digress
e Absicht, -en intention, purpose
absichtlich intentional
ab·streifen to get rid of
r Absturz, ˮe fall
ab·treten (i) a, e to resign
ab·tropfen drop off, to run down
ab·tun a, a to do away (with)
ab·tupfen to dab at, touch
abwärts downward(s)
achten (auf + *acc.*) to pay attention
 (to)
e Achtung respect, regard
r Acker, ˮ field
e Ackerkrume, -n top soil
e Ader, -n blood vessel, vein
r Affe, -n monkey
 Affe du! You ape!
ahnen to anticipate, sense
ähnlich similar
e Ahnung idea, suspicion
ahnungslos unsuspecting
e Akelei, -en columbine
alabastern made of alabaster

r Alkoholrausch, ˮe alcoholic stupor
allein alone, but, yet
allerdings to be sure
allerhand all sorts of things
allgemein general
allmählich gradually
r Ameiseneifer antlike zeal
an·beten to pray (to), adore
andauernd continuously
ändern to change
anders otherwise, different(ly)
e Änderung, -en change
aneinander·scheuern to rub against
 each other
s Aneinandervorbeisein lack of communication, alienation
an·ekeln to disgust
e Anerkennung, -en recognition, appreciation
an·fallen (ä) ie, a to attack, to fall
 upon
r Anfang, ˮe beginning
an·fangen (ä) i, a to begin
an·fassen to clutch
angenehm pleasant
angenommen accepted, assumed
s Angesicht face
angewiesen sein (auf + *acc.*) to be
 dependent (on)
an·gewöhnen (sich) to get accustomed to
e Angleichung, -en approximation
e Angst, ˮe fear, anxiety
ängstlich anxious, apprehensive
r Angstschweiß cold sweat
e Anklage, -n charge
an·kommen a, o to arrive
an·kommen auf (+ *acc.*) to depend
 on, be of importance
an·kündigen to announce
e Ankunft, ˮe arrival
e Anlehnung, -en dependence
an·nehmen (i) a, o to assume, sug-

gest; **sich an·nehmen** (+ *gen.*) to have mercy on, take care of
anscheinend apparently
an·sehen (ie) a, e to look at, tell by looking at
an·spannen to strain
an·sprechen (i) a, o to address
r **Anspruch, ⸚e** claim
e **Anstalt, -en** institution
anständig respectable
an·starren to stare at
anstatt instead
an·stecken to light
an·steigen ie, ie to mount
an·stoßen (ö) ie, o to nudge
e **Antiquitäten** (*pl.*) antiquities
an·wachsen (ä) u, a to grow
an·ziehen o, o to put, draw on; **sich an·ziehen** to get dressed
r **Anzug, ⸚e** suit
an·zünden to ignite, light up
e **Apfelsinenschale, -n** orange peel
e **Apotheke, -n** pharmacy
r **Ärger** annoyance
ärgerlich annoying
ärgern to annoy; **sich ärgern** to be annoyed
s **Ärgernis, -se** disturbance
ärmlich shabbily
e **Armut** poverty
armmutig poor
e **Art, -en** way, manner, kind, species
artig polite(ly)
r **Arzt, ⸚e** physician
s **Aschkastenspalier, -e** street lined with ash or dust bins
r **Atem** breath
r **Atemzug, ⸚e** breath
atmen to breathe
auf on, up, open; **auf und ab** to and fro; **auf und davon** up and away; **auf . . . zu** up to, toward
auf·bieten o, o to muster, summon

auf·brausen to rage
auf·brechen (i) a, o to break open
auf·fallen (ä) ie, a to be conspicuous, to attract attention
auf·fangen (ä) i, a to catch
e **Aufgabe, -n** task, assignment
auf·gehen i, a to open
aufgehoben sein to be well looked after
aufgelegt sein to be disposed
aufgeregt excited
auf·halten (ä) ie, a to stop
auf·hängen (sich) to hang o.s.
auf·hören to stop, cease
auf·machen to open up
aufmerksam attentive
auf·passen to watch out for, pay attention
auf·pusten to inflate
auf·regen to excite
e **Aufregung** excitement
auf·schäumen to bubble up
e **Aufschrift, -en** inscription
auf·seufzen to groan
auf·wachen to wake up
auf·zwingen a, u (+ *dat.*) to force upon (s.o.)
r **Augenblick, -e** moment
s **Augenpaar, -e** pair of eyes
e **Augenpflege** attention to eyes
aus·bürsten to brush out
aus·dörren to dry up
r **Ausdruck, ⸚e** expression
aus·drücken to express
auseinander separately
auseinander·platzen to burst apart
aus·füllen to absorb, fill up
ausgelaufen spilled
ausgeliefert sein to be reduced to, to be at s.o.'s mercy
r **Ausgelieferte, -en** outcast
ausgerechnet exactly, particularly
aus·halten (ä) ie, a to endure

aus·kosten to enjoy fully
aus·lachen to laugh at
aus·liefern to surrender
aus·machen to put out
aus·sehen (ie) a, e to look (like), appear
außen outside
außer except (for), besides
außerdem moreover
e **Aussicht, -en** prospect
aus·speien ie, ie to spit out
aus·spielen to lead (cards)
aus·spucken to spit out
aus·stopfen to stuff
aus·stoßen (ö) ie, o to expel
aus·strahlen to spread, radiate
aus·suchen to choose
aus·tragen (ä) u, a to endure
aus·üben to exercise
aus·weichen i, i (+ *dat.*) to avoid
auswendig by heart
aus·ziehen o, o (sich) to take off (clothes)
r **Autoschlosser, -** auto mechanic

B

s **Bad, ⁼er** bath
e **Bahn, -en** way, road, railway
r **Bahnhof, ⁼e** railway station
r **Bahnsteig, -e** platform
e **Bahre, -n** stretcher
bald . . . bald now . . . now
s **Ballettröckchen, -** short projecting skirt worn by a ballerina, "tutu" (*French*)
e **Bank, ⁼e** bench
e **Bank, -en** bank
barfuß barefoot
e **Barockkommode, -n** baroque chest (of drawers)
r **Bauch, ⁼e** belly, stomach
bauen to build, cultivate

r **Bauer, -n** peasant, farmer
r **Baum, ⁼e** tree
r **Bauunternehmer, -** building contractor
beachten to pay attention to
r **Beamte, -n** civil servant
bedeuten to signify
e **Bedeutung, -en** significance
e **Bedingung, -en** condition
bedruckt printed
bedürfen (+ *gen.*) to need
beenden to finish
r **Befehl, -e** order, command
befehlen (ie) a, o to command, order
befinden a, u (sich) to be located
befreien to relieve, to free
befühlen to examine by touch
begegnen to encounter, meet
e **Begegnung, -en** encounter
begehen i, a to commit; **Selbstmord begehen** to commit suicide
begleiten to accompany
begraben u, a to bury
begreifen i, i to comprehend
r **Begriff, -e** concept
begründen to justify, explain
behalten (ä) ie, a to keep
behaupten to maintain, assert
beheben o, o to make good
beherbergen to harbor
beherrschen (sich) to control one's feelings
behost clad (in pants)
behutsam careful(ly)
e **Behütung** protection
bei·bringen (+ *dat.*) to teach
beide both, two
s **Bein, -e** leg; **j-em ein Bein stellen** to trip s.o. up
s **Beispiel, -e** example
bekannt known
e **Beklemmung, -en** anguish
bekommen a, o to receive, get

belasten to weigh upon, burden
e **Beleuchtung** lighting
s **Bellen** barking
belohnen to reward
bemerken to notice, observe
benehmen (i) a, o (sich) behave, act
benennen a, a to call
s **Benzin** gasoline
r **Benzinfleck, -e** gasoline stain
r **Beobachter, -** observer
berauschen to intoxicate
bereit ready
bereiten to create
bereits already
berichten to report
r **Beruf, -e** profession
s **Berufssoldatengesicht, -er** face of a
  professional soldier
beruhigt with a feeling of relief,
  calmed
bescheiden unassuming, modest
beschlagen sheathed
beschreiben ie, ie to describe
beschwipst (*coll.*) intoxicated
besinnen a, o (sich) (auf + *acc.*) to
  remember, recall; ohne Besinnung unconscious
r **Besitz, -e** possession
r **Besitzer, -** owner
besoffen intoxicated
besonders particular, especially;
  das Besondere (an + *dat.*) the
  odd thing (about)
bestaunen to marvel (at)
bestehen a, a (aus) to consist (of)
bestehen (auf + *dat.*) to insist (on)
bestimmt certain, definite
r **Besuch, -e** visit, company
betäuben to stun
beten to pray
betören to fool, deceive
betrachten to regard, consider, observe

betreten (i) a, e to enter
betrüben to depress
beugen (sich) to bend
beurlaubt sein to be on leave
bewegen (sich) to move
e **Bewegung** movement
r **Beweis, -e** proof
beweisen ie, ie to prove
bewußt (+ *gen.*) conscious (of)
bezahlen to pay
bieder honest
biegen o, o to bend, turn
e **Bierflasche, -n** beer bottle
bieten o, o to offer, bid
s **Bild, -er** image, picture
bilden to constitute, form, educate,
  train
s **Billett, -e** ticket
billig cheap, fair (price)
e **Bindung, -en** commitment
bis . . . zu up to
bisher until now, previously
bißchen a little, a bit
bissig ferocious(ly)
e **Bitte, -n** request, plea
bitte please
bitten a, e to beg, plead, request
blähen to puff up
e **Blamage, -n** disgrace
blank bright, polished
blasiert blasé
blaß pale
s **Blatt, ⸚er** leaf, sheet, page
s **Blech, -e** tin
r **Blechofen, ⸚** tin stove
e **Blechschachtel, -n** tin box
e **Bleibe** shelter, repose, rest
bleiben ie, ie to remain
bleich faded
bleiern leaden, oppressive
r **Bleistift, -e** pencil
r **Blick, -e** glance, look
blicken to look, glance

blinken to gleam
blinzeln to blink, peek
r **Blitz, -e** lightning
blöd stupid, crazy
e **Blödheit** stupidity
blödsinnig silly
bloß mere(ly), bare(ly)
blühen to bloom
e **Blume, -n** flower, bloom
e **Bluse, -n** blouse
s **Blut** blood
blutdurstig bloodthirsty
bluten to bleed
e **Blutlache, -n** pool of blood
blutrünstig bloody
r **Boden, -** or **=** ground, floor, attic
s **Bodenlose** bottomless pit
r **Bombenangriff, -e** bombing
böse angry, bad, evil
e **Bosheit** wickedness
brach·liegen a, e to lie fallow
e **Bratkartoffel, -n** fried potato
brauchen to need, use
e **Braue, -n** eyebrow
brav good, well-behaved
e **Breite** breadth, width
bremsen to brake
brennen, a, a to burn
s **Brett, -er** board
r **Brief, -e** letter
e **Brille, -n** eyeglasses
s **Brot, -e** bread (loaf)
r **Brotkrümel, -** bread crumb
r **Brotteller, -** bread plate
e **Brücke, -n** bridge
brüllen to roar, scream
brummen to mutter, hum
r **Brummer, -** bluebottle
r **Buchstabe, -n** letter
bücken (sich) to bend
bucklig hunchbacked
r **Bückling, -e** bow
bummeln to stroll

bumsen to bang, bump
bunt gay, multicolored
s **Büro, -s** office
e **Büste, -n** bust

C

r **Chefarzt, =e** senior medical officer
r **Chor, =e** choir

D

da then, there, since, when
s **Dach, =er** roof
dachdurchlöchert leaky-roofed
e **Dachrinne, -n** gutter
r **Dachstuhl, =e** framework of a roof,
  rafters
daher′ (*emphatic:* **da′her**) conse-
  quently
dahin′ (*emphatic:* **da′hin**) there, to
  that place, gone
damals then, at that time
r **Damm, =e** dam, embankment
dampfdunstig steaming
r **Dampfer, -** steamer
daran·glauben (*coll.*) to lose one's
  life
darauflos eagerly
dar·bringen a, a to offer
dar·stellen to represent
darum′ (*emphatic:* **da′rum**) therefore, for that reason
s **Dasein** existence
e **Dauer** permanence
dauern to last, continue, take (to
  come)
davon·schlurfen to shuffle along
davon·stehlen (ie) a, o (sich) to
  steal away
e **Decke, -n** ceiling, cover
decken to cover
denn (*conj.*) for; (*adv.*) anyway

dennoch nevertheless
deshalb therefore
deuten to interpret, point (out)
dicht close-set, dense, close by
dichten to write (poetry)
r **Dichter, -** poet
e **Dichtung, -en** poetry, creative writing
dick fat, thick
r **Dieb, -e** thief
dienen (+ *dat.*) to serve
r **Diener, -** servant
r **Dienst, -e** service
r **Dienstag, -e** Tuesday
e **Diesigkeit** mistiness
doch yet, however; oh yes; on the contrary
r **Donner** thunder
donnern to thunder
r **Donnerstag, -e** Thursday
Donnerwetter! What do you know!
doof (*coll.*) stupid, dumb
s **Dorf, ∸er** village
r **Dorsch, -e** codfish
dösen to doze, to be sleepy
r **Draht, ∸e** cable, wire
drängen to press
d(a)rauf·gehen i, a to be lost
draußen outside, out there
drehen (sich) to turn, revolve
e **Drehung, -en** turn, rotation
dringen a, u to penetrate
drinnen within, inside
dröhnen to boom
r **Druck, ∸e** pressure
drucken to print
drücken to press, squeeze
duff dull
r **Duft, ∸e** scent
duften to smell sweetly
düngen to fertilize
dunkel dark
dünn thin

r **Dunst, ∸e** haze, veil
durch through, by (means of)
durchaus' by all means
durcheinander·rudern to move in confusion
durch·halten (ä) ie, a to endure
durchsichtig transparent
durch·streichen i, i to cross out
durch·ziehen o, o to draw through
dürr emaciated, withered, dry
r **Duschraum, ∸e** shower, bath stall
e **Düsterkeit** gloom

E

eben just, precisely, exactly, even
ebenfalls also
echt genuine
e **Ecke, -n** corner
edel noble
egal sein to be all the same
ehe (*conj.*) before
e **Ehe, -n** marriage
eher rather
e **Ehre, -n** honor
ehren to honor
ehrlich conscientious, straight, reliable, fair
s **Ei, -er** egg
r **Eifer** zeal, eagerness
eifrig eagerly
eigen own
eigens specially
eigentlich real, actual(ly)
s **Eigentum, ∸er** property
e **Eile** haste
eilen to hurry
eilig hurried, rushed
ein·bilden (sich) (*dat.*) to imagine
e **Einbildung, -en** conceit, imagination
r **Einfaltspinsel, -** simpleton
eingebildet imaginary

ein·gehen i, a to wither
ein·lassen (ä) ie, a (sich) (auf) to accede to (a request)
einmal once; auf einmal all at once; nicht einmal not even; noch einmal once more
ein·packen to pack up (and leave)
ein·richten to arrange
einsam alone, lonely
e Einsamkeit loneliness
ein·schlafen (ä) ie, a to fall asleep
ein·schlucken to swallow down
ein·schüchtern to intimidate
ein·spinnen, a, o (sich) to form a cocoon, seclude o.s.
einst once (*either past or future*)
ein·stellen (sich) (auf) to adjust (to)
e Einstellung, -en attitude
ein·teilen to divide
ein·treffen (i) a, o to come to pass
e Eintrittserklärung, -en declaration of membership
e Eintrittskarte, -n admission ticket
einzeln single, singly
einzig unique, sole, only
s Eisen iron (metal)
e Eisenbahn, -en railway
s Eisenblech, -e sheet-iron
eisig icy
r Eisschrank, ⸚e refrigerator
r Eiswagen, - refrigerated car
eitel conceited
elend wretched, miserable
e Eltern (*pl.*) parents
s Emaille enamel
r Empfang, ⸚e reception
empfangen (ä) i, a to receive, conceive (a child)
empfehlen (ie) a, o to recommend
empfinden a, u to feel, sense
empfindlich sensitive
s Endgültige definitive
eng narrow, tight

entblößen to expose
entdecken to discover
e Entdeckung, -en discovery
entfernen to remove, place at a distance
entgegen toward(s)
enthalten (ä) ie, a to contain
entlang along
e Entlausungsanstalt, -en delousing center
entscheiden ie, ie to decide
entschließen o, o (sich) to make up one's mind
r Entschluß, ⸚sse resolution
entschuldigen (sich) to excuse (oneself)
e Entschuldigung, -en excuse
entsetzen to shock
entsetzlich terrible
entspringen a, u to break away
entstehen a, a to arise, originate
entweder . . . oder either . . . or
entwickeln to develop
entwischen to escape
entwürdigen to degrade
s Erbarmen pity
erbauen to edify
e Erdbeere, -n strawberry
e Erde earth
s Erdgeschoß, -sse ground floor
erdig earthy
erdolchen to stab
r Erdteil, -e continent
ereifern (sich) to get excited
erfahren (ä) u, a (über) to learn, find out (about)
erfinden a, u to invent
r Erfinder, - inventor
e Erfindung, -en invention
r Erfolg, -e outcome, success
erfrieren o, o to freeze
erfüllen to fulfill
e Erfüllung fulfillment

erglimmern to glow faintly
ergreifen i, i to move, seize
erhalten (ä) ie, a to receive, maintain
erinnern (an + *acc.*) to remind of
erinnern (sich) (an + *acc.*) to remember
erkälten (sich) to catch a cold
erkennen a, a to recognize
erklären to explain, declare
erlauben to allow
erledigen to settle
e **Erleichterung, -en** relief
erleiden i, i to suffer, endure
ermorden to kill
ermüden to get tired
erreichen to attain, reach
erscheinen ie, ie to appear
e **Erscheinung, -en** appearance, phenomenon
erschießen o, o to shoot dead
erschlagen (ä) u, a to slaughter, slay
erschöpft exhausted
erschrecken to shock, frighten
erschrecken (i) a, o to be alarmed
erschüttern to move deeply
ersetzen to replace
erst first, not until, only
erstaunen to astonish
ertragen (ä) u, a to bear, endure
ertränken to drown (s.o. *or* s.t.)
erwachen to awaken (o.s.)
erwählen to choose
erwähnen to mention
erwarten to expect
erwidern to reply
erzählen to tell
e **Erzählung, -en** tale, story
erziehen o, o to educate, train
erzittern to tremble
r **Esel, -** donkey, ass
e **Esse, -n** funnel

essen (i) a, e to eat
s **Essen** food, meal
e **Etagentür, -en** apartment door
etwa (*adv.*) say, perhaps, approximately
ewig eternal
e **Ewigkeit, -en** eternity

F

e **Fabrik, -en** factory
r **Faden, ⸚** thread
fähig capable
fahl dimly, 'pale'
fahren (ä) u, a to go, drive, travel
r **Fahrradschlauch, ⸚e** tube or tire of a bicycle wheel
e **Fahrt, -en** trip, journey
r **Fall, ⸚e** case
e **Falte, -n** fold, wrinkle
falten to fold
fangen (ä) i, a to catch
e **Farbe, -n** color
r **Farbton, ⸚e** shade
fassen to take hold of, grasp
fast almost
fauchen to puff
faul lazy, rotten
faulig foul
e **Faust, ⸚e** fist
faustisch Faustian
e **Feder, -n** feather, pen
fehlen (+ *dat.*) to lack, be missing
r **Fehler, -** mistake
e **Feier, -n** ceremony
feiern to celebrate
feig(e) cowardly
e **Feile, -n** file
fein elegant, fine
r **Feind, -e** enemy
feixen (*coll.*) to grin
s **Feld, -er** field
r **Fels, -en** rock, cliff

s **Fenster, -** window
e **Fensterbank, ⸚e** window sill
s **Fenstergitter, -** window-grating
e **Ferien** (*pl.*) holiday(s)
 fertig through, ready
 fertig·bringen a, a to achieve
 Fertigmachen! Get ready!
 fertig·werden to make out well, manage
s **Fest, -e** festival, celebration, 'feast'
 fest firm, well-fastened
 fest·stellen to determine, find out
 fett fat
 fettig greasy
 feucht moist
 fischduftend smelling of fish
 flach shallow
e **Flasche, -n** bottle
 flau dull, slack
r **Fleck, -e** (*or*) r **Flecken, -** spot, patch
r **Fleckfieberverdacht** suspicion of typhus fever
 fleckig spotted
e **Flegeljahre** (*pl.*) adolescence
s **Fleisch** flesh, meat
 fleißig industrious
r **Fliederbusch, ⸚e** lilac bush
e **Fliege, -n** fly
 fliegen o, o to fly
 fliehen o, o to flee
e **Fliese, -n** tile
 fließen o, o to flow
 flimmern to shimmer
 florieren to flourish, strive
 flüchtig lightly
s **Flugfeld, -er** airfield
s **Flugzeug, -e** airplane
r **Fluß, ⸚sse** river
 flüstern to whisper
e **Flut, -en** flood

e **Folge, -n** consequence, sequence, sequel
 folgen (+ *dat.*) to follow
 folgsam obedient
 fordern to demand
 förmlich literally
 forschen to do research
r **Forscher, -** researcher
 fort away, gone, on
 freilich to be sure, of course
r **Freitag, -e** Friday
r **Freiwillige, -n** volunteer
 fremd strange, foreign
r **Fremde, -n** stranger, foreigner
 fressen (i) a, e to eat devour (for animals)
e **Freude, -n** joy
 freudig cheerfully
 freuen (sich) to be glad; **sich freuen (auf** + *acc.*) to look forward (to)
r **Friede(n)** peace
 friedhöflich graveyard-like
 frieren o, o to freeze, be cold
r **Friseur, -e** barber
e **Frisur, -en** hairdo
 froh cheerful, glad
e **Frucht, ⸚e** fruit
r **Frühling, -e** spring (season)
s **Frühstück, -e** breakfast
 fühlen (sich) to feel
 führen to lead
 füllen to fill
 furchig furrowed
e **Furcht** fear
 furchtbar terrible, fearful
 fürchten (sich) to be afraid
 fürchterlich horrible, terrifying
r **Fußballplatz, ⸚e** soccer field
r **Fußboden, -** *or* ⸚ floor
e **Fußspitze, -n** tip of toe
s **Futter** feed, 'fodder'
 füttern to feed

G

e Gabel, -n fork
gähnen to yawn
r Gang, ⸚e gait, corridor
e Gangart, -en pace, walking style
gar quite, even; gar′nicht not at all
r Gärtner, - gardener
r Gast, ⸚e guest
gebären a, o to give birth to
s Gebaren behavior
s Gebäude, - building
s Gebet, -e prayer
gebieten o, o to command, rule
s Geblinzel peek
geboren born
geborgen sheltered, secure
geborsten broken
r Gebrauch, ⸚e usage, use
gebrauchen to use
r Geburtstag, -e birthday
gedämpft damped (sound)
r Gedanke, -n thought, idea
s Gedärm, -e intestines
s Gedicht, -e poem
e Geduld patience
geduldig patient
gefährlich dangerous
gefallen (ä) ie, a (+ dat.) to be pleasing
e Gefangenschaft confinement, captivity
s Gefängnis, -se prison
s Geflute tide-stream
gefräßig voracious
s Gefühl, -e feeling
gegen against, toward, about
e Gegend, -en region
r Gegenstand, ⸚e object
gegenüber opposite, in relation to, face to face
e Gegenwart present, presence
gegenwärtig present

gegipst made of plaster
s Gehabe behavior
geheim secret
s Geheimnis, -se secret
geheimnisvoll secretive, mysterious
s Gehör hearing
gehören (+ dat.) to belong (to)
geigen to play the violin, fiddle
e Geilheit lechery
r Geist, -er spirit, mind, ghost; e geistige Gesundheit mental health
gekachelt tiled
e Gelassenheit composure
gelb yellow
s Geld, -er money
geleert void, empty
gelegen! lie down!
e Gelegenheit, -en opportunity
r Gelehrte, -n learned man
s Gelenk, -e joint
gelingen a, u (+ dat.) to succeed
gelöst sein to be relaxed
gelten (i) a, o to pass for, be valid, concern
s Gelüst, -e desire
gemein common, vulgar
gemeinsam in common
s Gemüse vegetable(s)
gemütlich comfortable
genarrt duped
r Genesende, -n convalescent
genial ingenious
s Genick, -e nape of neck
genießen o, o to enjoy
r Genießende, -n one who enjoys life
gerade just, precisely, straight, even
geräumig spacious
s Geraune murmur
s Geräusch, -e noise
s Gericht, -e court (of law); dish (of food)
gering slight, insignificant

gerissen torn
e Gerissenheit cunning
gern gladly
gern haben to like
gerötet reddened
r Geruch, ⸚e smell
s Gerüst, -e framework
geschehen (ie) a, e to happen
s Geschenk, -e present, gift
e Geschichte, -n story, history, affair
e Gesellschaft, -en society
s Gesetz, -e law
s Gesicht, -er face, power of sight
s Gespenst, -er ghost
e Gestalt, -en form, figure
gestehen a, a to confess
r Gestellungsbefehl, -e induction order
s Gestirn, -e star
s Gestöhn (coll.) moaning
gesund healthy
gewähren lassen (+ dat.) to let s.o. have his own way
e Gewalt, -en power, force
gewaltsam forcibly
s Gewehr, -e gun
gewiß certain, sure
s Gewitter, - storm
gewöhnen (sich) (an + acc.) to accustom oneself (to)
gewöhnlich ordinary
gewöhnt sein (an + dat.) to be accustomed (to)
gierig greedy
gießen o, o to pour
giftig spiteful, scathing, malicious
r Gipfel, - summit
s Gitter, - bars (of the prison fence)
r Glanz radiance, splendor, glare
glänzen to shine, be radiant
glanzlos lustreless
s Glas, ⸚er jar, lens
glasäugig glass-eyed

s Glasdach, ⸚er skylight
gläsern glassy
glasig glassy
glatt smooth, without a hitch
e Glatze, -n bald head
r Glaube, -n belief, faith
gleich (adv.) right away, soon, at once; (adj.) equal, same
gleichmäßig steadily, regularly, evenly
gleichmütig even-tempered
s Gleis, -e track
gleiten i, i to glide
s Glied, -er limb, member
e Gliedmaßen (pl.) limbs
glimmen o, o to glow
glimmern to shimmer, 'glimmer'
glotzen to stare
s Glück fortune (good or bad); happiness
glücklich happy, fortunate
glühen to 'glow', burn
s Glühwürmchen glow-worm
gönnen (+ dat.) to concede, not begrudge
gönnerhaft condescending
gottähnlich godlike
e Gottesanbeterin, -nen praying mantis
e Gottheit, -en divinity, deity
e Göttin, -nen goddess
r Götze, -n idol
s Grab, ⸚er grave
graben (ä) u, a to dig
r Graben, ⸚ moat, ditch
r Grad, -e degree
e Grammophonplatte, -n phonograph record
gräßlich horrible
grauenhaft horrible
gräulich greyish
grausam cruel
grausig gruesome

graziös gracefully
greifen i, i to seize, 'grip'
e **Grenze, -n** boundary, border, limit
greulich horrible
grinsen to grin
großartig grandiose
e **Großstadt, ⸚e** metropolis
großzügig generous
e **Grube, -n** ditch
grummeln (*coll.*) to grumble
r **Grund, ⸚e** ground, bottom, valley, reason
gründlich thoroughly
grundlos without reason
r **Gruß, ⸚e** greeting, salute
gucken (*coll.*) to look
s **Gut, ⸚er** property, estate; (*pl.*) goods
r **Güterwagen, -** freight-car
r **Güterzug, ⸚e** freight train

H

s **Haar, -e** hair
s **Haarbüschel, -** tuft of hair
s **Haargestrüpp** thicket of hair
haarscharf razor-sharp
r **Hacken, -** heel
r **Hafen, ⸚** harbor
e **Haferflocke, -n** rolled oats
r **Häftling, -e** prisoner
r **Haken, -** check mark
e **Hälfte, -n** half
r **Hals, ⸚e** neck, throat
halten (ä) ie, a to hold; stop (any motion); **halten für** to consider, take for
e **Haltung, -en** posture
hämmern to pound, 'hammer'
hampelig jittery
r **Hampelmann, ⸚er** jumping Jack
hampeln (*coll.*) to dither, flounder
r **Handel** trade, business deal

handeln to trade, deal, treat
e **Handlung, -en** action
r **Handschuh, -e** glove
s **Handtuch, ⸚er** towel
r **Hang, ⸚e** slope
r **Haß** hatred
hassen to hate
häßlich ugly
s **Haßlied, -er** song of hatred
hauen ie *or* **au, au** to 'hew', cut
r **Haufe(n)** crowd, pile
häufen to pile up
häufig frequently
s **Haupt, ⸚er** head
s **Haupthaar, -e** hair on the scalp
r **Hauptmann, -leute** captain
e **Hauswirtin, -nen** landlady
e **Haut, ⸚e** skin, 'hide'
e **Hebamme, -n** midwife
heben o, o to lift, 'heave'
s **Heer, -e** army
heftig violent
heilig holy, sacred
r **Heiligenschein, -e** halo
e **Heimat, -en** home(land)
e **Heimkehr** returning home
heimlich secret, mysterious
e **Heirat, -en** marriage
heiraten to marry
heiser hoarse, husky
heißen ie, ei to be named; mean; bid (to do)
r **Held, -en** hero
e **Heldengedenkfeier, -n** heroes' memorial day
hell clear, bright
hellwach wide-awake
s **Hemd, -en** shirt
e **Hemmung, -en** restraint, inhibition
heran·schieben o, o to move toward
heran·wälzen to roll in
heraus·fordern to provoke
heraus·kucken (*coll.*) to peep out

heraus·pendeln to roll outside
r **Herbst, -e** autumn
her·dammeln to hobble along
r **Herdentrieb, -e** herd-instinct
her·nehmen (i) a, o to take
herrlich splendid, lordly
herum·fummeln (*coll.*) to fumble
(with)
herum·schlagen (sich) (ä) u, a to
grapple with
herum·schwirren to fly, 'whir' about
herunter·sausen to dash down
s **Herzklopfen** palpitation (heart)
heulen to howl, cry
r **Himbeersaft** raspberry juice
r **Himmel, -** sky, heaven
himmlisch divine
hindurch through
hinein·gehören to belong (to), be
part of
hinein·saugen to breathe in (draw
in)
sich hinein·steigern to work o.s. up
into
hin·geben (i) a, e to indulge in
hingesunken collapsed
hinken to limp
hin·setzen (sich) to sit down
r **Hintere, -n** behind
hintereinander in succession
hinterher afterwards
hin und her back and forth
hinweg·schwemmen to carry away
s **Hirn** brain
hobeln to plane
r **Hochbunker, -** air-raid shelter
hochgemauert high-set
höchstens at most
hocken to cringe, squat
r **Hof, ⁼e** (court)yard, farm; (royal)
court
hoffen to hope
hoffentlich I hope, hopefully

e **Hoffnung, -en** hope
hoffnungsgrün green as hope
höflich polite(ly)
hohl hollow, empty
höhnisch sneering, mocking
holen to (go and) get
s **Holz, ⁼er** wood
hölzern wooden
e **Holzpantine, -n** wooden clog
r **Holzpantoffel, -** wooden clog
r **Honig** honey
horchen to listen
e **Hose, -n** pants
r **Hosenboden, ⁼** seat of trousers
hübsch pretty
e **Huldigung, -en** homage
humpeln to limp
hupen to honk
e **Hure, -n** 'whore', prostitute
r **Hut, ⁼e** hat
e **Hütte, -n** hut

I

immer ever, always; **immer wieder**
again and again; **immerzu** constantly, continuously, repeatedly
inbrünstig fervent
indem (*conj.*) while, as, by . . .-ing
r **Inhalt** content(s)
innen inside
innig deeply
insgeheim in secret
e **Instandsetzungskosten** (*pl.*) repair
costs
irgend any (at all)
irgendein any (at all), some
irgendwie somehow (or other)
irgendwo someplace (or other)
irren to 'err', wander off; **sich ir-**
ren to be mistaken, 'err'
e **Irrfahrt, -en** wandering(s) (*pl.*) vagaries

irrsinnig absurd, insane
r **Irrtum, -tümer** error
r **Iwan** popular name for Russians

J

e **Jagd, -en** hunt
je ever, each (*distributive*), per
je . . . je (desto/umso) the . . . the
jedenfalls in any case
jedermann everyone
jedoch´ however, yet, nevertheless
jemand someone
jener that (one)
jucken to itch
r **Juckreiz, -e** irritating itch
e **Jugend** youth
r **Junge, -n(s)** boy
r **Jüngling, -e** youth

K

r **Kabeljau, -e** codfish
e **Kachel, -n** tile
r **Käfig, -e** cage
r **Kai, -s** quay
e **Kaimauer, -n** wharf
s **Kalb, ⸚er** calf
e **Kälte** cold(ness)
e **Kammer, -n** chamber
r **Kampf, ⸚e** struggle, fight
kämpfen to struggle, fight
s **Kaninchen, -** rabbit
s **Kaninchenfutter** rabbit food
e **Kanonenorgel, -n** cannon-fire
e **Kanzel, -n** pulpit
kaputt broken, smashed, ruined
e **Karte, -n** card, ticket, map
e **Kartoffel, -n** potato
kaschiert pretended
kauen to chew
kaum scarcely
r **Kavalier, -e** gentleman

r **Kegel, -** bowling pin
e **Kegelbahn, -en** bowling alley
kegelförmig tapering
r **Kegler, -** bowler
kehren to (re)turn, sweep
keineswegs not at all
r **Keller, -** cellar
e **Kette, -n** necklace
keusch chaste, pure
r **Kienspanhalter, -** stick to hold pine-splinter (for lighting purposes)
r **Kinderspielplatz, ⸚e** playground
e **Kinderstube, -n** nursery
s **Kindsein** childhood
s **Kinn, -e** chin
e **Kirche, -n** church
Kirschsaft, ⸚e cherry juice
e **Kiste, -n** crate
r **Kitt** putty
r **Kittel, -** coat, smock
r **Klabautermann, ⸚er** hobgoblin, bogeyman
klaffen to bark
e **Klage, -n** lament
klagen to lament
klappern to rattle
klatschen to slap, clap
s **Klavier, -e** piano
r **Klavierunterricht** piano lessons
s **Kleid, -er** dress; (*pl.*) clothing
r **Kleinstadtbahnhof, ⸚e** small town railway station
klettern to climb, scramble
e **Klingel, -n** (door)bell
klingeln to ring
klingen a, u (nach, wie) to sound (like)
klirren to clash, clang
klopfen to knock, pound
klug clever
r **Knabe, -en** boy
knabbern to nibble
knarren to creak

e **Kneipe, -n** pub
s **Knie, -e** knee
r **Knöchel, -** knuckle
 knochig bony
 knurren to rumble, growl
 kochen to cook
r **Kochtopf, ⸚e** cooking pot
r **Kohlenwagen, -** coal car
 kokett flirtatious
e **Kokosnuß, ⸚sse** coconut
r **Kolibri, -s** humming-bird
 komisch funny, comical
r **Komödiant, -en** comedian
e **Komödie, -n** comedy
r **Kompanieführer, -** company leader
r **König, -e** king
r **Kopf, ⸚e** head
s **Kopfkissen, -** pillow
r **Kopschuß, ⸚sse** head wound
s **Kopfsteinpflaster, -** cobble stones
 kopfüber head over heels
e **Koralle, -n** coral
r **Korb, ⸚e** basket (bucket)
r **Körper, -** body
 kostbar precious
r **Kostenanschlag, ⸚e** estimate (of
  cost)
 krächzen to croak
e **Kraft, ⸚e** strength
 kräftig vigorously
 kraftlos without strength
e **Krähe, -n** crow
r **Krake, -n** octopus
 krank sick
s **Krankenbett, -en** sick-bed
e **Krankenschwester, -n** nurse
r **Kranz, ⸚e** wreath
r **Kreis, -e** circle
s **Kreuz, -e** cross
 kriechen o, o to crawl, creep
r **Krieg, -e** war; **Krieg führen** to
  wage war
 kriegen (*coll.*) to get, catch

s **Kriegsgericht, -e** court-martial
s **Kriegslazarett, -e** military hospital
 kriegstauglich fit for war
e **Krücke, -n** crutch
 krumm crooked, bent over, bowlegged
e **Küche, -n** kitchen
r **Kuchen, -** cake
r **Küchenschrank, ⸚e** pantry
e **Küchenuhr, -en** kitchen clock
 kucken (*coll.*) to look
e **Kugel, -n** ball
e **Kuh, ⸚e** cow
r **Kuhgeruch** smell of cows
e **Kuhle, -n** hole
e **Kühle** reserve, 'coolness', freshness
s **Kühlhaus, ⸚er** cold-storage house
e **Kunst, ⸚e** art
r **Künstler, -** artist
r **Kürbis, -se** pumpkin
 kurzgeschoren close-cropped
r **Kuß, ⸚sse** kiss
 küssen to kiss

L

 lächeln to smile
 lachen to laugh
 lächerlich ridiculous
r **Lack, -e** varnish
 lackieren to varnish, 'lacquer'
r **Laden, ⸚** store, shop
r **Ladentisch, -e** counter
e **Lage, -n** position, situation
s **Lämpchen, -** little lantern
e **Landschaft, -en** landscape
 langsam slow
 längst long since *or* ago
r **Lärm** noise
 lärmend noisy
 lästernd blasphemous
r **Lastträger, -** porter
r **Lastwagen, -** truck

e **Laterne, -n** lantern
e **Latsche, -n** slipper
 latschen shuffle
e **Latte, -n** board, lath
r **Lattenzaun, ⸚e** lath-fence
 laufen (äu) ie, au to run, walk
s **Laufgitter, -** playpen
r **Laut, -e** sound
 lauter (*adv.*) merely, nothing, but, pure
s **Lazarett, -e** military hospital
r **Lebemann, ⸚er** man of the world
e **Lebensversicherung, -en** life insur- ance
e **Lebensweisheit, -en** practical wis- dom
s **Lederkoppel, -n** holster
r **Lederriemen, -** leather strap
 leer empty
 leer·laufen (äu) ie, au to run dry
 legen to lay, place
r **Lehm** clay, loam
 lehnen (sich) to lean
 lehren to teach
r **Lehrer, -** teacher
r **Leib, -er** body
e **Leiche, -n** corpse
 leicht easy, light
s **Leichte** light, easy (reading)
s **Leid, -en** sorrow
 leiden i, i to suffer
 leiden mögen to like
e **Leidenschaft, -en** passion
 leider unfortunately
 leid tun (+ *dat.*): **es tut mir leid** I'm sorry
r **Leierkastenmann, ⸚er** organ-grinder
e **Leine, -n** rope
 leise softly, in a low voice, slight
 leisten to accomplish, afford
 lendenlahm weak-kneed
 lesen (ie) a, e to gather; read
 leuchten to shine, throw light

r **Leuchtturm, ⸚e** light-house
r **Lichtstrahl, -en** light beam
 lieb dear, beloved
 lieb haben to be fond of
 lieben to love; r (e) **Geliebte** lover
 lieber prefer(ably)
s **Liebeslied, -er** lovesong
s **Lied, -er** song
 liegen a, e to lie, be situated
 lindern to appease
e **Linie, -n** line
 links to the left
r **Lippenstift, -e** lipstick
 loben to praise
s **Loch, ⸚er** hole
r **Löffel, -** spoon
r **Lohn, ⸚e** wages, reward
 los loose, going on, wrong, rid of; **was ist los?** what's wrong? what's up?
 los·brechen (i) a, o to break off
 los·fahren (ä) u, a (**auf** + *acc.*) to rush upon
 los·reißen i, i to tear away
 los·schreien ie, ie to start screaming
r **Löwenzahn, ⸚e** dandelion
e **Luft, ⸚e** air
r **Luftballon, -s** balloon
 lügen o, o to (tell a) lie
s **Lungenhaschee** minced lung tissue
 lupfen to stick out
e **Lust, ⸚e** desire, pleasure; **Lust ha- ben** to care to, want to
 lustig jolly

M

 machen to make, do; **es macht nichts** it makes no difference
e **Macht, ⸚e** might, power
 mächtig mighty
s **Mädchen, -** girl
 mädchenheimlich girlishly mysteri- ous

r **Magen,** ⸚ stomach
e **Makrele, -n** mackerel
s **Mal, -e** (single) time; mark; **-mal** times; **mit einem Mal** all at once
malaiisch Malayan
malen to paint
r **Mammutkadaver, -** mammoth carcass
manchmal sometimes
r **Mangel,** ⸚ lack
mangeln (an + *dat.*) to be lacking
mani- und pediküren to manicure and pedicure
r **Mantel,** ⸚ coat, cloak
e **Manteltasche, -n** coat pocket
märchenhaft fantastically
r **Maschendraht,** ⸚e wire netting
s **Maschinengewehr, -e** machine gun
s **Massengrab,** ⸚er common grave
massieren to massage
s **Mathematikheft, -e** math notebook
matt dim
e **Mauer, -n** (outside) wall
mauern to risk nothing (cards)
r **Mauerrest, -e** remains of a wall
s **Maul,** ⸚er mouth (of an animal)
r **Maulwurf,** ⸚e mole
s **Meer, -e** ocean, sea
s **Mehl** flour
meinen to think, say, mean
e **Meinung, -en** opinion
meist most(ly)
meistens generally
melden to report
r **Melkschemel, -** milking stool
e **Menge, -n** crowd, multitude, (large) amount
r **Mensch, -en** person, human being
merken to notice; **sich** (*dat.*) **merken** to remember; **merken (an** + *dat.*) to tell by
merkwürdig strange, remarkable
messen (i) a, e to measure

s **Messer, -** knife
e **Meute, -n** pack
MG = s **Maschinengewehr, -e** automatic rifle
e **Miet(e)rechnung, -en** rent bill
s **Milchgeschäft, -e** dairy store
milchig milky (white)
mildernde Umstände extenuating circumstances
minder less
mindest least
mindestens at least
mischen to mix
r **Mitleidende, -n** fellow sufferer
mitleidig sympathetic
r **Mittag, -e** midday
e **Mitte, -n** middle
mit·teilen to tell, communicate, impart
s **Mittel, -** means, remedy
mitten in the middle of
r **Mittwoch** Wednesday
möglich possible
e **Möglichkeit, -en** opportunity
r **Monat, -e** month
r **Mond, -e** moon
mondblaß pale in the moonlight
r **Montag** Monday
montieren to assemble
r **Mord, -e** murder
r **Mörder, -** murderer
morgen früh tomorrow morning
morsch decaying
e **Mücke, -n** gnat
müde tired
muffig musty
e **Mühe, -n** effort
r **Mulatte, -n** mulatto
r **Mund,** ⸚er mouth
mürbe mellow, brittle, tender, full of dry rot
murmeln to murmur
e **Muschel, -n** shell

r **Mut** courage, spirit, disposition

N

na well
r **Nabel, -** navel
r **Nachbar, -n** neighbor
nach·helfen (i) a, o (+ *dat.*) to assist
nach·denken a, a to reflect, ponder, think about
nachdenklich pensive
nachher afterwards
nachmittags in the afternoon
nach·polieren to polish over
e **Nachricht, -en** report, news
nachsichtig indulgently
e **Nächstenliebe** love of fellow-men
nachträglich (*adv.*) subsequently
nach·tun to imitate
nach·ziehen o, o to pencil, copy
r **Nacken, -** (nape of the) neck
nackt naked
r **Nagel, ⸚** nail
e **Nähe** neighborhood, vicinity
nähern (sich) (+ *dat.*) to draw near (to)
e **Nähmaschine, -n** sewing machine
nämlich namely, you see, the same
nanu well now
e **Nase, -n** nose
naß wet
r **Nebel, -** fog
e **Nebelkrähe, -n** hooded crow
nebenan next door, close-by
nee (*coll.*) = **nein** no
r **Neffe, -n** nephew
r **Neid** envy
neidisch envious
neigen (sich) to incline, bend
nett nice
s **Netz, -e** net
e **Nichte, -n** niece

nicken to nod
nieder·schmettern to crush
niederträchtig vile
niemals never
noch still, yet, else, even; **immer noch** still; **noch ein** one more; **noch etwas** something else; **noch nicht** not yet
r **Nord(en)** north
e **Not, ⸚e** need, distress
nötig necessary
e **Null, -en** zero
e **Nuß, ⸚sse** nut
r **Nutzen, -** use
nützen to be of use
nützlich useful

O

ob whether
oben above, up, upstairs
r **Oberfeldarzt, ⸚e** head medical officer
r **Obergefreite, -n** private first class
obgleich although
s **Obst** fruit
e **Öde** desolation
r **Ofen, ⸚** stove
öffentlich public
ohnehin already
s **Ohr, -en** ear
e **Ohrfeige, -n** box on the ears
s **Öl, -e** oil
s **Opfer, -** sacrifice, offering, victim
r **Optiker, -** optician
ordinär vulgar
e **Ordnung, -en** order
e **Orgel, -n** organ (musical instrument)
orgeln to play the organ
originell original, peculiar
r **Ort, -e** *or* ⸚**er** place, spot
r **Ortsvorsteher, -** chief local magistrate, mayor

P

(ein) paar (a) few
s Pantoffelgekloppel (*coll.*) slipslop-
　ping of the clogs
r Panzer, - tank
r Papierhändler, - petty shopkeeper
r Papierkrämer, - petty shopkeeper
e Pappe, -n cardboard
r Pappkarton, -s cardboard box
　passen to fit; to pass (cards)
　passieren to occur, happen
r Personenwagen, - passenger-car
e Perücke, -n wig
r Pfarrer, - priest, clergyman
e Pfeife, -n pipe
s Pferd, -e horse
r Pfiff, -e whistle
e Pflanze, -n plant
s Pflaster, - pavement, 'plaster'
r Pflasterstein, -e cobble stone
e Pflege care
　pflegen to take care of, be used, ac-
　customed to (doing)
e Pflicht, -en duty
r Pflug, ⸚e plow
　pflügen to plow
　pilzig verschimmeln grow over with
　mold
s Plakat, -e poster, placard
e Planke, -n fence of boards
　platschen to make a splashing noise
r Platz, ⸚e place, square
　plötzlich suddenly
　pochen to pound, knock
r Pokal, -e cup, goblet
　poltern to rattle
　pompös splendid
e Positur, -en pose
e Pracht magnificence
　prächtig splendid
e Praline, -n chocolate-cream
e Pritsche, -n plank bed

e Probe, -n experiment
　prosten to drink to s.o.'s health,
　toast
　prüfen to test
e Prüfung, -en test
r Puder powder
r Puderhauch slight odor of powder
s Pulver, - powder
　pupen to poop
　pusten to blow

Q

e Qual, -en agony
　quälen to torment
　qualmend smoking
e Quelle, -n source, spring
r Querbalken, - cross-beam

R

s Rad, ⸚er wheel
r Ramsch, -e rubbish, jumble
r Rand, ⸚er rim, edge
　rasch quick
r Rasen, - lawn
　rasender Pulsschlag racing pulse
　rasseln to clank
r Rat, ⸚e councillor
　Rat, *pl.* Ratschläge advice
　raten (ä) ie, a to advise; guess
　ratlos helpless
e Ratte, -n rat
r Rauch smoke
　rauchen to smoke
r Raum, ⸚e room
e Raumforschung space research
r Rausch, ⸚e drunkenness, ecstasy
　rauschen to rustle
　(he)rausgeschlüpft slipped out
　(he)raus·sehen (ie) a, e to peer out
　reagieren (auf + *acc.*) to react (to)
　rechnen to 'reckon', calculate

e **Rechnung, -en** 'reckoning', bill

recht right, just; **recht haben** to be right (with personal subject)

s **Recht, -e** law, justice

rechtfertigen to justify

rechtzeitig opportunely

e **Rede, -n** speech

reden to speak

reell solid, sound

e **Regel, -n** rule

regnen to rain

regelmäßig regularly

r **Regen** rain

r **Regentropfen, -** rain drop

r **Regenwurm, ⸚er** earthworm

regieren to govern

e **Regierung, -en** government

e **Regung, -en** emotion, impulse, motion

s **Reich, -e** realm, empire, kingdom

reich rich

reichen to reach, extend; pass (an object); be enough

r **Reichtum, ⸚er** wealth

reif mature, 'ripe'

e **Reihe, -n** 'row', series

rein pure, clean

reißen i, i to tear

reiten i, i to ride (an animal)

r **Reiz** charm

reizen to stimulate, irritate, attract

reizend charming

rennen a, a to run

retten to rescue

reuig contrite, 'rueful'

r **Revolverträger, -** person who carries a revolver

r **Rhabarber** rhubarb

richten to direct, arrange

r **Richter, -** judge

richtig right, correct

e **Richtung, -en** direction (of compass)

riechen o, o to smell

r **Riesenschlüsselbund, ⸚e** gigantic bunch of keys

riesig gigantic

e **Rille, -n** furrow

rings(um) (all) around

r **Rinnstein, -e** gutter

r **Rock, ⸚e** coat, skirt

rostblind rust-tarnished

e **Rübe, -n** turnip

r **Ruck, -e** jerk

ruckartig jerky

r **Rücken, -** back

r **Rückfall, ⸚e** reversion

r **Ruf, -e** call, reputation

rufen ie, u to call, shout

e **Ruhe** rest, calm

ruhig calm(ly); go right ahead and . . .

ruhlos restless

ruhmreich famous

rühren to move

rumpeln to rumble

e **Runde** round

rundherum round and round

r **Russe, -n** Russian

s **Rußland** Russia

rutschen to slide

S

sachlich matter of fact

sacht softly, qietly

saftig succulent

sammeln to collect

r **Samstag** Saturday

samten velvety

sanft soft(ly)

r **Sanitäter, -** medical orderly

r **Sarg, ⸚e** casket, 'sarcophagus'

satt full, 'satiated'; **etwas satt haben** to be fed up with s.t.

r **Satz, ⸚e** sentence

e **Sau,** ⸚e sow
sauber clean, neat
r **Säufer,** - drunkard
schade too bad
schaden to harm
schaffen u, a to make, create
r **Schaffner,** - conductor
r **Schal,** -s shawl, scarf
r **Schalter,** - switch
schämen (sich) to be ashamed
r **Scharfschütze,** -n sharpshooter
r **Schatten,** - shade, shadow
r **Schatz,** ⸚e treasure, sweetheart
schauen to look
s **Schauspielhaus,** ⸚er theatre
e **Scheibe,** -n disk, orb, slice
scheiden ie, ie to separate
r **Schein,** -e light, appearance
scheinbar seemingly
scheinen ie, ie to shine, seem
schenken to give
scheren o, o to shear
scheu shy
r **Scheuerlappen,** - scouring-cloth
scheußlich horrible
schicken to send
s **Schicksal,** -e fate (what is sent)
schicksalsträchtig fate-wielding
schieben o, o to push, shove
schief cockeyed, amiss
r **Schienenstrang,** ⸚e track
e **Schießbude,** -n shooting gallery
schießen to shoot
s **Schießpulver,** - gunpowder
s **Schiff,** -e ship
s **Schild,** -er sign-board, shield
schillern to be iridescent, gleam
e **Schlacht,** -en battle
s **Schlachtfeld,** -er battlefield
r **Schlaf** sleep
schlafen (ä) ie, a to sleep
schläfrig sleepy
schlagen (ä) u, a to strike

schlammgrau mudgray
e **Schlange,** -n snake
schlank slender
schlau sly
schlecht bad, poor (in quality)
schlechtrasiert badly shaven
schleichen i, i to slip, slink
schleudern to fling
schließen o, o **(aus)** to conclude
(from); close
schließlich finally, in conclusion
r **Schlosser,** - locksmith
r **Schlot,** -e smokestack
schluchzen to sob
schmal slim, narrow
schmecken to taste, taste good
r **Schmerz,** -en pain
r **Schmied,** -e smith
e **Schmierseife,** -n soft soap
schmucklos unadorned
schmutzig dirty
r **Schnaps,** ⸚e liquor, hard liquor
schnarchen to snore
schnauzenähnlich snout-like
r **Schnee** snow
schneiden i, i to cut
r **Schneider,** - tailor
schneidig dashing, snappy
schnippen to flick
schnitzen to carve
r **Schnupfen** head cold
e **Schokolade,** -n chocolate
r **Schornsteinrest,** -e remains of a
chimney
r **Schoß,** ⸚e lap
r **Schrank,** ⸚e closet, cupboard
schrecklich terrible
r **Schrei,** -e cry, scream
s **Schreibheft,** -e note book, copy
book
schreien ie, ie to cry (out)
r **Schreier,** - crier
r **Schritt,** -e step

schubsen to push
schüchtern shy
schuld at fault
e **Schuld, -en** guilt, debt
schuldig guilty, at fault
r **Schulhof, ⸚e** school playground
r **Schulmeister, -** schoolmaster, teacher
e **Schulter, -n** shoulder
r **Schuppen, -** engine-house
r **Schutt** rubble, ruins, debris
r **Schuttacker, ⸚** rubbish heap
schütteln to shake
e **Schuttwüste, -n** desert of rubble
r **Schutz** protection
schützen to protect
schwach weak
r **Schwächling, -e** weakling
schwanken to roll, toss
schwarz black
schweigen ie, ie to keep silent
e **Schwelle, -n** tie
schwenken to swing
schwielig callous-faced
schwierig difficult
r **See, -n** lake
e **See, -n** sea
e **Seele, -n** soul
s **Seepferdchen, -** little seahorse
segnen to bless
sehnen (sich) (nach) to long (for)
e **Sehnsucht** longing
seidig silky
s **Seifenpulver, -** soap-powder
s **Seil, -e** line, rope
seit (*prep.*) since, for (a period of time)
seitdem (*conj.*) since
e **Seite, -n** side, page
r **Seitenblick, -e** side glance
r **Sekt** champagne
selbst (*after noun or pron.*) -self; (*before noun or pron.*) even

selbstgefällig self-complacent(ly)
r **Selbstmord, -e** suicide
selbstverständlich naturally
selig blissful, blest
s **Seuchenlazarett, -e** isolation hospital
seufzen to sigh
r **Sexualanfall, ⸚e** sexual attack
sicher certain, safe, sure
siech sickly
r **Sieg, -e** victory
silbern silver
r **Sinn, -e** meaning, sense, mind
sinnlos foolish, senseless, aimless
sobald als as soon as
sofort at once
sogar even
sogleich at once
solange wie as long as
r **Soldat, -en** soldier
sonderbar strange, unusual
sonderlich particularly
sondern (*conj.*) but
r **Sonnabend, -e** Saturday
s **Sonnenstäubchen, -** mote (in a sunbeam)
r **Sonnenstrahl, -en** sun ray
r **Sonntag, -e** Sunday
sonst otherwise, else
sonst (et)was anything else
e **Sorge, -n** care, worry
sorgen to worry, care; **dafür sorgen** to see about it
sorgfältig careful(ly), painstaking
sorgsam careful(ly), cautious
sowas (*coll.*) such things
e **Spannung** suspense
sparen to save
sparsam thrifty
r **Spaß, ⸚e** fun; **das macht Spaß** that's fun
r **Spatz, -en** sparrow
spazieren to walk, stroll

r **Spaziergang, ⸚e** walk, stroll
r **Speicher, -** granary, garret
  spiegeln to reflect, mirror
s **Spiel, -e** game
  spielen to play
e **Spinne, -n** spider
s **Spinnenbein, -e** spiderleg
s **Spinnengewebe, -** cobweb
e **Spitze, -n** tip, head; point, end
  springen a, u to jump
  spucken to spit
e **Spur, -en** track, footstep; trace
r **Staat, -en** state
r **Staatsbeamte, -n** civil servant
s **Staatsdenkmal, ⸚er** national monument
e **Stadt, ⸚e** city, town
  stählern to steel
r **Stahlhelm, -e** steel helmet
s **Stahlskelett, -e** steel skeleton
  stakig stiff, wooden
r **Stall, ⸚e** stable
  stampfen to crush, 'stamp'
s **Standbild, -er** statue
  ständig constantly
  stark strong; considerably
  starr rigid, motionless
  statt (anstatt) instead
  statt·finden a, u to take place
r **Staub** dust
s **Staubgewölk** dust cloud
  staubig dusty
  staunen to marvel
  stecken to put, thrust, stick
  stecknadelschlank as slender as a pin
  stehen·bleiben ie, ie to stop
  stehen lassen (+ *acc.*) to let s.o. cool his heels
  stehlen (ie) a, o to steal
  steif stiff
  steigen ie, ie to climb
  steilgereckt erect

r **Stein, -e** stone
  steinreich enormously rich
e **Stelze, -n** stilt
  stemmen to set (against)
  sterben (i) a, o to die
r **Stern, -e** star
  sternbestickt star-embroidered
r **Stiefel, -** boot
s **Stielauge, -n** protruding eye
  stieren (auf + *acc.*) to stare (at)
e **Stilart** style
e **Stille** silence
  stillvergnügt calm and serene
e **Stimme, -n** voice
  stimmen be correct; to tune (an instrument); **das stimmt** that's right
e **Stimmung** mood
r **Stint, -e** smelt
e **Stirn(e), -(e)n** forehead
r **Stock, ⸚e** stick, cane; floor, story (of building)
s **Stockwerk, -e** story (of building), floor
r **Stoff, -e** stuff, material, fabric
  stöhnen to groan
  stolpern to stumble
  stolz proud
  stören to disturb
  stoßen (ö) ie, o to push, shove
e **Strafe, -n** punishment, fine
  strafen to punish
r **Strand, ⸚e** beach
r **Strang, ⸚e** track, rail
e **Straßenbahn, -en** streetcar
  streben to press (toward), 'strive'
  strecken to stretch
r **Streich, -e** trick
  streicheln to stroke
  streichen i, i to stroke, cancel, eliminate
r **Streit, -e** strife, quarrel
  streiten i, i quarrel

streng severe, strict
r **Strich, -e** line, 'stroke'
r **Strom, ⸗e** stream
stromabwärts down-stream
r **Strumpf, ⸗e** stocking
e **Stube, -n** (living)room
e **Stubenfliege, -n** housefly
s **Stück, -e** piece, head (of cattle); play
r **Studienrat, ⸗e** high school teacher, assistant headmaster
e **Stufe, -n** step
stumm silent
r **Stumpfsinn** dullness
e **Stunde, -n** hour, class, lesson
stur (*coll.*) stubborn, obstinate(ly)
stürzen to rush, fall headlong, plunge
stützen to support
e **Suche, -n** search
suchen to look for, seek
r **Süden** South
r **Südseealligator, -en** South Sea alligator
summen to buzz, hum
e **Sünde, -n** sin
e **Suppe, -n** soup
süß sweet

T

e **Tafel, -n** blackboard
r **Tag, -e** day; **alle Tage** every day
tagelang for days·
täglich daily
tagsüber during the day
s **Tal, ⸗er** valley, dale
r **Talar, -e** robe
tappen to grope
e **Tarnung** concealment; **zur Tarnung** (in order) to hide
e **Tasche, -n** pocket, briefcase
e **Tasse, -n** cup

e **Tat, -en** deed
r **Tatort, -e** scene of the act
e **Tatsache, -n** fact
täuschen (sich) to be wrong
r **Teer, -e** tar
s (r) **Teil, -e** part
teil·nehmen (i) a, o (an + *dat.*) to participate (in)
r **Teller, -** plate
s **Tempo, -s** *or* **Tempi** speed
teuer dear, expensive
r **Theologe, -en** theologian
tief deep
s **Tier, -e** animal
s **Tierreich** animal kingdom
e **Tinte, -n** ink
r **Tintenfisch, -e** cuttle-fish
r **Tintenklecks, -e** inkblot
s **Tischtuch, ⸗er** table cloth
titanisch gigantic
r **Tod,** *pl.* **Todesfälle** death
e **Tomate, -n** tomato
r **Ton, ⸗e** tone, sound
e **Tonne, -n** barrel
s **Tor, -e** goal (football)
r **Tote, -n** corpse, dead person
r **Totenwurm, ⸗er** death-watch beetle
tot·machen (*coll.*) to kill dead
totsteif stiff
träge sluggish
r **Träger, -** stretcher-bearer
e **Träne, -n** tear
r **Trauerfall, ⸗e** bereavement
trauern mourn
traurig sad
s **Treffen, -** meeting
treffen (i) a, o to hit, meet
treiben ie, ie to drive (before one), do, carry on, drift
trennen to separate
e **Treppe, -n** stair(s)
s **Treppenhaus, ⸗er** well of a staircase

s **Treppengeländer,** - banisters (*pl.*)

treten (i) a, e to step, walk; (*trans.*) kick

treu loyal

r **Trinkbecher,** - drinking cup

trocken (*adj.*) dry

trocknen to dry

r **Tropfen,** - drop

tropfen to trickle

r **Trost** consolation, comfort

trösten to comfort, console

trotz (+ *gen.*) in spite of

trotzdem in spite of that, nonetheless

trüb(e) dim(ly)

trudeln to trundle

Trümmer (*pl.*) debris, wreck, ruin

r **Trumpf,** ⸚e trump (card)

r **Trupp, -s** troop

s **Tuch,** ⸚er cloth

tüchtig industrious, considerable

'türlich = natürlich naturally

r **Turm,** ⸚e tower

U

übel bad, evil

e **Übelkeit** nausea

üben to practice

überall everywhere

übereinander one on top of the other

über·gehen i, a to proceed to

überhaupt in every respect under consideration

über·lassen (ä) ie, a to leave

über·laufen (äu) ie, au to overflow

überlegen to reflect, deliberate

übernommen accepted

über·pudern to powder over

überraschen to surprise

übersetzen to translate

über·wachsen (ä) u, a to outgrow

überwältigen to overwhelm

überwinden a, u to overcome

überzeugen to convince

überzittern to vibrate over

übrig left over, remaining

übrigens by the way, incidentally

e **Uhr, -en** timepiece; o'clock

um around, about, for, at

um·bringen a, a to kill

um·drehen to turn upside down

um·drehen (sich) to turn around

um·fallen (ä) ie, a to topple over

umfangen (ä) i, a to embrace

umfassen to clasp, embrace

umgeben (i) a, e to surround

e **Umgebung, -en** surrounding(s)

s **Umgekehrte** reverse

umgekippt overturned

umgestürzt overturned

umher all around

umher·irren to wander about

um·sinken a, u to drop down

umsonst in vain

umspannen to clutch

r **Umstand,** ⸚e circumstance

um·stellen (sich) to switch

umwickelt bound up

umwildert sein to be disorderly surrounded

umwirbeln to whirl about

umwittern to smell of

umwogt surrounded

um·wühlen to move deeply

unablässig incessant

unaufhaltsam incessantly

unbedingt absolutely

unbefangen unaffected, naive

unbegrenzt unlimited

unbeholfen clumsy

unbequem disagreeable

unbewußt unconscious

undurchdringlich impenetrable

unecht false

unerbittlich merciless
ungeahnt never dreamt-of
ungefähr approximately
s **Ungeheuer, -** monster
s **Ungeheure** atrocity
ungeniert unabashedly
unmittelbar directly
unnahbar aloof
unscheinbar insignificant
unsicher uncertain
e **Unsicherheit** insecurity
r **Unsinn** nonesense
unten below, downstairs
r **Unterarzt, ∺e** junior surgeon
unterdrücken to suppress
s **Untergangslied, -er** song about the
     end of the world
unterhalten (ä) ie, a to entertain
unterhalten (sich) to talk, converse
unterhaltsam entertaining
unterlassen (ä) ie, a to abstain from
unterliegen a, e to be defeated
e **Unterlippe, -n** lower lip
s **Unternehmen, -** undertaking
r **Unterricht** instruction
unterrichten to instruct
unterscheiden ie, ie to distinguish,
     differentiate
unterscheiden (sich) to be different
r **Unterschied, -e** difference
unterschlagen (ä) u, a to embezzle
untersuchen to investigate
unterwegs on the way, 'underway'
unübersehbar immense
ununterbrochen uninterrupted
unverschämt brazen, impudent
e **Unversöhnlichkeit** implacability
unwahrscheinlich improbable
umwillkürlich (adv.) automatically
uralt primeval
e **Ursache, -n** cause
r **Ursprung** source, origin
s **Urteil, -e** judgment, sentence

r **Urvater, ∺** forefather

V

s **Vaterland** fatherland
r **Vati, -s** daddy
r **Verabschiedete, -n** the departed one
verachten to despise
e **Verachtung** contempt
verängstigt scared
verantwortlich responsible
verbergen (i) a, o to conceal
e **Verbeugung, -en** bow, reverence
verbeult battered
verbieten o, o to forbid
verbinden a, u to connect, bandage
s **Verbrechen, -** crime
verdämmernd fading out
verdammt damn(ed)
verdecken to hide
verderbt corrupt(ed)
verdienen to earn, deserve
verdorrt withered
verdrehen to turn up (eyes)
verdunkeln (sich) to cloud over, be-
     come overcast
verehren to worship
r **Verein, -e** society, club
vereinsamt isolated, solitary
r **Verfall** decay
verfallen (adj.) fallow
verfaulen to rot
verfinstern (sich) to become obscure
verflixt confounded
verfolgen to follow
verführerisch fascinating
e **Vergangenheit, -en** past
vergebens in vain
vergehen i, a to pass
vergiften to poison
r **Vergleich, -e** comparison
vergleichen i, i to compare
s **Vergnügen** pleasure

vergnüglich diverting
vergnügt pleased, happy
s **Verhältnis, -se** relationship
e **Verhandlung, -en** trial
verheiraten to marry
verheißen ie, ei to promise
verhindern to prevent
verhöhnen to mock
verhören to interrogate
verrinnen a, o to run away
verkaufen to sell
r **Verkäufer, -** salesman
verkneifen i, i (sich) (+ *dat*.) to deny
  s.o. s.t.
verkommen a, o to go bad
verlangen to demand, ask (for)
verlassen (ä) ie, a to leave, abandon,
  desert
verlegen (*adj*.) self-consciously; embarrassed
verleihen ie, ie to confer
verleugnen to renounce, disavow
r (e) **Verliebte, -n** lover
verlieren o, o to lose
verlogen untruthful
vernehmen (i) a, o to perceive, become aware of, hear
verneinen to negate
verpestet poisoned
verraten (ä) ie, a to betray
verraten (sich) to give oneself away
e **Verrenkung, -en** contortion
verrinnen a, o to elapse
verrosten to rust
verrotten to rot
verrückt insane, crazy
e **Versammlung, -en** gathering
verschandeln to vandalize
verschieden (*adj*.) different, various
verschlucken to swallow
verschweigen ie, ie to disregard
verschwimmen a, o to become blur-
  red

verschwinden a, u to disappear
versichern to assure, insure
versickern to seep away
versprechen (i) a, o promise
r **Verstand** mind
verständigen (sich) (mit) to come to
  an understanding (with s.o.)
verstaubt covered with dust
verstummen to become silent
r **Versuch, -e** attempt, trial, experiment
versuchen to attempt, try
vertragen (ä) u, a to digest, hold
  (alcohol)
vertrauen (+ *dat*.) to trust
vertraut familiar
vertrocknen to dry up
verunglücken to have an accident
verursachen to cause
verwandeln to transform
verwandt related
r (e) **Verwandte, -n** relative
verweigern to refuse
verwirrt tangled
verwunden to wound
verwundert astonished
verwüsten to ravage
e **Verzeihung** pardon, excuse
verzerren to distort
e **Verzweiflung** dispair
r **Vetter, -n** (male) cousin
s **Vieh** cattle, livestock
vielmehr rather
vielversprechend promising much
e **Visage, -n** snoot, mug
vollenden to complete
völlig thoroughly, completely
vollkommen complete(ly), perfect
vollständig complete
vor (+ *dat*.) before, in front of; (in
  time expressions) ago
voraus ahead, in advance
e **Vorbedingung, -en** precondition

vorbei sein to have passed, be over
vorbei·pfeifen i, i to whistle past
s **Vorderbein, -e** forelegs
r **Vorderfuß, ⁼e** forefoot
r **Vorgarten, ⁼** front yard
vorhanden on hand, present
vorher before(hand), previously
vorig last
vor·kommen a, o to occur, appear;
   wie kommt dir das vor? how does
   that seem to you?
vor·lesen (ie) a, e to read (to)
vorletzt second last
vor·musizieren to play music for
vorne in front
vornüber forward
r **Vorschlag, ⁼e** proposal
vor·schlagen (ä) u, a to propose
Vorsehung Providence
vor sich hin to oneself
e **Vorsicht** caution, 'foresight'
vorsichtig careful
e **Vorstadt, ⁼e** outskirts (of city)
vorstehend protruding
vor·stellen (sich) (+ *dat.*) to imagine
r **Vorteil, -e** advantage
vorwärts! (go) forward!
vorwärts·rumpeln to rumble forward
vorwurfsvoll reproachful
e **Vorzeit** ages past
vor·ziehen o, o to prefer

W

wach awake
wachen to be awake, awaken
r **Wachhund, -e** watch dog
wachsen (ä) u, a to grow; **gewachsen sein** (+ *dat.*) to be up to
   (doing) s.t.
wacklig shaky
e **Waffe, -n** weapons, arms

wagen to dare
wagen (sich) to venture
r **Waggon, -s** (rail) carriage
e **Wahl, -en** choice, selection
wählen to choose, elect; dial
r **Wahnsinn** madness
wahnsinnig insane
wahr true; **nicht wahr?** isn't it so?
während during
wahrscheinlich probably
r **Wald, ⁼er** forest
e **Wand, ⁼e** (inside) wall
wanken to stagger, tremble
e **Ware, -n** merchandise, 'wares'
e **Wärme** warmth
-wärts -ward(s)
r **Wäschekorb, ⁼e** clothesbasket
r **Wasserbecher, -** drinking mug
wasserleichig like a corpse in the
   water
s **Wasserrohr, -e** water pipe
r **Wechsel, -** change; (bank) check
wechseln to change
wedeln to wave
weder . . . noch neither . . . nor
r **Weg, -e** way
weg (*adv.*) away
wegen (+ *gen.*) because of
s **Weggehen** departure
s **Weh** pain, misery
wehen to drift
weh tun (+ *dat.*) to hurt
weich soft, yielding
weichen i, i to yield, give way
e **Weihnachten** (*pl.*) Christmas
e **Weile** while
weinen to weep, cry
e **Weise, -n** way, manner; melody
weise wise
weisen ie, ie to point, show
weiß white
weit far, wide
weitab far away

weiter! go on! continue!

r **Weizen** wheat

e **Welle, -n** wave

r **Weltuntergang** end of the world

wenden to turn

wenigstens at least

wenn auch even if, although

werfen (i) a, o to throw

e **Werkstatt, ⸚en** workshop

s **Wesen, -** being, essence, creature, system

r **Wesenszug, ⸚e** characteristic

wichtig important

wider (+ *acc.*) against, contrary to

widerstehen to withstand

wiederholen to repeat

wiegen o, o to weigh

e **Wiese, -n** meadow

r **Wilde, -n** savage

(ab·)wimmeln to try to get rid (of)

e **Wimper, -n** eyelash

e **Windel, -n** diaper

winzig tiny

wirken to (have an) effect

e **Wirkung, -en** effect

r **Wirt, -e** host, innkeeper

wischen to wipe

wissen (zu + *inf.*) to know (how to + *inf.*)

e **Wissenschaft, -en** science, learning

e **Wohnung, -en** dwelling, apartment

e **Wolke, -n** cloud

e **Wolljacke, -n** wool jacket

e **Wollust** voluptuousness

womöglich perhaps

worauf for what

wund sore, wounded, stricken

s **Wunder, -** miracle, wonder

wunderhübsch very pretty

wundern (sich) to be surprised

r **Wunsch, ⸚e** wish

wünschen to wish

e **Würde, -n** dignity

würdig worthy, dignified

wurmig wormy

e **Wurzel, -n** root

wüst desolate

e **Wüste, -n** desert

r **Wutausbruch, ⸚e** fit of rage

wütend furious

Z

zaghaft timid(ly)

zäh tough, tenacious

e **Zahl, -en** number

zahlen to pay

zählen to count

r **Zahn, ⸚e** tooth

r **Zahnarzt, ⸚e** dentist

zart tender, delicate

zärtlich tenderly, affectionate

r **Zauber, -** magic

r **Zaun, ⸚e** fence

s **Zeichen, -** sign, symbol

zeichnen to draw, sign (name)

e **Zeichnung, -en** drawing

r **Zeigefinger, -** index finger, trigger finger

zeigen to show

r **Zeiger, -** hand (of a clock)

e **Zeile, -n** line (of print)

s **Zeitalter, -** age

e **Zeitung, -en** news(paper), 'tiding'

e **Zelle, -n** cell

zerbröckeln to crumble away

zerfahren (*adj.*) absent-minded

zerfetzen to tear up

zerfranst fuzzy

zerknittern to wrinkle

zerreißen i, i to tear

zerschmettern to smash to pieces

zersplittern to break into pieces

zerstieben o, o to disperse, scatter

zerstören to destroy

zerwühlen to dishevel

r **Zettel,** - (scrap of) paper
r **Ziegelschornstein, -e** brick chimney
ziehen o, o (*trans.*) pull; (*intrans.*)
  move, go
s **Ziel, -e** aim, goal, target
zielen (auf + *acc.*) to aim (at)
s **Zielfernrohr, -e** telescope-sight
ziemlich fairly, rather
r **Zigeuner,** - gipsy
s **Zimmer,** - room
zitieren to quote
zittern to tremble, quiver
zögern to hesitate
e **Zopfperücke, -n** tie-wig
r **Zorn** anger
zornig angry
r **Zucker** sugar
r **Zufall, ⁺e** chance
zufällig by chance
zu·flüstern to whisper (to)
zufrieden contented, satisfied
r **Zug, ⁺e** train, feature, move, pro-
  cession; e **(Gesichts)züge** (*pl.*)
  (facial) features
zugedeckt covered
zugleich at the same time
zu·greifen i, i to grasp
zu·hören to listen (to)
zu·klappen to snap shut
zu·kommen a, o to approach
e **Zukunft** future
zuletzt at last, finally
zu·machen to close, shut

zumindest at least
zunächst first (of all)
e **Zungenspitze, -n** tip of the tongue
zu·nicken (+ *dat.*) to nod (to s.o.)
zu·plinken (+ *dat.*) to wink (at s.o.)
zurecht·streichen i, i to smooth out
zürnen (+ *dat.*) to be angry (at s.o.)
zurück·streichen i, i to stroke back
zusammengebrochen collapsed
zusammengesackt collapsed
r **Zusammenhang, ⁺e** relationship,
  connection, coherence
zusammen·klappen to collapse
zusammen·nehmen (i) a, o (sich) to
  summon up all one's strength
zusammen·zucken to wince, flinch
zu·schieben o, o to close
zu·schlagen (ä) u, a to bang shut
zuschneiden i, i to cut out
zu·sehen (ie) a, e to watch, look at
r **Zustand, ⁺e** condition
zuweilen at times
zu·wenden to turn toward
zu·werfen (i) a, o to throw toward
zu·ziehen o, o to draw shut
zwar it is true, specifically
zwar . . . aber (doch) it is true . . .
  but
r **Zweck, -e** purpose
r **Zweifel,** - doubt
zweifeln to doubt
r **Zweig, -e** branch, twig
zwingen a, u to compel, force

B Strong
unsorted
3/99